INSPIRE / PLAN / DISCOVER / EXPERIENCE

SOUTHWEST USA
AND NATIONAL PARKS

DK EYEWITNESS

SOUTHWEST USA
AND NATIONAL PARKS

CONTENTS

DISCOVER 6

EXPERIENCE 62

NEED TO KNOW 270

Left: Brightly colored Navajo rugs
Previous page: Delicate Arch in Arches National Park, Utah
Front Cover: The scenic Zion National Park, Utah

DISCOVER

The Strip, Las Vegas

WELCOME TO
SOUTHWEST USA

Deep, twisting canyons, towering rock arches and pinnacles, cactus-studded deserts, and rugged mountains – the Southwest and its national parks is as much a state of mind as it is a geographical region, where you can conjure up frontier legends and indulge that bit of cowboy in your soul. Whatever your dream trip to the Southwest USA includes, this DK Eyewitness Travel Guide is the perfect companion.

1 Havasu Falls, Grand Canyon National Park.

2 Sign at the Tinkertown Museum, Turquoise Trail National Scenic Byway.

3 Sunrise over the flame-colored hoodoos in Bryce Canyon National Park.

The Southwest is distinguished by its dramatic landscapes: the red sandstone mesas of Monument Valley; the sculpted hoodoos of Utah's Bryce Canyon; the tall saguaro cacti in Southern Arizona; the staggering scale of the Grand Canyon; and the adobe architecture of New Mexico. For more than 15,000 years, the region was inhabited exclusively by Native Americans, who left remarkable cliff dwellings and ancient sites. Many of these natural and man-made wonders are protected in stunning national parks, where you can hike, bike, and explore miles of spectacular terrain.

Today, the Southwest is a synthesis of Native American, Hispanic, and Anglo-American traditions, which make up its multicultural heritage. This is often best experienced in the region's cities. Phoenix, Tucson, Albuquerque, and Santa Fe are replete with superb museums and galleries that highlight the fascinating history, art, and culture of the region. Las Vegas, with its glittering casinos, is an oasis of non-stop entertainment. Everywhere, you can sample the Southwest's distinctive, delicious cuisine.

The Southwest can overwhelm with the sheer number of unmissable national parks, cities, and sights. We've broken the region down into easily navigable chapters, with detailed itineraries, expert local knowledge, and colorful comprehensive maps to help you plan the perfect trip. Whether you're staying for a weekend, a week, or longer, this Eyewitness guide will ensure that you see the very best the region has to offer. Enjoy the book, and enjoy Southwest USA.

REASONS TO LOVE
SOUTHWEST USA

This part of the USA is famous for its rich, multicultural history, abundant natural wonders, and sunny climate. Here are some of the many reasons that make the Southwest USA easy to love and fun to explore.

1 SCENIC DRIVES

Nearly every Southwest road is a scenic road. Colorful expanses of desert and grasslands against beautiful mountain backdrops make driving one of the region's greatest pleasures.

BRIGHT LIGHTS 2

For urban excitement, you can't beat glitzy Las Vegas (p244) with its non-stop entertainment. The themed hotels, gleaming casinos, and neon lights are a sight to behold.

3 SPICY FOOD

Ranging from mild to powerfully hot, chile peppers are at the heart of Southwestern cuisine (p40), flavoring salsas, stews, burgers, and steaks. Buy ristras (strings of red chiles) as souvenirs.

COWBOY CULTURE *4*

Throw off your inhibitions and get your cowboy on. Buy some tooled leather boots, a Western hat, and a snap-button shirt. Then head for a Western bar and enjoy a margarita.

THE GRAND CANYON *5*

A truly spectacular sight, the Grand Canyon *(p68)* is a symbol of nature's beauty and power. Spend at least a day here to experience the changing light, colors, and moods of the canyon.

RELAXING SPAS *6*

Fancy a bit of pampering? Throughout the region you'll find hotel spas that welcome day visitors. Try a treatment using desert botanicals or Native American healing rituals.

SAGUAROS 7

A symbol of the Southwest, the multiarmed saguaro cactus grows only in the Sonoran Desert. Walk among these giants and take some amazing snaps in Saguaro National Park *(p108)*.

TRAIL RIDES 8

Saddle up for a quintessential Southwestern adventure. Ranches and resorts offer an exciting variety of riding activities. You can even join a working cattle roundup *(p80)*.

9 GREAT GOLF COURSES

With more than 400 top golf courses in Arizona alone, the Southwest is a golfer's paradise. Tee off at one of the legendary golf resorts in Scottsdale *(p96)* or Las Vegas *(p261)*.

10 NATURE'S PLAYGROUND

The Southwest is a picturesque playground for outdoor pursuits. Hike a backcountry path, bike along a red-rock trail, or take a thrilling whitewater rafting trip through the Grand Canyon.

SANTA FE ART 11

This beautiful city, itself a work of art, is one of the top art destinations in the USA. You can spend hours browsing its fine galleries and acclaimed museums (p192).

NATIVE AMERICAN HERITAGE 12

From ancient dwellings to beautiful crafts, the Southwest is a showcase for Native American culture. Visit pueblos and reservations to witness tribal customs and lifestyles.

EXPLORE
SOUTHWEST USA
AND NATIONAL PARKS

This guide divides Southwest USA into seven color-coded sightseeing areas, as shown on this map. Find out more about each area on the following pages.

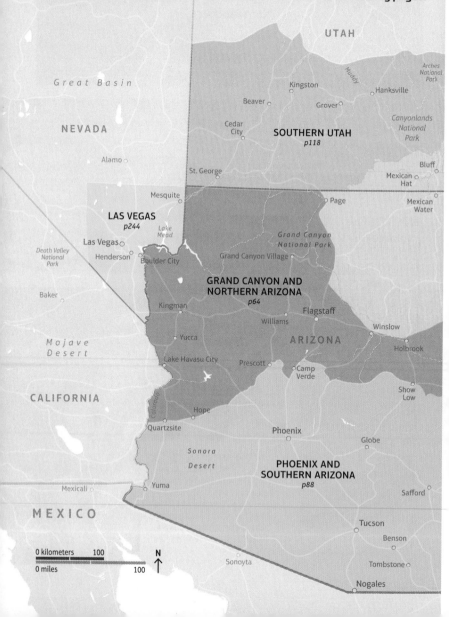

UTAH

Great Basin

Kingston

Hanksville

Beaver

Grover

Arches National Park

NEVADA

Cedar City

SOUTHERN UTAH
p118

Canyonlands National Park

Alamo

St. George

Bluff

Mexican Hat

Mesquite

Page

Mexican Water

LAS VEGAS
p244

Las Vegas

Lake Mead

Grand Canyon National Park

Death Valley National Park

Henderson

Boulder City

Grand Canyon Village

Baker

GRAND CANYON AND NORTHERN ARIZONA
p64

Kingman

Flagstaff

Williams

Winslow

Mojave Desert

Yucca

ARIZONA

Holbrook

Lake Havasu City

Prescott

Camp Verde

CALIFORNIA

Show Low

Hope

Phoenix

Quartzsite

Sonora Desert

Globe

Phoenix

PHOENIX AND SOUTHERN ARIZONA
p88

Mexicali

Yuma

Safford

MEXICO

Tucson

Benson

0 kilometers   100

N ↑

0 miles   100

Sonoyta

Tombstone

Nogales

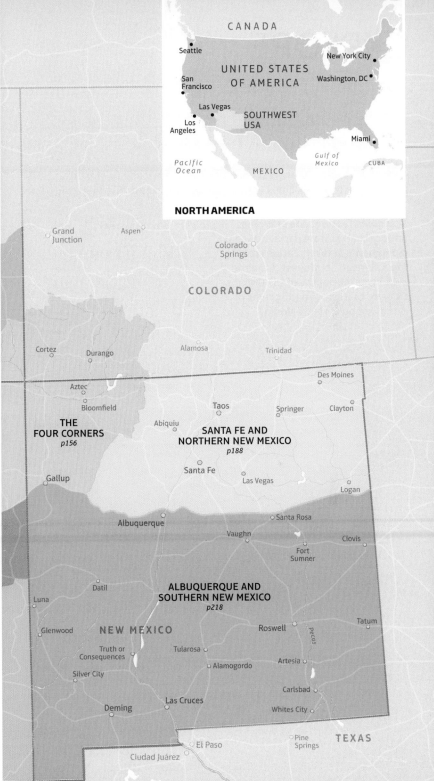

NORTH AMERICA

EXPLORE
PARKS AND
RECREATION
AREAS

This guide features the stunning national parks, state parks, national monuments, and recreation areas in the American Southwest, from the awe-inspiring depths of the Grand Canyon, to the fascinating ruins of cliff dwellings in Mesa Verde.

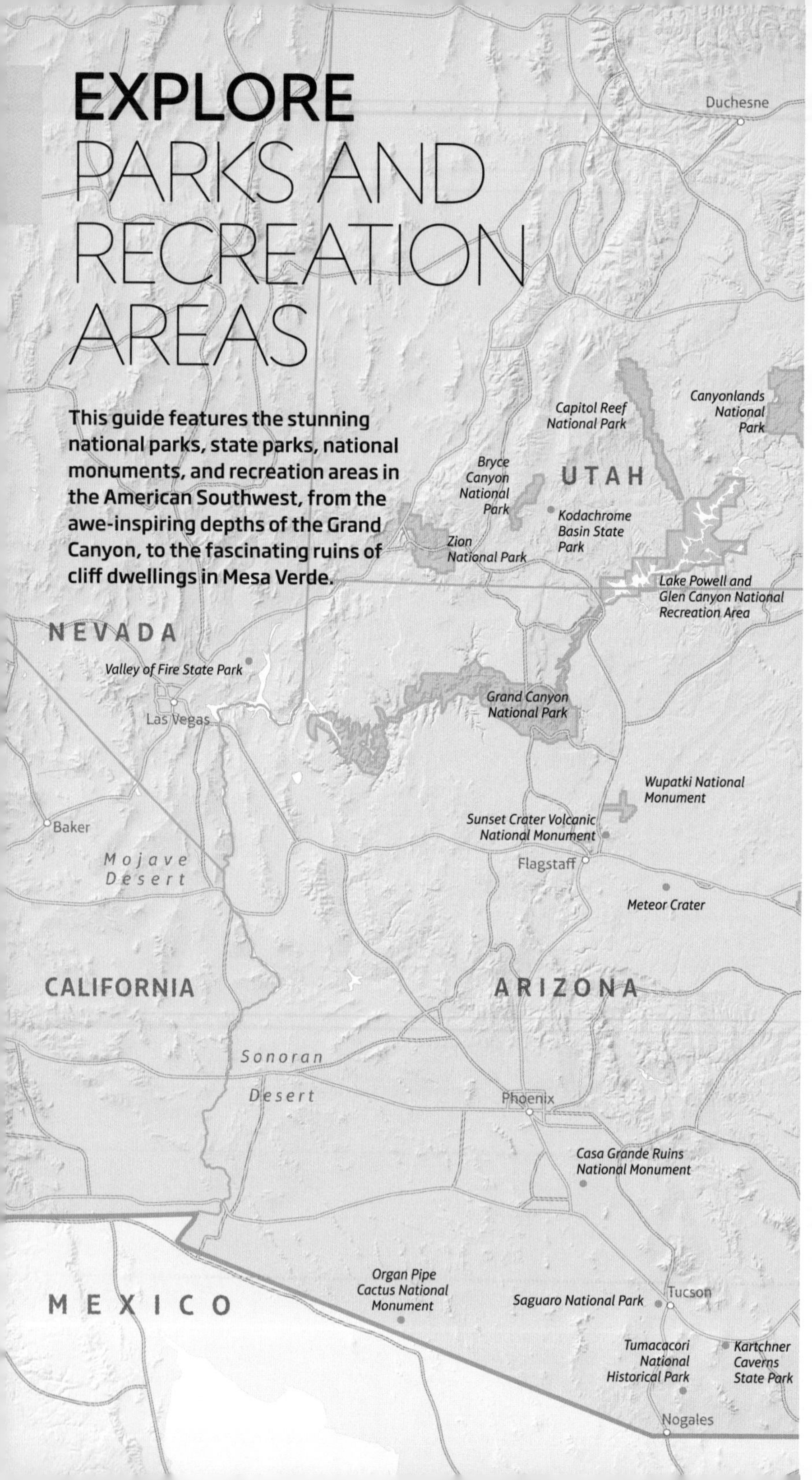

Duchesne

Capitol Reef National Park

Canyonlands National Park

UTAH

Bryce Canyon National Park

Kodachrome Basin State Park

Zion National Park

Lake Powell and Glen Canyon National Recreation Area

NEVADA

Valley of Fire State Park

Las Vegas

Grand Canyon National Park

Wupatki National Monument

Baker

Sunset Crater Volcanic National Monument

Flagstaff

Mojave Desert

Meteor Crater

CALIFORNIA

ARIZONA

Sonoran Desert

Phoenix

Casa Grande Ruins National Monument

MEXICO

Organ Pipe Cactus National Monument

Saguaro National Park

Tucson

Tumacacori National Historical Park

Kartchner Caverns State Park

Nogales

GETTING TO KNOW
SOUTHWEST USA

Awesome canyon landscapes, stunning rock formations, magical underground caverns: the natural wonders of Southwest USA sparkle like desert diamonds. Added to this is a wealth of cultural highlights, from Native American pueblos and historic Spanish ranches and missions to cities full of art and entertainment.

GRAND CANYON AND NORTHERN ARIZONA

PAGE 64

Defined by the magnificent spectacle of the Grand Canyon with its multicolored mesas, cliffs, and pinnacles stretching for hundreds of miles, this region has many smaller gems too. Discover natural marvels such as Sunset Crater, Meteor Crater, and the Petrified Forest. Beat the heat in the cool waters of Lake Havasu or Oak Creek Canyon. Explore historic buildings and art galleries in Jerome and Flagstaff and the New Age energy of Sedona with its stunning red rock vistas.

Best for
Spectacular canyon views

Home to
Grand Canyon National Park and Sedona

Experience
Hiking along the South Rim of the Grand Canyon

PAGE 88

PHOENIX AND SOUTHERN ARIZONA

From living legacies of the Old West to world-class spas and golf courses, Southern Arizona has a great variety of things to see and do. In Phoenix and Tucson, enjoy superb Southwestern cuisine and fascinating music and art museums. The cities are surrounded by the splendor of the Sonoran Desert, with its giant, multiarmed saguaro cacti. Visit old Spanish missions, the historic mining towns of Bisbee and Tombstone, the art colony at Tubac, wineries and more.

Best for
Desert beauty and Old West atmosphere

Home to
Phoenix and Tucson

Experience
A horseback ride through the Sonoran Desert

PAGE 118

SOUTHERN UTAH

A host of state and national parks sprawl across Southern Utah. Keep your camera at hand, ready to capture one stunning vista after another, from the red stone arcs of Arches National Park and the fascinating hoodoos of Bryce Canyon to the dramatic view of the Colorado River and Canyonlands National Park from Dead Horse Point. Relax with a boat trip on Lake Powell, or in laid-back towns such as Moab, which offer jeep trips, mountain biking, and other activities in the region's fabulous landscapes.

Best for
National parks and scenic views

Home to
Canyonlands, Capitol Reef, Bryce Canyon, Zion, and Arches national parks; Lake Powell and Glen Canyon National Recreation Area

Experience
Watching the sunset over Delicate Arch in Arches National Park

→

PAGE 156

THE FOUR CORNERS

The scenic junction of the states of Colorado, Utah, Arizona, and New Mexico contains the largest concentration of Native American heritage in the USA. This ranges from the ancient cliff dwellings and great houses of the Ancestral Puebloans at Mesa Verde, Chaco Canyon, and other key sites to the tribal lands and monuments of today's Navajo and Hopi communities. For stunning vistas, drive among the towering buttes of Monument Valley or along Colorado's breathtaking San Juan Skyway.

Best for
Native American heritage and Rocky Mountain scenery

Home to
Monument Valley, Canyon de Chelly National Monument, Chaco Culture National Historical Park, and Mesa Verde National Park

Experience
Riding the Durango and Silverton Narrow Gauge Railroad for spectacular mountain views

PAGE 188

SANTA FE AND NORTHERN NEW MEXICO

With its beautiful historic buildings, world-class art galleries and museums, and superb restaurants serving New Mexican cuisine, Santa Fe is the region's key draw. But Northern New Mexico offers much more to explore, from the peaceful Santuario de Chimayó church to the historic town and art colony of Taos. Visit Native American pueblos, explore ancient cliff dwellings at Puye and Bandelier National Monument, or take a scenic mountain drive along the Enchanted Circle forest scenic byway.

Best for
Southwestern art, architecture, and cuisine

Home to
Santa Fe and Taos

Experience
A river rafting trip down the Rio Grande

ALBUQUERQUE AND SOUTHERN NEW MEXICO

Southern New Mexico is a land of contrasts, ranging from Acoma Pueblo, the nation's oldest settlement, to busy Albuquerque, the state's largest city. Sights are scattered in this vast region. Take to the road to see the amazing dunes at White Sands National Park, the wondrous caves at Carlsbad Caverns, and the remote Gila Cliff Dwellings. Soak up legends of the Old West at the historic towns of Lincoln, Ruidoso, Mesilla, and Silver City.

Best for
Historic towns and villages, and natural wonders

Home to
Albuquerque and Carlsbad Caverns National Park

Experience
Soaring in a balloon over Albuquerque, the hot-air ballooning capital of the world

PAGE 244

LAS VEGAS

There's no place like Las Vegas – a glittering oasis dedicated to round-the-clock entertainment. The city is home to countless dazzling casino-hotels, known for their magical themed architecture, inventive restaurants, and unforgettable shows. Beyond the nightclubs and bars of the Strip, there are fascinating museums, such as the Mob Museum, dedicated to Las Vegas's legendary gangsters, and the Neon Museum, celebrating its glitzy signs. There's plenty to see outside the city, too, including the Hoover Dam and striking landscapes of the Red Rock Canyon.

Best for
Nightlife and entertainment

Home to
The Strip, Bellagio fountains, and The STRAT Tower

Experience
A bird's-eye view from the High Roller

←

1 Hiking in the Narrows gorge, Zion National Park.

2 Native American teepees at Capitol Reef Resort, Torrey.

3 Scenic Drive in Capitol Reef National Park.

4 Thor's Hammer in Bryce Canyon National Park, seen from the Navajo Loop Trail.

Southwest USA is a vast region, but the stunning scenery makes the miles fly by. These itineraries offer options that take in some of the top national parks, cities, and historical sights.

2 WEEKS

touring the Southwest

Day 1

Get an early start from Las Vegas on I-15 North. After 119 miles (192 km), stretch your legs in St. George *(p153)*. The Bear Paw Cafe *(75 N Main Street)* is a good place for coffee or a late breakfast. Continue 42 miles (68 km) to reach your lodgings at Zion National Park *(p138)* by lunchtime. If you're not staying at historic Zion National Park Lodge *(www.zion lodge.com)*, there are several options at Springdale. Ride the park shuttle buses the full length of the canyon, then follow the short River Walk to see the Virgin River emerge from the mouth of the Narrows.

Day 2

Tunnel your way east out of Zion via the extraordinary Zion–Mount Carmel Highway, then head north 75 miles (121 km) to spend the night near the fiery red-rock hoodoos of Bryce Canyon National Park *(p134)*. Hiking the Navajo Loop takes you into the heart of this labyrinth of towering pinnacles, while Sunset Point offers an evening vista of the vast desert ahead. The Lodge at Bryce Canyon *(www.bryce canyonforever.com)* has vintage rooms and cabins and a good restaurant.

Day 3

Continue east along Highway 12, a lovely route through the wilderness of Grand Staircase-Escalante National Monument *(p148)*. Hike to the iridescent waters of Calf Creek Falls; then, back on the road, cross the Hogsback, a knife-edge ridge of

rock with guardrails, to reach Torrey (116 miles/186 km), just west of the forbidding 100-mile (160-km) wall of rock at Capitol Reef National Park *(p126)*. The Capitol Reef Resort *(www.capitolreefresort.com)* has atmospheric accommodations in luxury cabins, teepees, and Conestoga wagons.

Day 4

Drive through the clay badlands that lie east of Capitol Reef on Highway 24 for 80 miles (129 km) to reach Goblin Valley State Park *(p147)*. The bizarre rock formations here resemble fairy-tale monsters. Another 50 miles (80 km) north, visit the museum dedicated to pioneer river-rafter John Wesley Powell in the town of Green River. Moab *(p146)*, 52 miles (84 km) southeast, makes a lively overnight base. The Gonzo Inn *(www.gonzoinn.com)* is a fun choice with eclectic, colorful rooms and a relaxing pool and hot tub. Moab is on the doorstep of Arches National Park *(p142)*, which holds the world's largest array of naturally formed stone arches. Hike to Delicate Arch for an unforgettable sunset.

Day 5

Stay another night in Moab, and visit the Island in the Sky district of Canyonlands National Park *(p122)*, about a half-hour's drive away. Hike the short trail to Mesa Arch, and take in sweeping views over the mighty canyons carved by the Green and Colorado rivers. Stop off on your way back at the dramatic viewpoints at Dead Horse Point State Park *(p146)*.

→

Day 6

Drive east into Colorado from La Sal Junction, south of Moab, to the Rocky Mountains. After 132 miles (212 km), stop at Telluride *(p184)* for lunch at Floradora Saloon *(www.floradorasaloon.com)*, a local favorite. Follow the San Juan Skyway *(p186)* north, which leads up amid the snow-crested peaks to the former mining town of Ouray *(p185)*. Then continue on the Million Dollar Highway over the 11,000-ft (3,350-m) Red Mountain Pass and drop back down to the Wild West outpost of Silverton. Drive 48 miles (77 km) to Durango *(p185)* for an overnight stay at the historic Strater Hotel *(www.strater.com)*.

Day 7

Spend the morning exploring the Victorian frontier town of Durango. Then head west for 56 miles (90 km), climbing into the forested tablelands above the Montezuma Valley to reach Mesa Verde National Park *(p172)*. Take a ranger-led tour to explore inside the fascinating ancient dwellings of Cliff Palace and Balcony House. Spend the night at Cortez, 31 miles (50 km) farther

west. Kelly Place *(www.kellyplace.com)* is a lovely B&B with prehistoric Native American sites on its grounds.

Day 8

Southwest of Cortez, 121 miles (195 km) away, Monument Valley Navajo Tribal Park *(p160)* represents the Wild West at its most majestic. Drive the scenic loop and take a Navajo-guided tour into the backcountry. The View Hotel *(www. monumentvalleyview.com)* makes an unforgettable stay.

Day 9

About an hour's drive southwest, take a tiny detour to see Navajo National Monument *(p179)*, where the ancient Betatakin pueblo can be visited on guided hikes. Then press on for 118 miles (190 km) to the South Rim of the Grand Canyon *(p70)*, where you'll enter the national park at Desert View. Visit sites along Desert View Drive, including Grandview Point overlook, then check into your hotel in Grand Canyon Village.

1 Cliff Palace, Mesa Verde National Park.

2 Jeep Tour around Monument Valley Navajo Tribal Park.

3 A weaver in a hogan, Navajo National Monument.

4 African display in the Musical Instrument Museum, Phoenix.

5 Watson Lake, Prescott.

Day 10

To make the most of a day on the South Rim, set off early to hike the Bright Angel Trail (p71) down into the canyon; don't try to reach the Colorado River, and turn back well before you're tired. Spend the afternoon touring the Hermit Road (p69), and try to catch the sunset at Hopi Point (p68).

Day 11

Head 80 miles (129 km) southeast to the lively university town of Flagstaff (p78). Visit the Museum of Northern Arizona, explore the historic downtown and venture 9 miles (15 km) east to see ancient ruins in Walnut Canyon National Monument (p81). Stay overnight at the historic Weatherford Hotel (www.weatherfordhotel.com).

Day 12

Drive 30 miles (49 km) on Highway 89A through Oak Creek Canyon (p80) to Sedona (p76), cooling off en route with a dip at Slide Rock State Park. Explore Sedona's galleries, tour the Red Rock Country, and relax in Amara Resort and Spa (www.amararesort.com).

Day 13

Head 27 miles (44 km) southwest to the old mining town of Jerome (p83); stop off on the way to see the pueblo ruins at the Tuzigoot National Monument (p84). In Jerome, browse the numerous art galleries and have lunch at the Haunted Hamburger (www.thehauntedhamburger.com). Less than an hour's drive south and set among the cool woodlands of the Prescott National Forest, the charming town of Prescott (p86) is the site of beautiful Watson Lake, where you can take a hike before seeing American Western art at the Phippen Museum. Stay overnight at the landmark Hassayampa Inn (www.hassayampainn.com).

Day 14

Drive to Phoenix, about 100 miles (160 km) away. En route, make a short detour to visit the experimental town of Arcosanti (p84) to see its ecological landscape-inspired architecture. In Phoenix, visit the Heard Museum (p94) to see Native American art, and the Musical Instrument Museum (p98), the largest museum of its type in the world.

7 DAYS
in New Mexico

Day 1

Starting at Albuquerque (p222), take the Turquoise Trail (Highway 14) north for 52 miles (84 km) to Santa Fe. This National Scenic Byway (p242) runs along the flanks of the Sandia Mountains. Linger in the old mining towns of Golden, Madrid, and Cerillos for photos and shopping. In Santa Fe, explore the streets around the plaza as the setting sun lights up St. Francis Cathedral (p194). Have a drink on the rooftop cantina at Coyote Cafe (www.coyotecafe.com) before retiring to one of the colorful hotels in the area (p195).

Day 2

Spend a full day in Santa Fe, soaking up the art and history of this beautiful town. Visit the Palace of the Governors, the Georgia O'Keeffe Museum (p192), and the Museum of Indian Arts and Culture (p197). Browse the art galleries on Canyon Road (p196) and treat yourself to dinner at Geronimo (p197).

Day 3

Head north into the hills for 28 miles (45 km) to the adobe pilgrim chapel at Chimayó (p212). Continue to picturesque Taos (p202), 49 miles (79 km) beyond. Stroll around its historic plaza, and visit Taos Pueblo (p206) with its striking adobe dwellings. For dinner, enjoy superb regional fare in a historic adobe inn at Doc Martin's Restaurant (p205). A lovely place to stay is the Sagebrush Inn (www. sagebrushinn.com), another historical landmark, with its rustic rooms, an atmospheric cantina and great restaurant.

Day 4

Get an early start for the 182-mile (293-km) drive to Chaco Culture National Historical Park (p168). The site is very remote and no food can be purchased, so bring a packed lunch and fill the car's fuel tank before you leave. Follow Highways 68 and 84 through Abiquiu (p213) and the dramatic red-rock country that inspired artist Georgia O'Keeffe. The impressive

① St. Francis Cathedral in Santa Fe. ↑

② Adobe dwellings in Taos Pueblo.

③ Luminarias at San José de los Jémez Mission, Jemez Springs.

④ A casing for the B-61 nuclear bomb, Bradbury Science Museum.

⑤ A mosaic of Billy the Kid on the wall of the visitor center in Ruidoso.

remains of the pre-Columbian settlement at Chaco Canyon are worth the long drive. Camp in or near the park itself, or drive 90 minutes to the nearest accommodations at Farmington (p184), 72 miles (116 km) away.

Day 5

Begin the day with a 196-mile (395-km) drive Los Alamos (p207) on Highways 550 and 4 via Jemez Springs (p207). Stretch your legs with a hike to see the ancient cliff dwellings of the Ancestral Puebloans in Bandelier National Monument (p211). Once in Los Alamos, visit the Bradbury Science Museum (p207), which has exhibits on the Los Alamos National Laboratory, a leading defense facility.

Day 6

Head for cowboy country. Lincoln Historic Site (p241) is a half-day's drive (226 miles/ 364 km) southeast via Highways 285 and 54. Explore its rustic buildings dating to the late 1800s and soak up tales of Billy the Kid at the Lincoln County Courthouse, where he was imprisoned. As the sun

starts to set, drive 30 miles (48 km) to Ruidoso (p240), a popular resort town perched high in the Rocky Mountains. Spend the night in one of the simply furnished yet comfortable rooms at the Hotel Ruidoso (www. hotelruidoso.net), in the town's historic Midtown district.

Day 7

Wander along Ruidoso's main street, which is lined with art galleries, shops, and restaurants before visiting the fascinating Hubbard Museum of the American West (p241), which is full of Western art and memorabilia. As you leave the museum, don't miss the striking sculpture Free Spirits at Noisy Water, which depicts seven galloping horses. From here it's a three-hour drive (180 miles/290 km) back to Albuquerque.

←

1 Natural arch, El Malpais National Monument.

2 Retro 66 Diner in Albuquerque.

3 The Colorado River seen from Hoover Dam.

4 The historic Hotel Monte Vista in Flagstaff.

3 DAYS

on Route 66

Day 1

Morning After breakfast at 66 Diner (www.66diner.com) in Albuquerque (p222), take the I-40, which runs parallel to the original Route 66. Drive 65 miles (105 km) southwest to Acoma Pueblo (p232). Take a tour of one of the oldest continuously inhabited villages in the USA on the mesa top; the views are amazing. Continue west on I-40 and stop at Grants (30 miles/48 km) for lunch (p232). El Cafecito (820 E Santa Fe Ave, Grants) on Historic Route 66 is a good spot for genuine Mexican food.

Afternoon After lunch, stretch your legs with a hike in the volcanic landscape of El Malpais National Monument (p232), just 4 miles (6 km) away. Back on I-40, drive to Gallup (65 miles/105 km), where there is a choice of overnight accommodations.

Day 2

Morning From Gallup, the I-40 crosses the border into Arizona. Stop to explore the Petrified Forest National Park (p85), 70 miles (113 km) away. In Holbrook, 18 miles (29 km) farther on, Brad's Desert Inn (www.bradsdesertinnaz.com) captures the historic spirit of Route 66 with its stylish themed rooms. Grab a bite to eat at Tom and Suzie's Diner (2001 Navajo Boulevard).

Afternoon Head to Winslow, 33 miles (53 km) west, where music fans may want to stop for a photo by the mural at Standin' on the Corner Park, a reference to the Eagles' song "Take It Easy", which mentions the town. Drive to Flagstaff (p78), 58 miles

(93km) farther on. Explore its historic downtown and dine at foodie favorite Tinderbox Kitchen (www.tinderboxkitchen. com). Stay overnight at the historic Hotel Monte Vista (www.hotelmontevista.com), dating to 1926, whose antiques-furnished rooms are named for Hollywood stars who were previous guests.

Day 3

Morning Get an early start and drive 40 minutes (33 miles/53 km) to Williams for breakfast at Goldie's Route 66 Diner (p81). Walk off your breakfast at Seligman, a 43-mile (69-km) drive, set among Arizona's mountains, with scenery that evokes the days of the westward pioneers. You'll find several Route 66-themed shops and diners here, where you can have lunch.

Afternoon Drive to the Grand Canyon Caverns, 25 miles (40 km) northwest on Historic Route 66, and explore stalagmites and seams of sparkling crystals on a 45-minute underground tour. Kingman (62 miles/100 km) is about an hour's drive farther along old Route 66. Here you can visit the Arizona Route 66 Museum (route 66museum.net), which also has a historic electric vehicle museum attached. From Kingman, follow Highway 93 for 76 miles (122 km) to Hoover Dam (p269) and enjoy a stroll around the marinas of Lake Mead National Recreation Area (p268). Then head on to Las Vegas, 37 miles (60 km) from here, for an evening of entertainment at Bellagio (p258) or Caesars Palace (p259).

←

1 Venetian resort illuminated at night.

2 The imposing Hoover Dam across the Colorado River.

3 The lights of downtown Las Vegas at night.

4 The STRAT Tower, with its observation deck.

3 DAYS
in Las Vegas

Day 1

Morning Start exploring the central Strip (*p252*) by visiting the elegant Bellagio casino (*p258*), and marvel at the floral displays in its Conservatory. Then catch the Aria Express CityCenter tram to see the contemporary sculptures in the Aria (*p256*), and shop at the stylish Crystals retail mall. Now head north across the Strip to Paris Las Vegas (*p257*), and enjoy a panoramic view from atop the Eiffel Tower. Eat lunch in one of the city's all-you-can-eat buffets.

Afternoon Visit Caesars Palace (*p259*), admiring its version of Michelangelo's *David* and browsing beneath the artificial sky of the Forum Shops. Cross the Strip to the LINQ Hotel + Experience (*p260*) and ride its High Roller observation wheel for stupendous views over the city and valley. Then move on to the Venetian (*p260*) and cruise along the Grand Canal in a gondola.

Evening Take in a Cirque du Soleil® show, then treat yourself to a gourmet dinner at Restaurant Guy Savoy (*p259*). Join the after-dark crowds on the Strip sidewalk to see free attractions such as the erupting volcano outside the Mirage (*p261*) and the dancing fountains of the Bellagio (*p258*).

Day 2

Morning Start by touring the mega-casinos at the southern end of the Strip. Enter the pyramid of the Luxor (*p254*) between the paws of the giant Sphinx, and visit its Bodies and Titanic exhibitions. Then walk through Excalibur castle (*p253*) to reach

New York New York (*p253*); take a swooping ride on its roller coaster. Head north to the other end of the Strip, where The STRAT Tower (*p263*) offers more thrilling rides and amazing views.

Afternoon Continue to the city's original downtown core for a taste of classic Las Vegas lunch at Siegel's 1941 in the El Cortez Hotel and Casino (*p267*). It's a five-minute walk from here to the Mob Museum (*p266*), which reveals Vegas's crime-ridden history in detail. As the sun sets, take a cab to the Neon Museum (*p267*) for a retro tour.

Evening Return to downtown's Fremont Street Experience (*p266*) and watch the amazing light shows on the overarching canopy. Venture into the historic casinos along this stretch of "Glitter Gulch." Dine at Oscar's Steakhouse (*p267*).

Day 3

Morning Pack a picnic lunch, and head 10 miles (16 km) west to Red Rock Canyon (*p268*). Drive the scenic loop road along the escarpment, and take a short hike into one of the winding canyons.

Afternoon It's about an hour's drive back across the city and east to Hoover Dam (*p269*). Take a tour, which includes impressive views over the dam's huge generators from the observation deck.

Evening Return to the city for an early dinner at Picasso (*p259*). Take in a star-studded musical, then party away in one of the Strip's glamorous bars.

Just Deserts

Each desert in the Southwest has its own distinctive features. The Sonoran Desert *(p108)* is home to the multi-armed saguaro cactus; the Mojave to unique Joshua Trees. In the Chihuahuan Desert you'll find the dunes of New Mexico's White Sands National Park, the world's largest gypsum dune field *(p239)*.

←

A multiarmed saguaro cactus, native to the Sonoran desert

SOUTHWEST USA'S
AMAZING
LANDSCAPES

The amazing landscapes and natural wonders of the Southwest will stay with you forever. From vast expanses of cactus-studded desert and snowcapped mountain peaks to jaw-dropping canyons and stunning natural stone arches, the Southwest has an abundance of photogenic panoramas.

Craggy Canyons

The Grand Canyon *(p68)* may be the best known, but there are many other breathtaking ravines in the region. The Horseshoe Canyon's *(p122)* Green River creates its awesome curved gorge, while the walls of Arizona's Canyon de Chelly *(p164)* shelter centuries of Native American heritage.

Ancient Rock

The Southwest is home to some of the most incredible natural arches in the world. Red-tinged Utah is particularly photogenic. There are more than 2,000 of them in Arches National Park *(p142)* alone, while Bryce Canyon *(p134)* holds an army of fascinating formations called hoodoos.

→

Delicate Arch, located in Arches National Park

Below Ground

Awesome subterranean landscapes mirror the beauty of the Southwest above ground. Carlsbad Caverns *(p228)* is a magical kingdom of soda straws, stalactites, stalagmites, and other magnificent cave formations. In Kartchner Caverns *(p117)*, you can walk amid the huge mineral columns of a living cave.

←

Stalactites hang from the roof of one of the region's many caves

Montane Vistas

The Rocky Mountains of Colorado and northern New Mexico make a breathtaking backdrop for scenic road trips. Drive the San Juan Skyway *(p186)* for some spectacular panoramas, or chug through the mountains on the historic Durango and Silverton Narrow Gauge Railroad *(p181)* to take in fabulous views from the gondola cars.

↑ The stunning Spider Rock at sunset, Canyon de Chelly

→

The tree-lined Durango and Silverton rail route

A Night at the Opera

It might seem surprising but opera has long been a popular entertainment in the Southwest. In the early days, a town wasn't a town until it could boast an opera house. Today, the acclaimed Santa Fe Opera *(p199)*, with its striking, open-sided theater, is a unique chance to take in an opera in a modern setting that is as dramatic as anything on stage.

←

The state-of-the-art auditorium of the Sante Fe Opera

SOUTHWEST USA
ON THE TOWN

The Southwest has some of the best entertainment in the world. From state-of-the-art sports stadiums through old-fashioned bars and star-studded Las Vegas shows to opera beneath the night sky, the region offers plenty of options for when the sun goes down.

Viva Las Vegas

There's no place like Vegas for fabulous shows *(p248)*. Mega-stars like Lady Gaga, Celine Dion, and Diana Ross have previously performed here, as has the thrilling Cirque du Soleil®, whose gravity defying acrobatic shows astound.

→

Cirque du Soleil® performers putting on a colorful, mesmerizing show

Home of the Diamondbacks

Chase Field in Phoenix, home ground for the Diamondbacks baseball team, offers sports fans a real all-American treat: watching a night-time game. The stadium roof can be open to the stars, or closed during inclement weather, but either way, the roar of the fans adds to the rousing spectacle. If baseball's not your thing, you can watch occasional concerts and international soccer matches here too *(www.mlb. com/dbacks/ballpark)*.

→

Unveiling of the US flag before a soccer game at Chase Field

Did You Know?

Chase Field's roof can be opened or closed in just over four minutes using 4 miles (6.5 km) of cables.

Bet on Fun

Casinos aren't only in Las Vegas *(p244)*, and aren't just for gambling. They exist throughout the Southwest, often on Native American land as revenue earners. Many have fine restaurants and concert halls hosting big-name acts – check out the Fire Rock Casino in New Mexico, or Tucson's two casinos: the Casino del Sol and Desert Diamond.

←

Gambling chips, used throughout the Southwest's wealth of casinos

Cinematic History

Downtown Tucson *(p102)* has two historic theaters: the Rialto and the nearby Fox Theatre. These early 20th-century movie houses are now on the National Register of Historic Places, and offer guided tours so you can get a closer look at the historical features. KiMo Theater *(p224)* in Albuquerque is another Art Deco gem that shows local music, theater, and movies.

→

The eye-catching exterior of Fox Theatre in Tucson

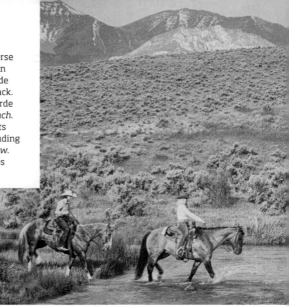

Home on the Range

There's no better way to immerse yourself in the Southwest than to stay on a guest ranch and ride through the desert on horseback. Some, like Tucson's Tanque Verde Ranch *(www.tanqueverderanch.com)* provide cowboy cook-outs and poetry, while others, including the White Stallion Ranch *(www.whitestallion.com)* offer rodeos and shooting lessons.

→
Horseback riders following a trail through the rolling scenery of Utah

SOUTHWEST USA FOR
THE WILD WEST

The Old West is alive and well in today's Southwest. Visit places where Billy the Kid and Wyatt Earp became notorious, hit the trail on ranches that stretch into the sunset, or sample a traditional rodeo. Whatever you get up to, embrace your inner cowboy with a pair of tooled leather boots and a Stetson.

Wild West Legends

There are plenty of places to trace the footsteps of Old West outlaws and frontiersmen. Watch a reenactment of the OK Corral gunfight in Tombstone, Arizona *(p116)*, or follow the trail of famous outlaw Billy the Kid from his childhood haunts in Silver City, New Mexico *(p234)*.

Val Kilmer and Kurt Russell starring in *Tombstone*, ↑ © 1993 Warner

All the Gear...

Spruce up your wardrobe Southwest-style with a great pair of cowboy boots, a Western hat, and tooled leather belt – or just add a snap-front shirt to your favorite jeans. Alternatively, treat yourself to some Native American-made jewelry featuring turquoise stones and fine silverwork. Top places to shop for these items include Phoenix *(p92)*, Scottsdale *(p96)*, Santa Fe *(p192)*, and Albuquerque *(p222)*.

← An array of well-worn cowboy boots lining the shelves of a store

Traditional Rodeos

Since Buffalo Bill's first Wild West shows in the 1880s, the Southwest has been a mecca for Western-style entertainment. You'll be amazed at the skills of today's cowboys and cowgirls. The most popular rodeos are Tucson's Fiesta de los Vaqueros, *(p54)*, in February, the New Mexico State Fair and Rodeo in Albuquerque in September, and the world's oldest, Prescott's Frontier Days Rodeo, *(p55)*, on July 4.

↑ A woman guiding a bucking horse in the paddock

TOP 5 STORES FOR WESTERN GEAR

Az-Tex Hats
W aztexhats.com
The largest selection of cowboy hats in the Southwest.

Saba's Western Wear
W sabasofchandler.com
A family-run store since 1927 with branches throughout Arizona.

Espinoza Boot Maker
W espinozabootmaker.com
Head here for custom, handmade boots and fine-quality leather belts.

Double Take
W santafedoubletake.com
New Mexico's biggest consignment store has plenty of vintage and second-hand cowboy apparel.

Back at the Ranch
W backattheranch.com
This old adobe store in Santa Fe provides a one-stop shop for those seeking luxury, bespoke cowboy boots.

Go West

Traditional Western art, from the lively paintings of William Robinson Leigh to the intricate work of Frederic Remington, is complemented by exciting contemporary artists at the Tucson Museum of Art *(p102)* or the Amerind Foundation's Fulton-Hayden Memorial Art Gallery *(p117)*. The Georgia O'Keeffe Museum *(p192)* hosts some of her best-loved works.

←

Visitors wandering through the galleries of Santa Fe's Georgia O'Keeffe Museum

SOUTHWEST USA FOR
ART LOVERS

The clear quality of the light in the Southwest, especially in its dramatic desert landscapes, has long drawn artists and photographers here. Among the best known are the Taos Society of Artists and Georgia O'Keeffe, who settled at Abiquiu. Santa Fe is one of the country's leading art centers.

HIDDEN GEM
Harwood Museum of Art

Located in Taos *(p202)* this is New Mexico's second-oldest gallery (after the New Mexico Museum of Art in Santa Fe). It features works by original members of the Taos Society of Artists and by contemporary local artists.

Discover Native American Art

The Heard Museum *(p94)* in Phoenix has the finest collection of Native American arts and crafts in the Southwest, including kachina dolls, pottery, textiles, silver pieces, and fine art. Its shop sells a large range of Native American arts and crafts. In Santa Fe, you can see an impressive selection of works by today's Native American artists at the IAIA Museum of Contemporary Native Arts *(p193)*.

→

The Heard Museum's impressive collection of kachina dolls

Tubac Art Colony

A half-hour drive from the Mexican border, the little town of Tubac *(p115)* is a thriving art colony whose streets are lined with galleries and studios that showcase the vibrantly colored artworks of Southern Arizona and northern Mexico. The Tubac Center of the Arts hosts constantly changing exhibitions and hands-on workshops by local artists.

→

La Entrada de Tubac, home to an artists' community in Arizona

Hispanic Art

The Hispanic art created by both Spanish settlers and Mexican immigrants is a potent part of the Southwest's rich arts scene. Santa Fe's annual Spanish Market *(www. spanishcolonial.org)*, held over the last weekend of July on the historic Santa Fe Plaza, showcases Hispanic art, with opportunities to buy. Albuquerque's Old Town Plaza *(p226)* also has galleries displaying Hispanic art.

←

Colorful Mexican ceramics on sale at Santa Fe's annual market

Canyon Road Treasures

Canyon Road *(p196)* in Santa Fe's historic district is a half mile (0.8 km) of art heaven. Contemporary, traditional, and Native American fine art galleries, often set in historic adobe buildings, display paintings, sculptures, rugs, glassworks, folk art, and more. Art lovers will find the colorful contemporary collections particularly inspiring.

→

A visitor walking past one of the many art galleries that line Canyon Road

City of Gastronomy

Tucson *(p102)* was the first of only two US cities to be declared a UNESCO Creative City of Gastronomy in 2015 (followed by San Antonio Texas in 2018). Its food heritage dates back 4,000 years to when Native Americans first cultivated adapted crops to the arid climate. Delicacies include edible cacti such as *nopales* (prickly pear pads), mesquite pancakes, and Sonoran white wheat tortillas.

$\longrightarrow$

Typical Mexican dishes served at restaurants in Tucson

SOUTHWEST USA FOR
FOODIES

It's worth visiting the Southwest for the food alone. You'll discover the mouthwatering flavors of Mexican dishes, the subtly different New Mexican cuisine, a hint of Tex-Mex, and the gourmet creations of top chefs in the region's resorts and hotels, especially Las Vegas.

TOP 3 REGIONAL DISHES

Carne Seca
This spicy dried beef is a signature dish in Tucson's El Charro restaurant *(p104)*.

Posole
A traditional Mexican soup or stew of pork, hominy and chile, *posole* is best sampled at The Shed in Santa Fe *(www.sfshed.com)*.

Pollo en Mole
The classic Mexican dish of chicken in a spicy chocolate sauce is a staple at the Barrio Café in Phoenix *(www. barriocafe.com)*.

Santa Fe Style

New Mexico has its own distinctive cuisine. It is strongly influenced by Mexican cooking but uses local ingredients such as blue corn for tortillas. Sample it in Santa Fe *(p192)*, with its sophisticated dining scene and excellent cooking school.

$\longrightarrow$

Santa Fe Farmers' Market in the Santa Fe Railyard district

Native American Food

While it's hard to find true Native American food outside private homes, Native American fry bread – a flat, fried dough served with sweet or savory toppings – is often sold at tourist attractions or events. Festivals are the best places to taste indigenous dishes such as fried rabbit meat or Three Sisters Stew, made with corn, beans, and squash.

→ A tempting pile of golden Native American fry bread

Red or Green?

You'll often hear this question when you order food in the Southwest. Chile is a staple here, and many dishes can be served with either green or red peppers on top. One is not necessarily hotter than the other; the heat depends on the variety of chile and how many seeds it contains. To try a little of each on the side, just ask for "Christmas."

← An arrangement of drying chiles at a New Mexico market

Did You Know?

There are more than 100 types of chile, including jalapeño, poblano, chipotle, and spicy serrano.

A Taste of Mexico

The chile pepper is at the heart of Southwestern cuisine. Other main ingredients are similar to those found in Mexican cooking: corn, beans, cheese, and tomatoes. Local additions include ingredients such as nuts from the *piñon* pine, chayote (a squash similar to zucchini), and tomatillos, a walnut-sized green berry fruit.

↑ Santa Fe soup with beans, corn, cheese, and chiles

Margarita Bars

The margarita is the go-to cocktail in the Southwest. The mix of tequila, triple sec, and lime juice is usually served in a glass with salt around the rim. Maria's New Mexican Kitchen has a margarita list with over a hundred choices and is part of the Santa Fe Margarita Trail *(www.santafe.org/ Margaritatrail)*.

→

Bar at the top of La Fonda on the Plaza hotel in Santa Fe, and a margarita cocktail *(inset)*

SOUTHWEST USA
BY THE GLASS

You may be in the desert but you won't die of thirst in the Southwest. You can even enjoy award-winning wines made locally, as well as tasty craft beers. New distilleries are opening too, featuring unique spirits, while popular bars serve inspired cocktails made from local ingredients.

Craft Beers

While lighter Mexican brews have traditionally been the beers of choice in the hot climate of Southwest USA, there's a booming craft beer scene throughout the region that suits beer lovers of all stripes. Try a Serrano Seduction, a wheat beer with chiles from Dillinger Brewing in Tucson *(www.dillinger brewing.com)* or the equally spicy El Heffe (hefeveizen with roasted peppers) from Banger Brewing in Las Vegas *(www.bangerbrewing.com)*.

←

The tap room of Dillinger Brewing Company micro-brewery in Tucson

↑ Sparkling wines, made at the New Mexico-based Gruet winery

Southwest Wine
Sonoita Vineyards *(www.sonitavineyards. com)* in Arizona has received national recognition for its Pinot Noir and Cabernet wines. Among New Mexico's 60 wineries, the Gruet winery *(www.gruetwinery.com)* is known for its excellent sparkling wines.

↑ Pure agave tequilas being poured for a bar tasting

TOP 3 BARS FOR SOUTHWEST DRINKS

Barrio Café
w barriocafe.com
Over 300 tequilas and a range of margaritas are served at this Phoenix venue.

Lon's Last Drop Bar
w hermosainn.com
The bar at the Hermosa Inn in Paradise Valley creates superb cocktails with Southwest-made spirits and ingredients from its kitchen garden.

El Pinto
w elpinto.com
The Tequila Bar at this acclaimed New Mexican restaurant features more than 160 blue agave tequilas and 35 different mezcals.

Tequila Tasting
Discover the subtleties of this popular Mexican spirit, served widely in Southwest USA. The Cabo Wabo Cantina in Planet Hollywood in Las Vegas *(p257)* offers tasting flights of its own brand tequila, while 89Agave restaurant in Sedona *(www. 89agave.com)* stocks 89 tequilas with several tasting options. At Santa Fe's La Fonda on the Plaza hotel *(p195)*, the La Fiesta Lounge serves flights of tequila and mezcal.

Adobe Architecture

The traditional building material of the Southwestern desert is adobe, a mixture of mud or clay and sand, with straw or grass as a binder. It's formed into bricks that harden in the sun; they are then built into walls, cemented with a similar material, and plastered over with more mud. Modern adobe-style buildings ("fauxdobe") often substitute cement for mud, and are painted to look like adobe.

←

Typical burnt-orange adobe exterior of a traditional building

SOUTHWEST USA'S
ARCHITECTURE

Across the Southwest, you'll see historic adobe buildings in many old town districts. Other popular architectural styles include Spanish Colonial and Mission Revival, while wooden storefronts, Victorian mansions, and miners' cottages lend an additional rustic charm to many mountain towns.

Into the Future

The Southwest's wide open spaces have given visionary architects room to design some remarkable eco-friendly dwellings, such as the Biosphere 2 *(p113)* in Southern Arizona and Paolo Soleri's Arcosanti *(p84)*. Just outside Taos *(p202)*, a community of 70 "Earthships" uses upcycled materials to build artistic and sustainable homes.

The light-filled expanse of a building in Taliesin West

Did You Know?

Adobe (meaning "sun-dried brick") needs to be replastered every couple of years.

Frank Lloyd Wright

Perhaps the USA's leading architect, Frank Lloyd Wright (1867-1959) practiced in the Southwest. Wright's "organic architecture" advocated the use of local materials and the importance of the setting. Visit his architectural complex at Taliesin West *(p97)* to see a key example of his work. It was built from desert stones and sand, and the expansive proportions reflect the Arizona desert.

Revival Residences

In the 17th and 18th centuries, Spanish Colonial missions combined the Baroque style of Mexican and European religious architecture with indigenous design. The early 20th-century Mission Revival style is similiar in spirit, characterized by stucco walls made of white lime cement, often with graceful arches and flat roofs. A fine example is the 1906 J. Knox Corbett House in Tucson's Historic District *(p102)*.

← The 1929 Old Pima County Courthouse, with its distinctive Mission Revival style

↑ The striking design of Arcosanti, an eco-housing project

Ancient Dwellings

The Southwest is peppered with cliff dwellings, built by the Ancestral Puebloans *(p176)* around AD 750-1300. Some of the best can be viewed in Mesa Verde National Park *(p172)* or the Canyon de Chelly National Monument *(p164)*.

↑ Long House, a key cliff dwelling at Wetherill Mesa in Mesa Verde National Park

45

The Navajo

Covering more than 25,000 sq miles (64,750 sq km) in New Mexico, Arizona, and southern Utah, the Navajo Nation is the largest reservation in the Southwest. Its spiritual center is Canyon de Chelly *(p164)*, but the terrain of Monument Valley Tribal Park *(p160)* is also sacred, with some areas accessible only with a Navajo guide.

←

Three Navajo sisters, pictured in Monument Valley Tribal Park

SOUTHWEST USA'S
INDIGENOUS CULTURES

Meeting indigenous peoples and exploring their rich heritage is one of the highlights of a visit to the Southwest. There are more than 50 Native American reservations in the region, offering insight into the history of the peoples, while feast days and local arts and crafts provide a window into their cultures.

HOPI SPIRITUALITY

The Hopi are the only Pueblo tribe in Arizona. They have cultivated the arid, rocky land that today makes up the Hopi Reservation *(p178)* for over a millennium. Deeply religious, the Hopi's ceremonies focus on kachina spirit figures that symbolize all forms of nature. These are represented by intricately carved wooden dolls and ceremonial kachina dancers.

The Pueblo Peoples

New Mexico's 19 Pueblo tribes share religious and cultural beliefs, but speak five different languages. Most trace their lineage to the Ancestral Puebloans who once lived at Mesa Verde *(p172)*, Chaco Canyon *(p168)*, and other sites in the Southwest. Most pueblos produce distinctive arts and crafts, and tourism is an important source of income. Among the most visited are Taos Pueblo *(p206)*, with its multistoried dwellings, and Acoma Pueblo with its sweeping views *(p232)*.

→

Members of a Pueblo tribe in Acoma, New Mexico in the early 1900s

Ceremonial Dancing

Native American ceremonies often include spectacular displays of drumming, dancing, and traditional costumes. These take place during tribal feast day celebrations (often open to visitors) or at powwows such as the Gathering of Nations, when tribes meet from around the country *(p55)*.

←

A tribal member performing a Native American ceremonial dance in Santa Fe

> 🔍 HIDDEN GEM
> ### Amerind Foundation
> This fascinating museum in Southern Arizona *(p117)* houses an exquisite collection of Native American artifacts. Regular programs give insights into the culture of these tribal communities today.

The Tohono O'odham

Along with their close relatives, the Pima people, the Tohono O'odham live in Southern Arizona's Sonoran Desert. Due to the harsh nature of the environment here, neither tribe has ever been moved off its ancestral lands. Today, the Tohono O'odham are largely Christian – the mission church of San Xavier del Bac *(p110)* is on Tohono O'odham land south of Tucson.

→

The white walls of San Xavier del Bac Mission, on the Tohono O'odham Nation San Xavier Indian Reservation

Arts and Crafts

Each tribal community has an artistic heritage that dates back centuries. Look for beautiful woven baskets, silver jewelry inlaid with precious stones, colorful textiles, and pottery with traditional motifs. Good places to buy crafts include museum shops, and in pueblos, markets, or reservations, where you can buy directly from the artists.

←

Native American pottery, featuring traditional patterns

▽ The Coen Brothers

Well aware of the power provided by the vast backdrops of the Southwest, the Coen Brothers shot their second film, *Raising Arizona* (1987), in lively Tempe *(p100)*. One of their biggest hits, *No Country for Old Men* (2007), was filmed in New Mexico around the small town of Las Vegas, where the sparse landscapes made a perfect setting for this atmospheric cowboy noir.

△ Beyond the Western

They may be synonymous with the Southwest, but Westerns aren't the only genre filmed in New Mexico's diverse landscapes. Over 240 films and TV series have been made here. A Movie Trails map from Santa Fe's tourist office *(p192)* will help you track down locations.

SOUTHWEST USA
ON SCREEN

The Southwest's red rock formations have played a starring role in countless Hollywood movies, while many hit TV series were made at Old Tucson Studios. From the wide spaces of New Mexico to the mystical landscapes of Utah's national parks, the region continues to attract award-winning productions.

△ Red Rocks

Spectacular canyons are a natural draw for filmmakers. *The Space Between Us* (2017) used the red rocks of Southern Utah to stand in for Mars. *The Lone Ranger* (2013) was largely filmed in Monument Valley.

▽ The Wild West's Golden Age

Stagecoach (1939) director John Ford's first movie in Monument Valley *(p160)* so enthralled audiences that it brought the Western back into vogue and made the young John Wayne a star. Ford brought the grandeur of the West to the big screen, and ignited a "studio stampede" of directors keen to utilize the beauty of the area.

▷ Breaking Bad Making Good

The groundbreaking TV series *Breaking Bad* (2008–13) put Albuquerque *(p222)* and Northern New Mexico firmly on the movie map. Despite the controversial subject matter, the show, which some critics called the best TV series of all time, still draws visitors to see the city and the surrounding dramatic desert landscapes. You can even book tours with Breaking Bad RV Tours *(www.breaking badrvtours.com)*.

◁ Bright Lights, Big City

The glittering casinos and lavish resorts of Las Vegas and its arid surroundings have landed the city a starring role in many a Hollywood blockbuster. *Jason Bourne* (2016) had an exciting car chase right along The Strip *(p252)*, while sequences in *Now You See Me* (2013) were filmed at the MGM Grand *(p255)*. Morgan Freeman starred alongside Michael Douglas, Kevin Kline, and Robert de Niro in *Las Vegas* (2013), which featured such locations as the Aria *(p256)* and Binion's *(p266)*.

Whitewater Thrills

The Green, San Juan, and Colorado rivers are among the world's top destinations for whitewater rafting. These rivers run fast and deep, offering white-knuckle rides through breathtaking canyons. The dams along the Colorado River have created huge recreation areas where you can relax after your trip.

←

A team taking on Lava Falls on the Colorado River, which runs through the Grand Canyon

SOUTHWEST USA FOR
THE GREAT OUTDOORS

The unrivaled landscapes of the Southwest are made for outdoor adventures. Tramp along hiking trails deep into the backcountry, soar down ski runs under sunny blue skies, or plunge into exhilarating whitewater. The Southwest is also one of the best areas in the USA for golfing.

By the Boots

The best way to soak up the scenery of the Southwest is on foot. State and national parks have excellent, well-marked trails of varying difficulty, from easy day hikes to challenging wilderness routes for hardy backpackers. Check out ranger-led hikes for fascinating insights into the local wildlife and environment.

A family of hikers on the Emerald Pools Trail through Zion Canyon ↑

Did You Know?

New Mexico's diverse landscapes mean you can ski in the morning and golf in the afternoon.

Hit the Slopes

There's superb skiing to be had in the mountains of the Southwest. Head for the black diamond runs of chic Telluride *(p180)*, or the world-class pistes of Santa Fe Ski Area *(p199)* and Taos Ski Valley *(p207)*. For cross-country skiers, the Arizona Snowbowl *(p79)* near Flagstaff is a deservedly popular spot.

→

A skier spraying up powder on the slopes of Telluride, Colorado

On the Greens

With more than 300 golf courses in Arizona alone, the Southwest is a golfer's paradise. This is particularly true of Southern Arizona with its year-round warm weather. Scottsdale *(p96)* is considered to be America's premier golf spot, while Tucson *(p102)* is also a putter's paradise. New Mexico, too, has excellent courses and affordable greens fees.

←

Oak Creek Country Club golf course in Sedona, Arizona, overlooked by red rock formations

Off-Road Rides

Those who like their thrills behind a wheel will enjoy this region. Moab *(p146)* is one of the top centers for off-road drivers. Canyonlands National Park *(p122)* and Sedona's *(p76)* red-rock canyons are other top spots. Monument Valley *(p160)* is a prime location for 4WD tours, often led by Navajo guides.

→

A Jeep traveling the Shafer Trail Road in Canyonlands National Park

◁ Arts and Crafts

Hispanic folk art often combines religious belief with artistic expression, such as in the carved, painted wooden figures of saints, known as *bultos* and *santos*. Bold ceramics and tin decorations are also popular. The latter originated in Mexico, where tin was a cheap substitute for silver, and are cut into shapes and punched with designs or brightly painted.

SOUTHWEST USA'S
HISPANIC CULTURE

Hispanic culture is a vivid thread in the tapestry of the Southwest. The merging of Spanish traditions brought by missionaries and the Mexican culture from across the border has brought colorful, joyful accents to music, art, festivals, and everyday life throughout the region.

MARIACHI RECORDINGS

Singer Linda Ronstadt produced two Grammy-winning albums of mariachi songs from her Tucson childhood: *Canciones de mi Padre (Songs of my Father, 1987)* and 1991's *Mas Canciones (More Songs.)*

△ Red-Hot Ristras

Colorful garlands of dried red chiles are known as chile *ristras*. They make delightful decorations, and you'll see them throughout New Mexico. They can be bought as an unusual souvenir at markets in Santa Fe *(p192)* and in Hatch, where most chiles are grown.

▽ Let There Be Light

One of the most beautiful and moving sights in the Southwest is the decoration of walls and buildings with hundreds of *luminarias*. Also called *farolitos*, these simple ornaments consist of a candle set in sand in a paper bag, but they create a warm and wondrous atmosphere. They are often displayed during religious festivals, especially in the build-up to Christmas.

△ Colorful Celebrations

Vibrant fiestas showcase Hispanic culture at its liveliest. These celebrations take place throughout the year, particularly on saints' days or at the annual Cinco de Mayo *(p54)* festivities. There's Mexican music, traditional dance performances, festive foods such as tamales, and fun activities for all the family.

▷ Heating up the Hornos

Hornos are unusual outdoor ovens made of mud and adobe in the shape of a beehive, and are used for baking bread. They were originally introduced in Spain by the Moors, and in turn the Spanish missionaries and settlers brought them to the Southwest USA, where they were also adopted by Native Americans. They are still used today, and you can see demonstrations at El Rancho de las Golondrinas *(p196)* in Santa Fe.

△ Mariachi Music

You're bound to hear a mariachi band on your visit to the Southwest. This lively style of music comes from Mexico, and the musicians play trumpets, violins, and traditional Mexican instruments such as the *guitarrón* (base guitar).

A YEAR IN
SOUTHWEST USA

The Southwest's stunning landscapes form the backdrop to an exciting range of events. Spring craft fairs give way to summer music festivals and winter sports events, while celebrations of cowboy culture and Native American heritage are sprinkled throughout the year.

Spring

With sunny skies, balmy temperatures, and blooming cacti, spring is the perfect time to visit the desert. Events blossom across the area: browse for treasures at craft fairs and Native American markets, sample traditional dishes at local food festivals, or hear your favorite authors speak at the Tucson Festival of Books. Spring also sees colorful Cinco de Mayo festivities take place across the area, while cities such as Las Vegas celebrate their cowboy past with parades and concerts.

Flowers carpeting the desert near Phoenix, Arizona

Summer

Desert temperatures soar during summer – when they get too hot, head for higher ground and the sounds of music. Telluride hosts outdoor bluegrass and jazz festivals beneath its Rocky Mountain peaks, Taos features chamber music concerts under

CINCO DE MAYO

The Cinco de Mayo (May 5) is a vibrant celebration of Mexican-American culture. It commemorates the triumph of the smaller Mexican army over invading French forces at the Battle of Puebla in 1862. Expect bright traditional costumes, lively music and dancing, delicious food, parades, and fireworks.

the stars, and the Santa Fe Opera stages productions in its outdoor arena. On July 4, the Wild West comes alive in northern Arizona at Prescott Frontier Days, the world's oldest rodeo.

Musicians performing at the Telluride Bluegrass Festival

Fall

Fall is all about eye-catching colors. The forests of the Four Corners region and northern Arizona begin to turn brilliant orange and gold, and, further south in southern Mexico, September's Hatch Chile Festival sees the annual harvest of multicolored chiles take place. In October, meanwhile, hundreds of brightly colored hot-air balloons fill the skies at the International Balloon Fiesta in Albuquerque.

Multicolored hot-air balloons at Albuquerque's International Balloon Fiesta

Winter

As winter draws in, thousands of migrating birds descend on wildlife refuges in southern New Mexico and Arizona. Then, as Christmas approaches, traditional *luminarias* (paper lanterns) light up the region's cities and towns. When snow begins to fall, locals hit the slopes at ski resorts near Flagstaff, Santa Fe, Taos, and Telluride, before heading to the prestigious Phoenix Open golf tournament in the New Year.

Luminarias *decorating the* Santuario de Chimayó *and* (inset) *birds at a wildlife refuge in Arizona*

TOP 3 ARTS AND CRAFT MARKETS

Heard Museum Guild Indian Fair and Market
Arts and crafts by hundreds of indigenous artisans are showcased during March at this renowned art museum.

Roosevelt Row
Downtown Phoenix's hip arts district offers a monthly arts market dedicated to fine art, handmade crafts, and vintage items.

Santa Fe Indian Market
Taking place in August, this celebrated event features exquisite jewelry and traditional crafts by Native American artists from across North America.

3

4

A BRIEF
HISTORY

Ever since the arrival of the first nomadic people in prehistoric times, diverse immigrants have made the Southwest their home. Native American tribes, Hispanic colonizers, Mormon communities, and Anglo-American settlers have given this desert landscape a rich, multicultural heritage.

Ancient Cultures

The earliest known people in the Southwest were the nomadic Clovis culture in New Mexico around 10,000 BC. By AD 100 three dominant cultures had emerged – the Hohokam, Mogollon, and Ancestral Puebloans (also called Anasazi). The Hohokam farmers of southcentral Arizona, forefathers of today's Tohono O'odham and Pima peoples, created sophisticated irrigation systems in the desert. In southern New Mexico, the Mogollon developed distinctive pottery, particularly in the Mimbres Valley. The Ancestral Puebloans lived in extended family groups, first in below-ground pithouses and later in elaborate

1 A 19th-century engraving showing Pueblo peoples dancing.

2 Illustration of Ancestral Puebloans carrying water pots.

3 Painting re-creating life in an ancient cliff dwelling.

4 Coronado's expedition to the Southwest.

Timeline of events

800 BC
Corn is brought to the Southwest from Mexico and agriculture begins.

200 BC–AD 1400
Ancestral Puebloan culture in Four Corners region; Mogollon culture in southwestern New Mexico and southeastern Arizona.

1020
Chaco Canyon is at its height as a trading and cultural center.

10,000–8,000 BC
The nomadic Clovis people hunt in New Mexico.

300 BC–AD 1400
Hohokam civilization in southcentral Arizona.

56

pueblos and cliff dwellings in the Four Corners region. These ancient cultures reached their height between 800 and 1250. Large pueblos with round ceremonial chambers called kivas were built at Chaco Canyon and Mesa Verde. But by 1400 these ancient sites were mysteriously abandoned. It is thought the people migrated to new pueblos along the Rio Grande, where their descendants live today. Between 1100 and 1500, the Navajo, who were primarily hunters, and the Apache, who were skillful warriors, arrived in the Southwest from their native homelands, Canada and Alaska.

The Arrival of the Spanish

Driven by dreams of gold and the desire to convert the indigenous population to Christianity, the Franciscan priest Fray Marcos de Niza led the first Spanish expedition into the Southwest in 1539. A year later, Francisco Vázquez de Coronado returned with soldiers and livestock, overwhelming the trading center of Zuni Pueblo. His treatment of the people was brutal, sacking homes and burning villages, as he spent two years searching in vain for the fabled riches of the Seven Cities of Cíbola.

↑ The painting *Black Knife, an Apache Warrior* by John Mix Stanley (1846)

1150
Acoma Pueblo and Hopi Mesa villages are established.

c 1250
Many ancient sites are mysteriously abandoned; new pueblos are established along Rio Grande.

1400
The Navajo and Apache migrate from Canada to the Southwest.

1539
The Spanish make their first expedition to the Southwest, headed by Fray Marcos de Niza.

1540–42
Francisco Vázquez de Coronado leads a search for gold in New Mexico.

The Colony of New Mexico

Not finding riches, the Spanish lost interest in this region until conquistador and explorer Juan de Oñate established the colony of New Mexico in 1598. It stretched into Arizona, parts of Colorado, and Utah and beyond. Under Governor Don Pedro de Peralta, Santa Fe became the capital in 1610. Colonists seized farmlands and created huge ranches for themselves, the Puebloans resisted, and bloody battles ensued. Rising up in the Pueblo Revolt of 1680, they drove the settlers south across the Rio Grande. But in 1692, Don Diego de Vargas reclaimed Santa Fe, and the Spanish extended their reach in the Southwest throughout the next century.

Anglo-American Settlement

In 1803, Napoleon sold the vast Louisiana Territory to the United States, bringing its border to New Mexico. After a long war, Mexico declared independence from Spain in 1821. That same year, William Becknell led traders from Missouri along the Santa Fe Trail. Wagon trains followed. By the 1840s, the United States had embarked on a vigorous expansion westward. As

THE MISSIONS

In the late 17th century, Jesuit missionary and explorer Father Eusebio Kino brought beef livestock and seeds for wheat crops to the Pima people of Southern Arizona to help them diversify their agriculture. By the time he died in 1711, he had established a number of missions across the area, including the churches at Tumacácori (p114) and San Xavier del Bac (p110).

Timeline of events

1598
Juan de Oñate founds a permanent colony in New Mexico.

1680
The Pueblo Revolt.

1803
The Louisiana Purchase extends US boundaries to the New Mexico border.

1810–21
Mexican War of Independence.

1846–48
The Mexican War; Treaty of Guadalupe-Hidalgo cedes Mexican territory to US.

3

Anglo settlers encroached on Mexican lands, war broke out in 1846. Two years later, most of the Southwest and California was ceded to the US for $18.25 million in the Treaty of Guadalupe-Hidalgo. The Gadsden Purchase of 1854 brought Southern Arizona into the fold. Meanwhile, Mormon pioneers built settlements in southern Utah and Las Vegas.

Ranchers and Miners

After the Civil War (1861–5), Anglo settlement of the West rapidly increased. Rich lodes of gold, silver, and copper were discovered, and boomtowns flourished at Tombstone, Jerome, Bisbee, and Silver City. In Colorado, the towns of Silverton, Ouray, and Telluride also grew up around the mining industry. Vast areas of the Southwest became huge cattle and sheep ranches. "Range wars" between farmers and ranchers were common, such as the Lincoln County War (1878 81), known for its infamous protagonist Billy the Kid. As Anglo ranchers seized land, the New Mexicans' tradition of communal land use was overturned and many indigenous farmers lost their livelihoods.

1 Conquistador and explorer Juan de Oñate.

2 Anglo-American settlers journeying westward in the 19th century.

3 Miners in the Southwest in the 19th century.

Did You Know?

Tubac Presidio was the first Spanish settlement built in Arizona in 1752.

1861–5
US Civil War.

1854
The US acquires Southern Arizona with the Gadsden Purchase.

1869
John Wesley Powell leads an expedition on the Colorado River through the Grand Canyon.

1868
Navajo Reservation established in the Four Corners region.

1877
Copper found at Bisbee, Arizona; silver discovered at Tombstone, Arizona.

The Long Walk

Native Americans suffered as the government set about clearing more land for settlers. In 1864, more than 8,000 Navajo were forced from their lands and made to march "The Long Walk" of 400 miles (644 km) to a reservation in New Mexico. Many died en route. The Chiricahua Apache continued to fight against forced settlement until the surrender of their leader, Geronimo, in 1886.

The End of the Frontier

By the 1880s, four major railroads crossed the region, bringing new Anglo settlers in search of prosperity. They came believing it was their destiny to expand across the continent and exploit its resources. New industries emerged. The opening of the Grand Canyon Railroad in 1901 brought tourists, and national parks were declared at Mesa Verde, Zion, and Bryce Canyon.

The Atomic Age

The legacy of World War II changed the economic course of the Southwest. Military research and its industrial offshoots led to a post-war population boom. New Mexico's remote desert areas

1 Navajo peoples in the 19th century.

2 Santa Fe Railroad.

3 A Virgin Galactic space shuttle flying over Spaceport America.

4 Phoenix's skyline, Arizona.

Did You Know?

Trinity was the code name for the first detonation of a nuclear weapon.

Timeline of events

1886
American Indian Wars end with the surrender of Geronimo.

1889
Phoenix becomes the territorial capital of Arizona.

1901
Grand Canyon Railroad opens, bringing tourists to the region.

1912
New Mexico and Arizona become the 47th and 48th states of the Union.

1917
The US enters World War I.

provided secret research, development, and testing sites for the atomic bomb at Los Alamos and the Trinity test site southeast of Socorro. The Southwest also became a major center for space travel. In 1982, Space Shuttle Columbia landed at White Sands Space Harbor, and the base for the first commercial space flights, Spaceport America, was built in 2011 near Las Cruces.

The Southwest Today

The Southwest continues to be a major center for defense research and development and space travel. In 2018, the Phoenix and Las Vegas metropolitan areas ranked among the nation's fastest-growing cities. Water supply remains a serious issue in the region, as does the growing number of migrants seeking entry to the US across the Mexican border. Meanwhile, tourists visit the region's cities and beauty spots in ever-increasing numbers. The national parks encourage a heightened awareness of indigenous cultures and conservation issues, which will help guard the Southwest's precious heritage for generations to come.

WATER SUPPLY

Enormous dams were built to channel water to the burgeoning cities of the Southwest. Hoover Dam was completed in 1936, the tallest dam in the country at the time, but soon even that proved inadequate. In 1963, Glen Canyon Dam created the huge reservoir of Lake Powell, flooding permanently an area of great beauty and destroying ancient Native American ruins.

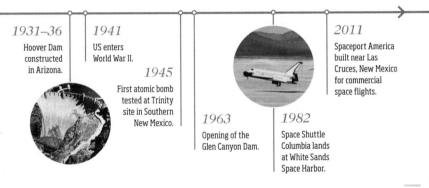

1931–36
Hoover Dam constructed in Arizona.

1941
US enters World War II.

1945
First atomic bomb tested at Trinity site in Southern New Mexico.

1963
Opening of the Glen Canyon Dam.

1982
Space Shuttle Columbia lands at White Sands Space Harbor.

2011
Spaceport America built near Las Cruces, New Mexico for commercial space flights.

EXPERIENCE

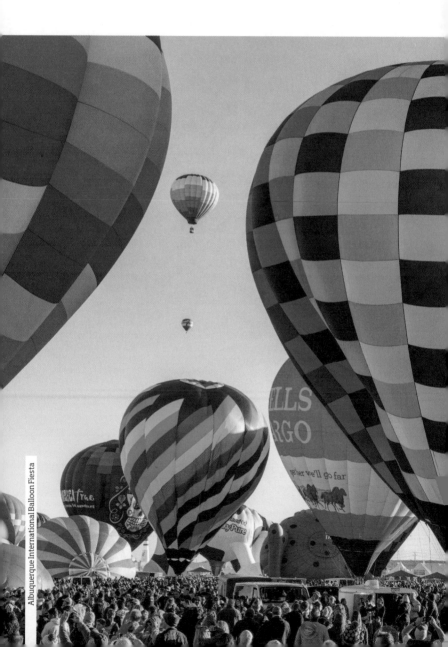

Albuquerque International Balloon Fiesta

GRAND CANYON AND NORTHERN ARIZONA

For most people, Northern Arizona is famous as the location of the Grand Canyon, a gorge of breathtaking proportions carved out of rock by the Colorado River as it flows southwest across the state towards the Gulf of Mexico.

The Grand Canyon forms just a part of the high desert landscape of the Colorado Plateau, with its sagebrush and amazingly colored rock formations. Here you'll find the lively city of Flagstaff as well as for the charming towns of Sedona and Jerome. This region is also dotted with fascinating mining ghost towns such as Chloride and Oatman, a reminder that Arizona won its nickname, the Copper State, from the mineral mining boom that took place in the first half of the 20th century.

More than 25 percent of Arizona is Native American reservation land. The state is also home to several centuries-old Puebloan ruins, most notably the hilltop village of Tuzigoot and the hillside remains of Montezuma Castle.

GRAND CANYON AND NORTHERN ARIZONA

Must Sees
1 Grand Canyon National Park
2 Sedona

Experience More
3 Flagstaff
4 Wupatki National Monument
5 Oak Creek Canyon
6 Sunset Crater Volcano National Monument
7 Walnut Canyon National Monument
8 Williams

9 Lake Havasu City
10 Montezuma Castle National Monument
11 Jerome
12 Grand Canyon Skywalk/ Grand Canyon West
13 Prescott
14 Tuzigoot National Monument
15 Arcosanti
16 White Mountains
17 Meteor Crater
18 Petrified Forest National Park

Grand Staircase-Escalante National Monument

Lake Powell

Wahweap

Marble Canyon

Page

Colorado River

THE FOUR CORNERS *p156*

Cameron

Kykotsmovi Village

Keams Canyon

Gray Mountain

GRAND CANYON AND NORTHERN ARIZONA

HOPI RESERVATION

4 WUPATKI NATIONAL MONUMENT

Dilkon

Houck

6 SUNSET CRATER VOLCANO NATIONAL MONUMENT

Sanders

FLAGSTAFF **3**

7 WALNUT CANYON NATIONAL MONUMENT

17 METEOR CRATER

OAK CREEK CANYON **5**

Joseph City

18 PETRIFIED FOREST NATIONAL PARK

2 SEDONA

Holbrook

A R I Z O N A

Volcanic Mountain 5,958 ft (1,816 m)

10 MONTEZUMA CASTLE NATIONAL MONUMENT

Snowflake

St Johns

Zeniff

Taylor

PHOENIX AND SOUTHERN ARIZONA *p88*

Kohls Ranch

Payson

Apache-Sitgreaves National Forest

Show Low

Young

Pinetop-Lakeside

WHITE MOUNTAINS

16

Tonto Basin

Theodore Roosevelt Lake

FORT APACHE RESERVATION

ALBUQUERQUE AND SOUTHERN NEW MEXICO *p218*

Mesa

Claypool

0 kilometers 40

0 miles 40

N

1

GRAND CANYON NATIONAL PARK

⚑B3-C4 ✈ 🚌From Williams 🚌From Flagstaff and Williams 🕐South Rim: year-round daily; North Rim: mid-May-mid-Oct daily 🌐ps.gov/grca

One of the world's great natural wonders, the Grand Canyon offers awe-inspiring beauty on a vast scale and is an instantly recognizable symbol of the Southwest. Its beauty is revealed in the ever-shifting patterns of light and shadow and the colors of the rock, bleached white at midday, but bathed in red and ocher at sunset.

An iconic World Heritage Site, the Grand Canyon National Park covers 1,904 sq miles (4,930 sq km) and is made up of the canyon itself, which starts where the Paria river empties into the Colorado, and surrounding lands that stretch from Lees Ferry to Lake Mead (p268). The area gained national park status in 1919. The park has two main entrances, on the North and South rims of the canyon. The southern section of the park receives the most visitors and can become very congested during the summer season. Visitors can park in nearby Tusayan and take a free shuttle bus to the South Rim.

The canyon is 277 miles (446 km) long, an average of 10 miles (16 km) wide, and around 5,000 ft (1,500 m) deep. It was formed over a period of six million years by the Colorado River, whose

> **GREAT VIEW**
> **Hopi Point**
>
> Projecting far into the canyon, the tip of Hopi Point offers one of the best spots for viewing sunsets along Hermit Road. As the sun sets, it highlights the canyon's many beautiful sculpted peaks.

↑ A ranger leading tourists on a mule ride along the narrow trails of the South Rim

HERMIT ROAD

Running from Grand Canyon Village west to Hermits Rest, this 7-mile (11-km) road follows the canyon rim and provides some of the best canyon views from anywhere. It is closed to all private vehicles from March through November, when a free shuttle bus takes visitors between eight stunning overlooks along the way, including Trailview Overlook, Maricopa Point, and Hopi Point. You can also walk between the viewpoints on the Rim Trail, and catch the shuttle at any time. Hermit Road is also a great cycle route.

fast-flowing waters sliced their way through the Colorado Plateau, which includes the gorge and most of northern Arizona and the Four Corners region. The plateau's geological vagaries have defined the river's twisted course and exposed vast cliffs and pinnacles that are ringed by rocks of different color, variegated hues of limestone, sandstone, and shale (p74). The magnificent rock formations with towers, cliffs, steep walls, and buttes recede as far as the eye can see, their bands of rock varying in shade, as light changes through the day. The park's main roads, Hermit Road and Desert's View Drive, start at Grand Canyon Village and encompass a selection of the choicest views of the gorge. Walking trails along the North and South rims offer staggering views, but to experience the canyon at its most fascinating, explore the more challenging trails that lead to the canyon floor.

Did You Know?

The temperature at Grand Canyon varies by about 20° F (11° C) from top to bottom.

↑ Rock formations of the Grand Canyon with the Colorado River at sunset

The South Rim

Most of the Grand Canyon's 6.3 million annual visitors come to the South Rim, since, unlike the North Rim, it is open year-round and is easily accessible along Highway 180/64 from Flagstaff or Williams. Hermit Road (p69) is closed to private vehicles from March to November, but there are free shuttle buses. The longer Desert View Drive (Highway 64) is open all year, winter snows permitting, and leads 60 miles (97 km) in the opposite direction to Cameron. After winding for 12 miles (20 km) from Grand Canyon Village it reaches Grandview Point, where the Spaniards may have had their first glimpse of the canyon in 1540. Ten miles (16 km) farther on lie the pueblo remains of Tusayan Ruin, where a small museum has exhibits on the Ancestral Puebloans. After a few miles, the road leads to Desert View with a fanciful Watchtower, its upper floor decorated with early 20th-century Hopi murals. It was designed by ex-schoolteacher and trained architect Mary E.J. Colter, who drew on Native American and Hispanic styles and is responsible for many of the historic structures that grace the South Rim, including the 1914 Lookout Studio and Hermits Rest, and the rustic 1922 Phantom Ranch on the canyon floor.

Did You Know?

Kolb Studio, the former home of the Kolb brothers, exhibits their stunning photos of the Grand Canyon.

The North Rim

Sited at about 8,000 ft (2,400 m), the North Rim is higher, cooler, and greener than the South Rim, with dense forests of ponderosa pine, aspen, and Douglas fir. Visitors are likely to spot wildlife, such as mule deer, Kaibab squirrel, and wild turkey. The North Rim is reached via Highway 67, off Highway 89A, ending at Grand Canyon Lodge, where there is a campground, a gas station, a restaurant, and a general store.

STAY

El Tovar
With a perfect location right on the canyon rim, this luxurious landmark lodge, built in 1905, incorporates natural stone and Douglas fir. The restaurant serves excellent Southwestern cuisine.

🏠 1 El Tovar Rd
🌐 grandcanyon lodges.com

$$$

Bright Angel Lodge
The famed architect Mary Elizabeth Jane Colter designed this rustic, log-and-stone lodge and cabins in 1935. Accommodations range from basic lodge rooms to historic cabins with fireplace and TV.

🏠 9 North Village Loop Dr
🌐 grandcanyon lodges.com

$$$

←

The Lookout Studio, also known as the Lookout, on the South Rim

↑ Wotans Throne,
seen from Cape Royal
on the North Rim

The North Rim is twice as far from the river as the South Rim, and the canyon really stretches out from the overlooks giving a sense of its massive width. There are about 30 miles (48 km) of scenic roads, as well as hiking trails to high viewpoints or down to the canyon floor (of particular note is the North Kaibab Trail that links to the South Rim's Bright Angel Trail.) The picturesque Cape Royal Drive starts north of Grand Canyon Lodge and travels 23 miles (37 km) to Cape Royal on the Walhalla Plateau. From here, several famous buttes and peaks can be seen, including Wotans Throne and Vishnu Temple. There are also several short, easy walking trails around Cape Royal. A 3-mile (5-km) detour leads to Point Imperial, the highest point on the canyon rim, while along the way the Vista Encantada has delightful views and picnic tables overlooking the gorge.

The Bright Angel Trail

The most popular of all Grand Canyon hiking trails, the Bright Angel trail begins near the Kolb Studio at the western end of Grand Canyon Village on the South Rim. It then continues via a series of switchbacks down the side of the canyon for 9 miles (14 km). The trail crosses the river over a suspension bridge, ending a little further on at Phantom Ranch. Do not attempt to walk all the way to the river and back in one day. Temperatures at the bottom of the canyon can reach 110° F (43° C) or higher during the summer. It is essential for day hikers to carry plenty of water and salty snacks in summer.

CALIFORNIA CONDORS

The California Condor is America's largest bird, with a wingspan of over 9 ft (2.7 m). The species was on the edge of extinction in the 1980s, when the last 22 condors were captured for breeding in captivity. In 1996 the first captive-bred birds were released in Northern Arizona. Today, over 80 condors fly the skies over Northern Arizona. They are frequent visitors to the South Rim, though visitors should not approach or feed them.

EXPLORING GRAND CANYON NATIONAL PARK

The park's main roads, Hermit Road and Desert View Drive, both accessible from the south entrance, overlook the canyon. Stop at the excellent visitor center at the south entrance, where you can pick up detailed maps of drive routes and hiking trails, see a video-enabled relief map, study exhibits of artifacts, and rent a bike or book a guided bike ride. Grand Canyon Village is located on the South Rim and offers a wide range of hotels, restaurants, and stores. It is also the starting point for most of the mule trips through the canyon and the terminus for the vintage Grand Canyon Railway from Williams. Visitors can also enter the park from the north, although this route (Highway 67) is closed during winter. The Bright Angel Trail on the South Rim and the North Kaibab Trail on the North Rim descend to the canyon floor and are tough hikes involving an overnight stop.

North Rim Entrance Station

Kaibab Plateau

67

Perched above the canyon at Bright Angel Point, the **Grand Canyon Lodge** *has rooms and a number of dining options.*

67

North Rim Visitors Center

Grand Canyon Lodge

Crystal Creek

Point Sublime
7,459 ft
(2,274 m)

Granite Gorge

Shiva Temple

Bright Angel Creek

Bright Angel Trail *starts from the South Rim. It is well maintained but demanding.*

Isis Temple

Diana Temple

Colorado River

Phantom Ranch
2,400 ft (730 m)

Bright Angel Canyon

Hoppy Point

BRIGHT ANGEL TRAIL

Hermits Rest

Yavapai Point

Hermit Road

Grand Canyon Village

Grand Canyon Visitors Center

Yaki Point

DESERT VIEW DRIVE

64

Situated 5 miles (8 km) north of the canyon's South Entrance, along a stretch of the Rim Trail, is **Yavapai Point**. *Its observation station offers stunning views of the canyon, and a viewing panel identifies the central canyon's main landmarks.*

Grand Canyon National Park Airport Tusayan

↑ A hiker on the Bright Angel Trail in winter

At 8,803-ft (2,683-m) high, **Point Imperial** is the highest point on the North Rim and offers views of Mount Hayden and the Painted Desert (p85).

→

Point Imperial, the highest overlook on the North Rim

Point Imperial
8,803 ft
(2,683 m)

Nankoweap Creek

Colorado River

Vista
Encantada

Kwagunt Creek

Kwagunt
Butte

Atoko Point

Chuar
Butte

*Walhalla
Plateau*

Grand Canyon

Little
Colorado River

National Park

Cape Solitude
6,135 ft
(1,870 m)

Walhalla
Overlook

Colorado River

roaster
emple

Cape Royal

Venus Temple

Comanche
Point

The uniquely shaped rock formation known as **Wotans Throne** lies closer to the North Rim, but can be seen from both sides of the canyon.

Wotans Throne

Vishnu Temple

Granite Gorge

Cardenas Butte

Horseshoe Mesa

Lipan Point

Desert View
Visitors Center

Desert View Drive connects Grand Canyon Village with Desert View and offers breathtaking views of both the central and eastern canyon.

Moran Point

DESERT VIEW DR

64

Grandview
Point

64

Tusayan
Ruin

0 kilometers   5
0 miles   5

N
↑

Tusayan Ruin was a pueblo abandoned by the Ancestral Puebloans around 1150. The Tusayan Museum now sits next to the site.

At 7,400 ft (2,250 m), **Grandview Point** is one of the highest places on the South Rim. It is one of the stops along Desert View Drive (p70).

THE GEOLOGY OF THE GRAND CANYON

The Grand Canyon's multicolored layers of rock provide the best record of the Earth's formation anywhere in the world. Each stratum of rock reveals a different period in the Earth's geologic history beginning with the earliest, the Precambrian era, which covers geologic time up to 570 million years ago. Almost two billion years of history have been recorded in the canyon, although the most dramatic changes took place relatively recently, five to six million years ago, when the Colorado River began to carve its path through the canyon walls. The sloping nature of the Kaibab Plateau has led to increased erosion in some parts of the canyon.

THE ASYMMETRICAL CANYON

The North Rim of Grand Canyon is more eroded than the South Rim. The entire Kaibab Plateau slopes to the south, so rain falling at the North Rim flows toward the canyon and over the rim, creating deep side canyons and a wide space between the rim and the river.

HOW THE CANYON WAS FORMED

While the Colorado River accounts for the canyon's depth, its width and formations are the work of even greater forces. Wind rushing through the canyon erodes the limestone and sandstone a few grains at a time. Rain pouring over the canyon rim cuts deep side canyons through the softer rock. Perhaps the greatest canyon-building force is ice. Water from rain and snowmelt works into cracks in the rock. When frozen, it expands, forcing the rock away from the canyon walls. The layers vary in hardness. Soft layers erode quickly into sloped faces. Harder rock resists erosion, leaving sheer vertical faces.

RECORD OF LIFE

The fossils found in each layer tell the story of the development of life on Earth. One of the oldest layers in the canyon, the Vishnu Schist, was formed in the Proterozoic era, when the first bacteria and algae were just emerging. Many of the layers were created by billions of small marine creatures, whose hard shells eventually built up into thick layers of limestone.

The North Rim, with the Colorado River running through the canyon ↑

↑ The spectacular cliffs and pinnacles of the Grand Canyon's beautiful South Rim

THE COLORADO RIVER

About five million years ago the Colorado River changed its course. According to one theory, it joined with another, smaller river that flowed through the Kaibab Plateau. The force of the combined waters carved out the deep Grand Canyon. The South Rim of the canyon lies closer to the Colorado River than to the North Rim.

Did You Know?

The three main types of sedimentary rocks at the Grand Canyon are sandstone, shale, and limestone.

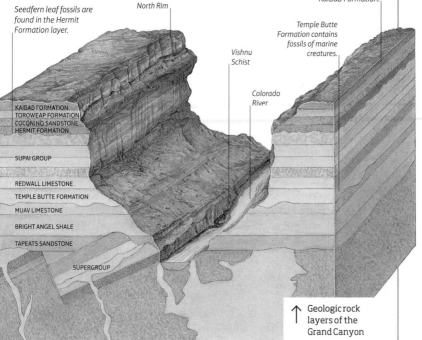

Fish plate fossils are found in the Kaibab Formation.

Seedfern leaf fossils are found in the Hermit Formation layer.

North Rim

Temple Butte Formation contains fossils of marine creatures.

Vishnu Schist

Colorado River

KAIBAB FORMATION
TOROWEAP FORMATION
COCONINO SANDSTONE
HERMIT FORMATION

SUPAI GROUP

REDWALL LIMESTONE

TEMPLE BUTTE FORMATION

MUAV LIMESTONE

BRIGHT ANGEL SHALE

TAPEATS SANDSTONE

SUPERGROUP

↑ Geologic rock layers of the Grand Canyon

SEDONA

⚠ C4   ℹ 331 Forest Rd; www.visitsedona.com

Sedona sits amid the magnificent red-rock cliffs and canyons south of Flagstaff. Its awesome scenery has formed the backdrop for dozens of Hollywood Westerns, but the town shot to fame in the 1980s when psychics identified "vortexes" in the area, which they believed emanated electromagnetic energies that invigorate the soul, and it became a spiritual destination for upscale New Agers.

Today Sedona is so popular that parking in uptown, which is lined with boutiques, art galleries, restaurants, and tourist shops, can be a challenge. The real attraction, however, is the breath-taking landscape surrounding the town. Head through West Sedona on Highway 89A to reach Red Rock State Park and the Red Rock Loop Road, where a gentle, wooded stretch of Oak Creek offers hikes and lovely picnic spots. Or drive south along the Red Rock Scenic Byway (Highway 179) to access stunning landmarks such as the Chapel of the Holy Cross, Bell Rock, Courthouse Butte, and Cathedral Rock. The wealth of activities includes relaxing spas, jeep tours, backcountry hikes, mountain biking, horseback riding, and hot-air balloon rides. Sedona Trolley tours take in highlights of the town and surroundings.

SPIRITUAL SEDONA

The Red Rock Country around Sedona is said to be full of mystical "vortexes". These are swirling centers of energy, where the earth's cosmic forces are especially strong and conducive to healing, meditation, and spiritual practices. Four major vortexes are located at Bell Rock, Airport Mesa, Cathedral Rock, and Boynton Canyon. Each is said to emanate its own particular energy, attracting people seeking enlightenment.

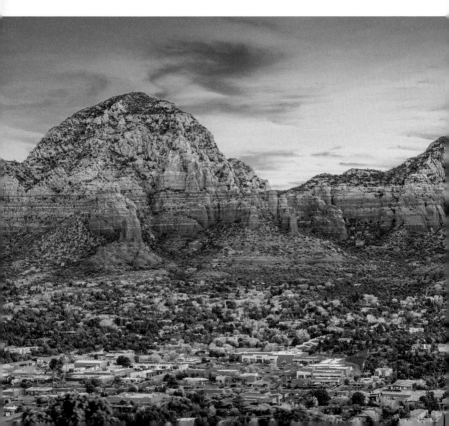

Giant dinosaur skull in front of a New Age shop in Sedona

Drive south along the Red Rock Scenic Byway (Highway 179) to access landmarks such as the Chapel of the Holy Cross or Bell Rock.

The town of Sedona sitting amid striking red-rock cliffs

Chapel of the Holy Cross

△ This Roman Catholic chapel, built into the buttes of Sedona in 1957, was commissioned by local sculptor Marguerite Brunswig Staude.

Bell Rock

Resembling a giant red bell, this butte is a key landmark just north of Oak Creek Village, south of Sedona. The rock is claimed by some to be a "vortex" - a center of spiritual energy.

Cathedral Rock

▷ About 2 miles (3 km) south of Uptown Sedona, this sandstone rock is one of the most photographed formations in the area. The climb to the top along a steep trail is somewhat challenging, but worth the effort for the breathtaking views.

Courthouse Butte

Just east of Bell Rock, this butte can easily be viewed up close due to its proximity to the road and is one of Sedona's most beautiful rock formations.

Snoopy Rock

Named for the *Peanuts* character Snoopy, this rock resembles his reclining profile. It is visible from Uptown Sedona - you will find a good view of it anywhere from Main Street, where there are shops, restaurants, and galleries.

Uptown Sedona

▷ With its many art galleries (there are at least 40), shops selling crystals, fossils, and jewelry, and spa facilities, the town of Sedona is the perfect place to unwind.

EXPERIENCE MORE

❸
Flagstaff

🅰C4 ✈Pulliam, 4 miles (6 km) S of town 🚆Amtrak Flagstaff, 1 E Route 66 🚌800 E Butler Ave ℹ️Amtrak depot, 1 E Route 66; www.flagstaff arizona.org

Nestled deep among the pine forests of Northern Arizona's San Francisco Peaks, Flagstaff is a lively, easy-going town with a maze of old red-brick buildings that make up its compact downtown. Flagstaff's first permanent settlers were sheep ranchers, who arrived in 1876. The railroad came in 1882, and the town quickly developed as a lumber center. Flagstaff is the home of Northern Arizona University and is a good base for visiting the Grand Canyon's South Rim, just under two hours' drive away. The surrounding mountains attract hikers in summer and skiers in winter.

Just ten minutes' walk from end to end, Flagstaff's historic downtown dates mainly from the end of the 19th century. Many buildings sport decorative stone and stucco friezes and are occupied by cafés, bars, and stores. There are several standout pieces of architecture, particularly the Babbitt Building and the 1926 train station that today houses the visitor center. Perhaps the most attractive is the Weatherford Hotel, which opened in 1900, and has a sunroom and a grand wraparound veranda.

> **Just ten minutes' walk from end to end, Flagstaff's historic downtown dates mainly from the end of the 19th century.**

Did You Know?

Flagstaff is situated within the world's largest ponderosa pine forest.

Atop a hill about a mile (2 km) northwest of the town center, the **Lowell Observatory**, founded in 1894, is named for its benefactor, Percival Lowell, a member of one of Boston's wealthiest families. He financed the observatory to look for life on Mars and chose the town because of its high altitude and clear mountain air. The Lowell Observatory went on to establish an international reputation by documenting evidence of the expansion of the universe. One of its astronomers, Clyde Tombaugh, discovered Pluto in February 1930. The observatory continues to build upon this legacy today. Visitors have access to the main rotunda, the exhibition halls, and the John Vickers McAllister Space Theater, which shows presentations on the night sky and current research at Lowell. Tours are available daily, and telescope viewings nightly.

Flagstaff's lively café society owes much to the 22,000 or so students of **Northern Arizona University** (NAU), just southwest of downtown. NAU has green lawns, stately trees, and several historic buildings. There are two campus art galleries: the Beasley Gallery in the Fine Art Building, housing temporary exhibitions and student work, and the Old

→

The wraparound veranda of the iconic Weatherford Hotel in downtown Flagstaff

Main Art Museum and Gallery in the Old Main Building, which features the permanent Weiss collection, including works by the Mexican artist Diego Rivera.

Located a little south of the university is the grandiose **Riordan Mansion State Historic Park**, which was built in the 1880s by brothers Michael and Timothy Riordan, wealthy lumber merchants. The 40-room log mansion has a rustic, timber-clad exterior and two wings (one for each brother) containing arts and crafts furniture.

A little north of downtown is Flagstaff's **Pioneer Museum**, occupying an elegant stone building, which was originally a hospital in 1908. On display in the grounds are a 1929 steam locomotive and a Santa Fe Railroad caboose. Inside, a particular highlight is a selection of Grand Canyon photographs taken in the early 1900s by photographers Ellsworth and Emery Kolb.

The **Museum of Northern Arizona**, a little farther north of the Pioneer Museum, holds significant collections of Southwestern artifacts, as well as fine art and natural science exhibits. The Archaeology Gallery is a good introduction

← The huge telescope inside the main rotunda of the Lowell Observatory

to the region's history, while the Ethnology Gallery documents some 12,000 years of Native American culture on the Colorado Plateau. Exhibits on the plants and animals found in the region through the ages are displayed in the courtyard.

Just 7 miles (11 km) north of town, the **Arizona Snowbowl** offers downhill skiing. The San Francisco Peaks receive an average of 260 inches (660 cm) of snow every year, enough to supply the ski runs that pattern the lower slopes of the Agassiz Peak. In summer, there is a hiking trail up to the peak. For those less inclined to walk, the Arizona Scenic Chairlift offers great views of the scenery.

Lowell Observatory
🌐 📷 🏛 1400 W Mars Hill Rd 🕐 10am-10pm Mon-Sat, 10am-5pm Sun 🅦 lowell.edu

Northern Arizona University
🏛 620 S Knoles Dr 🅦 nau.edu

Riordan Mansion State Historic Park
🌐 🎫 🏛 🚻 409 W Riordan Rd 🕐 May-Oct: 9:30am-5pm; Nov-Apr: 10:30am-5pm Thu-Mon 🅦 azstateparks.com

Pioneer Museum
🌐 🏛 🚻 2340 N Fort Valley Rd 🕐 9am-5pm Mon-Sat (Sep-May: 10am-4pm), 10am-4pm Sun 🅦 arizonahistorical society.org

Museum of Northern Arizona
🌐 🏛 🚻 3101 N Fort Valley Rd 🕐 10am-5pm Mon-Sat, noon-5pm Sun 🅦 musnaz.org

Arizona Snowbowl
🏛 Snowbowl Rd 🅦 arizonasnow bowl.com

EAT

Downtown Diner
Car license plates, hubcaps, and photos of local landscapes line the walls of this archetypal diner, a neighborhood favorite for breakfast. The impressive lunch menu includes giant burgers and fresh trout.

🅐C4 🏛 7 E Aspen Ave ☎ (928) 774-3492

$$$

Black Bart's Steakhouse
A family-owned hangout named after a notorious 1870s stagecoach robber, Black Bart's serves high-quality corn-fed steaks and fresh seafood. A musical revue of Disney and Broadway songs is performed by the staff every evening.

🅐C4 🏛 2760 E Butler Ave 🕐 Lunch 🅦 blackbartssteak house.com

$$$

4

Wupatki National Monument

🅰 C4 **🚗 Hwy 545 off Hwy 89 at mile marker 444, Flagstaff** **🚂🚌 Flagstaff** **🗓 Dec 25** **🌐 nps.gov/wupa**

Covering more than 56 sq miles (145 sq km) of sun-scorched wilderness to the north of the city of Flagstaff, the Wupatki National Monument incorporates about 2,700 historic sites once inhabited by the Sinagua, ancestors of the Hopi people.

The area was first settled after the eruption of Sunset Crater in 1064. The Sinagua people, a pre-Columbian culture, and their Ancestral Puebloan cousins realized that the volcanic ash had made the soil more fertile and consequently favorable for farming. The power of the volcanic eruption may also have appealed to their spirituality. They left the region in the early 13th century, but no one really knows why (p176). The largest site here is the Wupatki Pueblo consisting of red sandstone structures built in the 12th century around a natural rock outcrop amid miles of prairie overlooking the desert. Once a four-story pueblo complex of 100 rooms, housing more than 100 Sinagua, it was a meeting place where different cultures traded goods. A trail explores the remains of the buildings, including a kiva. The most unusual structure is a Central American-style ballcourt. It is believed that the Sinagua may have used this to play at dropping a ball through a stone ring without using hands or feet.

5

Oak Creek Canyon

🅰 C4 **ℹ (800) 288-7336 or (928) 203-2900**

Just south of Flagstaff, Highway 89A weaves a charming route, which makes for a very pleasant drive through Oak Creek Canyon on the way to the town of Sedona (p76). In the canyon, dense woods shadow the road, and the steep cliffs are colored in bands of red and yellow sandstone, pale limestone, and black basalt. This is a popular summer vacation area crisscrossed by many day-hiking trails, including the East Pocket Trail, a steep wooded climb to the canyon rim. At nearby Slide Rock State Park, containing an apple farm and one of the USA's top swimming holes, visitors can enjoy sliding over the red rocks that form a natural water chute – a great way to cool off.

TRAIL RIDES

Saddle up for a ride among the saguaros and experience Arizona like a cowboy. Ranches throughout the state offer trail rides for all ages and levels. You can even stay at a ranch. Tanque Verde Ranch in Tucson offers lessons, trail rides, barbecues, and other activities. At rustic ranches like Sprucedale Guest Ranch in the White Mountains you can join an authentic horse or cattle drive.

↑ Visitors resting by a stream in Slide Rock State Park, near Oak Creek Canyon

↑ Hiking through the ashy landscape of Sunset Crater Volcano National Monument

followed by a spur track to the Grand Canyon's South Rim in 1901, Williams became established as a tourist center. By the late 1920s, it was also a popular rest stop on Route 66 (p28).

Today, the town retains its frontier atmosphere, complete with Stetson-wearing locals. Here you can step back in time to the heyday of Route 66. Visitors can explore more than six blocks of historic buildings, many containing interesting shops and art galleries. Most hotels and diners are arranged around a loop that follows Route 66 on one side and its replacement, Interstate Highway 40, on the other. Traditional diners evoke the 1950s and are filled with Route 66 memorabilia, including original soda fountains, posters, and car license plates.

 6

Sunset Crater Volcano National Monument

🅰C4 🚗Hwy 545 off Hwy 89 at mile marker 430, 6082 Sunset Crater Rd 🚉🚌Flagstaff ⏰Sunrise-sunset daily 🚫Dec 25 & Jan 1 🌐nps.gov/sucr

In 1064, a volcanic eruption formed the 400-ft- (122-m-) deep Sunset Crater, leaving a cinder cone overlooking the surrounding lava field. The one-mile (1.6-km) self-guided Lava Trail offers a stroll around the ashy landscape with its lava tubes, bubbles, and vents.

 7

Walnut Canyon National Monument

🅰C4 🚗Hwy I-40, exit 204 🚉🚌Flagstaff ⏰9am-5pm daily (Jun-Oct: 8am-5pm) 🚫Dec 25 🌐nps.gov/waca

Located about 10 miles (16 km) east of Flagstaff, off Interstate Highway 40, Walnut Canyon houses an intriguing collection of cliff dwellings.

These were inhabited by the Sinagua, in the 12th and 13th centuries. The Sinagua were attracted to the canyon by its fertile soil and plentiful water from nearby Walnut Creek.

Today, visitors can tour 25 cliff dwellings huddled underneath the natural overhangs of the canyon's eroded sandstone and limestone walls. The Sinagua left the canyon abruptly early in the 13th century, possibly as a result of war, drought, or disease (p176). Sinagua artifacts are on display in the Walnut Canyon Visitor Center.

8

Williams

🅰C4 🚂 🛈200 W Railroad Ave; www.experience williams.com

This distinctive little town was named in 1851 for Bill Williams (1787–1849), a legendary mountain man and trapper who lived for a time with the Osage tribe in Missouri. The town grew up around the railroad that arrived in the 1880s, and when this was

EAT

Twisters Soda Fountain & The Route 66 Place
With a black-and-white checkerboard floor and vinyl chairs, Twisters has a 1950s vibe. On the menu are burgers, chili dogs, and banana splits.

🅰C4 🚗417 E Route 66, Williams 🚫Sun 🌐route66place.com

$$$$$$$$$

Goldies Route 66 Diner
Sip coffee at the counter with the regulars or choose a booth and enjoy classic diner fare such as burgers, fries, and tuna melts.

🅰C4 🚗425 E Route 66, Williams 📞(928) 635-4466

$$$$$$$$$

← Hot-air balloons flying over London Bridge in Lake Havasu City

⑨ Lake Havasu City

🅰B5 �️ 🚌 ℹ314 London Bridge Rd; www.golake havasu.com

California businessman Robert McCulloch founded Lake Havasu City in 1964. The resort city he built on the Colorado River was popular with the landlocked citizens of Arizona. However, his real brainwave came four years later, when he bought London Bridge and transported it from England to Lake Havasu. Some mocked McCulloch, suggesting that he had thought he was buying London's Gothic Tower Bridge, not this much more ordinary one. There was more hilarity when it appeared that there was nothing in Havasu City for the bridge to span. Undaunted, McCulloch simply created the waterway he needed. Today this is one of Arizona's most popular areas for outdoor recreation.

⑩ Montezuma Castle National Monument

🅰C4/5 🚗Hwy I-17, exit 289 🕐8am–5pm daily 🌐nps. gov/moca

Dating from the 1100s, the pueblo remains that make up Montezuma Castle occupy an idyllic location, built into the limestone cliffs high above Beaver Creek, a few miles to the east of Interstate Highway 17. Once home to the Sinagua people, this cliff dwelling originally contained 20 rooms spread over five floors. Montezuma Castle was declared a National Monument in 1906 to preserve its condition. The visitor center has a display on Sinaguan life and is found at the start of a trail along Beaver Creek, with views of the ruins.

The National Monument also incorporates Montezuma Well, situated about 11 miles (18 km) to the northeast. This natural sinkhole, 50 ft (15 m) deep and 470 ft (143 m) in diameter, had great religious significance for the Native Americans, with several tribes believing it was the site of the Creation. Over 1,000 US gallons (3,785 liters) of water flow through the sinkhole every minute, an inexhaustible supply that has long been used to

> 💬 INSIDER TIP
> **Hualapai Legacy Pass**
>
> Three viewpoints and transportation on the hop-on-hop-off shuttle service are included in the basic entry pass to Grand Canyon West. There is an additional fee for the Skywalk.

irrigate the surrounding land. A narrow trail leads around the rim before twisting its way down to the water's edge.

⑪ Jerome

🅰C4 ℹ310 Hull Avenue, Jerome; www.jerome chamber.com

Approached from the east along Highway 89A, Jerome is easy to spot in the distance, its old brick buildings perched high above the valley, clinging to the steep slopes of Cleopatra Hill. Silver mining began here in the 1870s, but the boom times really started in 1912, when the first big vein was discovered, and continued as the price of copper exploded during World War I. The Wall Street Crash of 1929 brought things to a halt, although the mines limped along until 1953. To make matters worse, underground dynamiting had made the area unstable, and the town began to slide downhill at a rate of 4 inches (10 cm) a year. By the early 1960s, Jerome had become virtually a ghost town. However, its fortunes were revived by an

→ The Grand Canyon Skywalk, suspended over the Colorado River at Grand Canyon West

influx of artists and artisans. Today Jerome is busy with day trippers who come to see the late 19th- and early-20th-century brick buildings that make up the town's historic center, and enjoy its art galleries, coffeehouses, and restaurants.

Grand Canyon Skywalk/Grand Canyon West

⊞B3 **🕓8am–6pm daily (to 7pm in summer)**
ⓦgrandcanyonwest.com

The Grand Canyon Skywalk – a 70-ft (21-m) glass walkway cantilevered beyond the rim and 4,000 ft (1,220 m) above the floor of the Grand Canyon – is managed by the Hualapai tribe. Located near their modest resort, the Hualapai Ranch, the Skywalk and Grand Canyon West are situated much closer to Las Vegas than to the famous South Rim of the canyon (p72), which is nearly 250 miles

(402 km) away by road. All-inclusive package tours can be booked from Las Vegas – most visitors fly – and on site. Tours include demonstrations of cowboy skills, horseback riding, helicopter flights, and pontoon boat rides on the Colorado River, in addition to the Skywalk itself. A Native American Village features re-created dwellings of the Hualapai and three other Arizona tribes. Native American cultural performances and presenta-tions are put on daily in the village's amphitheater. A shuttle bus operates within the Grand Canyon West area, as no private vehicles are permitted.

Prescott

❓B5 **🏠117 W Goodwin St**
ⓦvisit-prescott.com

Founded in 1864 as Arizona's first territorial capital, Prescott was a boisterous frontier town of farmers, ranchers, gold miners, and adventurers. In its

historic downtown lies Whiskey Row, whose characterful buildings once housed saloons. The street is still known for its bars, and also has galleries, shops, hotels, and restaurants.

Nearby, you'll find the **Sharlot Hall Museum**, which details Prescott's pioneer history, and the **Museum of Indigenous People**, which displays a variety of artifacts. There's also the **Phippen Museum**, showcasing the art and heritage of the American West.

Prescott's higher elevation and surrounding lakes and forests make it ideal for hiking, kayaking, and other outdoor activities. The Peavine National Recreation Trail follows a former rail bed through the Granite Dells, a landscape of giant, rippled boulders.

Sharlot Hall Museum
⊛⊛ 🏠 415 W Gurley St
ⓦsharlothallmuseum.org

Museum of Indigenous People
⊛ 🏠 147 N Arizona Ave
ⓦmuseumofindigenouspeople.org

Phippen Museum
⊛⊛ 🏠 4701 Hwy 89 N
ⓦphippenartmuseum.org.

> **Tours include demonstrations of cowboy skills, horseback riding, helicopter flights, and pontoon boat rides on the Colorado River, in addition to the Skywalk itself.**

14

Tuzigoot National Monument

📍 C4 🚗 Follow signs from Hwy 89 past Cottonwood 🕐 8am–5pm daily 🚫 Dec 25 🌐 nps.gov/tuzi

Set on a slender limestone ridge, the Tuzigoot National Monument ruins offer splendid views of the Verde River Valley. The pueblo was built by the Sinagua people between the 12th and 15th centuries and, at its peak, had a population of around 300. It was later abandoned in the early 15th century, when it is believed the Sinagua migrated north to join the Ancestral Puebloans.

Tuzigoot was partly rebuilt by a local and federally funded program in the 1930s. This emphasized one of the most unusual features of pueblo building, the lack of doorways. The normal pueblo room was entered by ladder through a small hatchway in the roof. Sinaguan artifacts and art are on display at the visitor center.

15

Arcosanti

📍 C5 🏠 13555 S Cross L Rd, Mayer 🕐 10am–4pm daily 🌐 arcosanti.org

Italian architect Paolo Soleri (1919–2013) established this educational housing project in 1970 to test his concept of "arcology." Combining architecture and ecology, it aims to reduce urban sprawl and human impact on the environment while improving quality of life. Residents live in structures that combine work and leisure space. You can see the striking architecture and learn about the ethos behind it on a guided tour. Tours, workshops, and overnight stays are also available.

16

White Mountains

📍 D5

Rising over 11,000 ft (3,353 m) high, the White Mountains of east-central Arizona are often overlooked by visitors. For Arizonans, this region of cool ponderosa pines, lakes, and reservoirs is a popular escape from the summer heat, and a top area for outdoor activities. **Fool Hollow Lake Recreation Area** offers fishing, camping, and swimming.

The White Mountain Trail System, with loop trails of varying lengths, takes hikers, horse riders, and mountain bikers through beautiful stretches of forest. It begins near the village of **Pinetop-Lakeside**, a tourism hub. Snowflake and Show Low, both on the trail route,

> **Did You Know?**
>
> US-60 offers a scenic drive from Show Low to Globe along winding roads above Salt River Canyon.

↑ The distinctive structures of Arcosanti, balancing architecture and ecology

↑ A visitor taking in the vast scale of the Meteor Crater from the rim

also have restaurants and accommodations. Sunrise Park Resort is a winter playground for skiers and snowboarders.

From Pinetop-Lakeside, head east on SR 260 past lakes, forests, and meadows beneath the slopes of Mount Baldy (11,409 ft/3,477 m), the state's second-highest peak. Watch for pronghorn, deer, elk, bighorn sheep, and wolves.

Fool Hollow Lake Recreation Area
♿ 🏕 ⏰ 5am–10pm daily
🌐 azstateparks.com

Pinetop-Lakeside
🚹 102-C W White Mountain Blvd, Lakeside 🌐 pinetop lakesidechamber.com

Meteor Crater

🅰 C4I ⏰ Off Hwy I-40, exit 233 ⏰ Jun–Aug: 7am–7pm daily; Sep–May: 8am–5pm daily 🗓 Dec 25
🌐 meteorcrater.com

The Barringer Meteor Crater, a meteorite impact crater, was formed nearly 50,000 years ago. The crater is 550 ft (167 m) deep and 2.4 miles (4 km) in circumference, and so closely resembles a moon crater that NASA astronauts trained

here in the 1960s. Guided rim tours are available, and the visitor center tells the story of the crater through exhibits and a film.

Petrified Forest National Park

🅰 D4 ⏰ Off Hwy 180
⏰ Times vary, check website 🗓 Dec 25
🌐 nps.gov/pefo

This national park is one of Arizona's most unusual attractions. Millions of years ago rivers swept trees downstream Into a vast swamp that once covered this area. Groundwater transported silica dioxide into downed timber, eventually turning it into the quartz stone logs seen today, with colored crystals preserving the trees' shape and structure. Running the length of the forest is the Painted Desert, an area of colored bands of sand and rock changing from blues to reds as light catches mineral deposits.

From the Painted Desert Visitor Center, a road travels the length of the park. There are nine overlooks on the route, including Kachina Point, where the Painted Desert Wilderness trailhead is located.

The **Rainbow Forest Museum** is by the south end of the road.

Rainbow Forest Museum
♿ 🚹 (928) 524-6228
⏰ Times vary, call ahead
🗓 Dec 25

STAY

Hon Dah Resort-Casino & Conference Center
Owned by the White Mountain Apache tribe, this resort has a heated pool, restaurant, spa, and live entertainment.

🅰 D5 ⏰ 777 Hwy 260, Pinetop
🌐 hon-dah.com

$ $ $

La Posada Hotel
This former railroad hotel resembling a Spanish hacienda was a retreat for stars like Bob Hope and John Wayne.

🅰 C4 ⏰ 303 E Route 66, Winslow
🌐 laposada.org

$ $ $

A DRIVING TOUR
HEART OF ARIZONA LOOP

Distance 85 miles (137 km) **Recommended route** From Sedona, take Hwy 89A to Tuzigoot, Jerome, and Prescott. Hwy 69 runs east from Prescott to the I-17, which connects to Camp Verde, Fort Verde, and Montezuma Castle

The Verde River passes through the wooded hills and fertile meadows of central Arizona before opening into a wide, green valley between Flagstaff and Phoenix. The heart of Arizona is full of charming towns such as Sedona, hidden away among stunning scenery, and the former mining town of Jerome. Over the hills lies Prescott, once the state capital and now a busy, attractive little town with a center full of dignified Victorian buildings. The area's ancient history can be seen in its two beautiful pueblo ruins, Montezuma Castle and Tuzigoot.

*A popular relic of Arizona's mining boom, **Jerome** (p92) is known for its 1900s brick buildings that cling to the slopes of Cleopatra Hill.*

*The charming historic town of **Prescott** (p83) is set among the rugged peaks and lush woods of Prescott National Forest, making it a popular center for many outdoor activities.*

Jerome

Willow Creek Reservoir

89A

Prescott Valley

Watson Lake

Prescott Forest

89

69

Yavapai Hills

169

Prescott

Dewey-Humboldt

69

0 kilometers 10

0 miles 10

N ↑

← A mining shaft in Jerome, a leading former copper mining town, founded in 1876

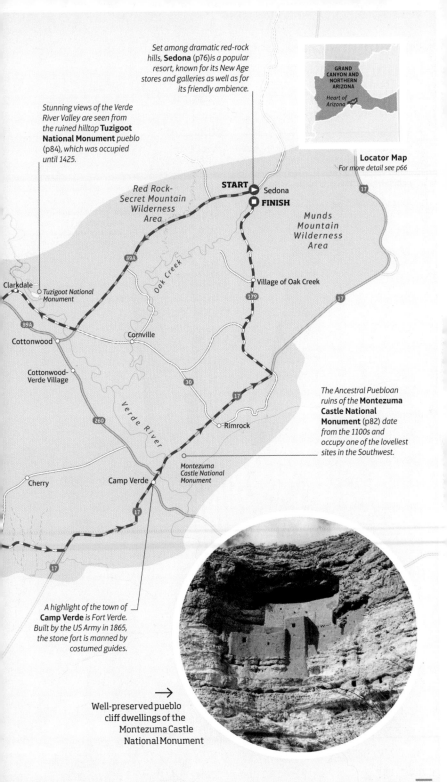

Set among dramatic red-rock hills, **Sedona** (p76) is a popular resort, known for its New Age stores and galleries as well as for its friendly ambience.

Locator Map
For more detail see p66

GRAND CANYON AND NORTHERN ARIZONA

Heart of Arizona

Stunning views of the Verde River Valley are seen from the ruined hilltop **Tuzigoot National Monument** pueblo (p84), which was occupied until 1425.

Red Rock-Secret Mountain Wilderness Area

START Sedona

FINISH

Munds Mountain Wilderness Area

Oak Creek

89A

Clarkdale   Tuzigoot National Monument

Village of Oak Creek

179

89A

Cornville

Cottonwood

30

17

Cottonwood-Verde Village

Rimrock

260

Verde River

The Ancestral Puebloan ruins of the **Montezuma Castle National Monument** (p82) date from the 1100s and occupy one of the loveliest sites in the Southwest.

Cherry   Camp Verde

Montezuma Castle National Monument

17

17

A highlight of the town of **Camp Verde** is Fort Verde. Built by the US Army in 1865, the stone fort is manned by costumed guides.

→ Well-preserved pueblo cliff dwellings of the Montezuma Castle National Monument

PHOENIX AND SOUTHERN ARIZONA

The land in Southern Arizona was first farmed around 400 BC by the Hohokam people, who carefully used the meager water supplies to irrigate their crops. When the Spanish settled here in the 18th century, they built fortified outposts throughout the region. This Hispanic heritage is recalled by the beautiful mission churches of San Xavier del Bac and Tumacácori, and in the popular historic city of Tucson, which grew up around the 1776 Spanish fort.

When silver was discovered nearby in the 1870s, the scene was set for a decade of rowdy frontier life. Today, towns such as Tombstone, famous for the Gunfight at the OK Corral, re-create this Wild-West era. The influx of miners also spurred the growth of Phoenix, a farming town established on the banks of the Salt River in the 1860s. Phoenix is now the largest city in the Southwest, known for its warm winter climate and recreational attractions.

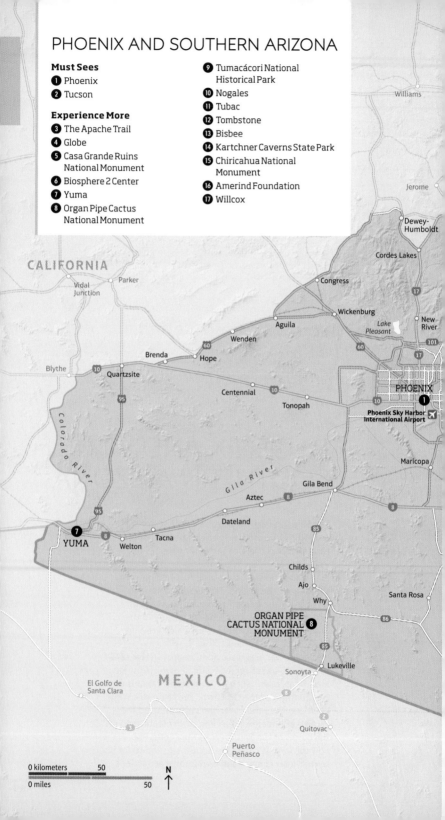

PHOENIX AND SOUTHERN ARIZONA

Must Sees

1. Phoenix
2. Tucson

Experience More

3. The Apache Trail
4. Globe
5. Casa Grande Ruins National Monument
6. Biosphere 2 Center
7. Yuma
8. Organ Pipe Cactus National Monument
9. Tumacácori National Historical Park
10. Nogales
11. Tubac
12. Tombstone
13. Bisbee
14. Kartchner Caverns State Park
15. Chiricahua National Monument
16. Amerind Foundation
17. Willcox

CALIFORNIA

Williams

Jerome

Dewey-Humboldt

Cordes Lakes

Congress

Vidal Junction

Parker

Wickenburg

New River

Aguila

Lake Pleasant

Wenden

Blythe

Quartzite

Brenda

Hope

PHOENIX

Centennial

Tonopah

Phoenix Sky Harbor International Airport

1

Colorado River

Gila River

Maricopa

Gila Bend

Aztec

Dateland

YUMA

7

Welton

Tacna

Childs

Ajo

Santa Rosa

Why

El Golfo de Santa Clara

ORGAN PIPE CACTUS NATIONAL MONUMENT

8

Lukeville

Sonoyta

MEXICO

Quitovac

Puerto Peñasco

0 kilometers   50

0 miles   50

N

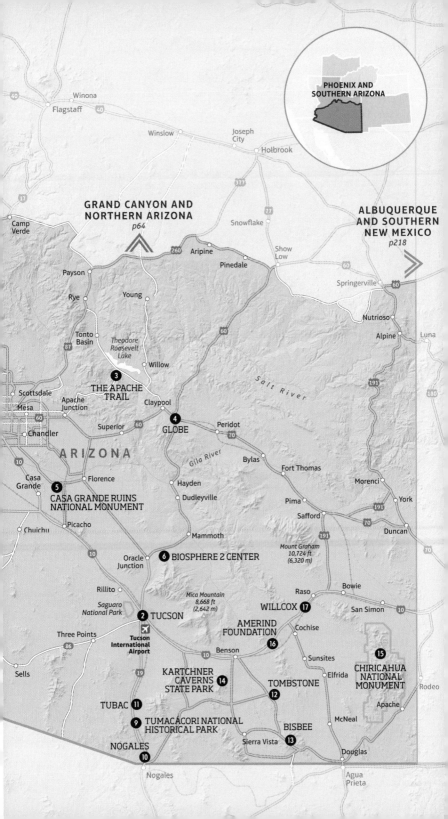

❶

PHOENIX

🅰C5 🛫2.5 miles (4 km) E of downtown 🚌2115 E Buckeye Rd 🛈125 North 2nd St; www.visitphoenix.com

Phoenix is a huge metropolis, stretching across the Salt River Valley. Farmers and ranchers settled here in the 1860s, and by 1912 the city had developed into the political and economic focus of Arizona, becoming the state capital. As it grew, it absorbed surrounding towns, although each district still maintains its identity. Downtown Phoenix is home to many historic attractions, including Heritage Square and the Heard Museum.

① 🖥 🏛

Arizona Capitol Museum

🏛1700 West Washington St 🕒9am–4pm Mon–Fri (Sep–May: also 10am–2pm Sat) 🚫Public hols 🌐azlibrary.gov/azcm

Completed in 1900, the Arizona Capitol houses the legislative and executive branches of the state government, as well as the museum. Spread over four stories, the museum covers the region's political, social, economic, and cultural history using high-tech and traditional displays.

② 🎨 🖥 🏛

Children's Museum of Phoenix

🏛215 N 7th St 🕒9am–4pm Tue–Sun 🌐childrens museumofphoenix.org

This is not so much a museum as a wonderful indoor play-ground designed for kids up to the age of ten. Kids can run, build, and learn freely in a safe environment. Highlights include hands-on art activities, a room designed for fort-building, and a forest made of bright green and orange noodles. There is a special area for children under three years of age.

③ 🍴 🖥 🏛

Roosevelt Row

🌐rooseveltrow.org

Affectionately known as RoRo, this earthy arts district, which neighbors downtown Phoenix to the north, lies between 7th Avenue and 12th Street with Roosevelt Street at its heart. The formerly run-down houses and abandoned buildings have been transformed by artists into colorful galleries and studios. There is also a range of eateries, and you can find every kind of shop from chic to grungy. Stroll around and you'll see vibrant murals at almost every turn (you can download a map from the website). Celebrities such as

← Cityscape of downtown Phoenix against a mountain backdrop at dusk

Billie Holliday and Marilyn Monroe compete for wall space with skeletons, rainbows, boxers, giant roosters, and all manner of graffiti. A great time to visit is during downtown's First Friday Art Walk or RoRo's Third Friday events (both open 6–11pm), when museums and galleries do not charge an entrance fee and stay open until late. These events include an arts market with local handmade crafts, Hot Box Galleries with art exhibitions by cutting-edge artists set in pop-up shipping containers, street performers, food stalls, and live music.

Must See

STAY

The Wigwam Resort
Opened in 1929, this sprawling adobe-and-timber complex is set in lush grounds and offers elegant suites and casitas. It also has a luxurious spa, four pools, three restaurants, two bars, and three championship golf courses.

🏠 300 E Wigwam Blvd, Litchfield Park
Ⓦ wigwamarizona.com
Ⓢ Ⓢ Ⓢ

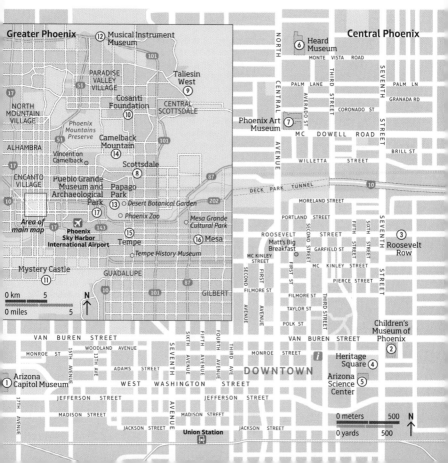

④
Heritage Square

📍 115 N 6th St
🌐 heritagesquarephx.org

Phoenix is a thoroughly modern city, which grew rapidly after World War II. Many of its older buildings did not survive this expansion. However, a few late 19th- and early 20th-century buildings remain, and the most interesting of these are found on tree-lined Heritage Square, which also has numerous cafés and restaurants, and makes for a pleasant stroll. Rosson House, a handsome wooden mansion on Monroe Street, dates from 1895 and has a wraparound veranda and distinctive hexagonal turret. Visitors may tour the house, which is furnished in period style (call 602 262-5070). Next door is the Burgess Carriage House, constructed in an

expansive colonial style rare in the Southwest. The 1900 Silva House features exhibits detailing Arizona's history.

---

⑤
Arizona Science Center

📍 600 E Washington St
🕐 10am–5pm daily
🚫 Thanksgiving, Dec 25
🌐 azscience.org

This ultramodern facility has over 300 interactive science exhibits, covering everything from physics and energy to the human body, spread over four levels. There is something for everyone here. The popular "All About Me" gallery on Level One focuses on human biology. Here, visitors can take a virtual-reality trip through the body. Level Three has "Forces of Nature," where you can experience simulations of earthquake tremors, fierce hurricane winds, and the heat of a forest fire. There is also a large-screen cinema that is popular with children.

⑥
Heard Museum

📍 2301 North Central Ave
🕐 9:30am–5pm Mon–Sat (6–10pm first Fri every month except Mar), 11am–5pm Sun 🚫 Dec 25 🌐 heard.org

The Heard Museum was founded in 1929 by Dwight Heard, a wealthy rancher and businessman, who, with his wife, Maie, assembled an extraordinary collection of Native Southwestern American art in the 1920s. Several benefactors later added to the collection, including Senator Barry Goldwater of Arizona and the Fred Harvey Company, who donated their kachina dolls.

The museum's wide-ranging collection contains more than 40,000 works, but the star attraction is its

Did You Know?

In the Hopi tradition kachinas are the spirits of nature deities, animals, or ancestors.

← Traditional Hopi kachina doll, typically carved from cottonwood roots

display of more than 500 kachina dolls (p46). Additionally, the museum showcases baskets, pottery, textiles, and fine art, as well as sumptuous silverwork by the Navajo, Zuni, and Hopi peoples.

⑦ ⊘ ▱ 🏛

Phoenix Art Museum

🏛 1625 N Central Ave
🕙 10am–5pm Tue–Sat (to 9pm Wed), noon–5pm Sun
🚫 Thanksgiving, Dec 25
🌐 phxart.org

The largest art museum in the Southwest US, the highly acclaimed Phoenix Art Museum has an enviable reputation for the quality of its temporary exhibitions. The equally impressive permanent collection includes more than 19,000 works of American, Asian, European, and Latin American art, as well as modern art, contemporary art, fashion, and photography galleries. Works from the 14th to 19th centuries form the European collection. The Asian galleries feature archaeological artifacts, sculptures, scrolls, and manuscripts. The large Latin American collection encompasses Colonial Spanish pieces, including furniture and decorative arts, as well as works by Mexican painters from the 18th to 20th centuries. The American collection has works by 18th- and 19th-century American artists, with a focus on painters connected to the Southwest. The exhibits here include first-rate work from the Taos art colony of the 1900s and Georgia O'Keeffe (p213), who was the most distinguished member of the group, as well as works by Frederic Remington and Ernest Blumenschein.

EAT & DRINK

Pizzeria Bianco
Foodies flock to this restaurant for the gourmet pizza pies. A menu of salads and wood-fired pizzas incorporates local, seasonal ingredients such as fennel sausage and smoked mozzarella.

🏛 623 E Adams St
🌐 pizzeriabianco.com.

⑤⑤⑤

Matt's Big Breakfast
Locals line up early to get into this excellent little diner with 1950s dinette tables and vintage artwork. The breakfast menu has only grain-fed meats, free-range eggs, and organic produce.

🏛 825 N 1st St 🕙 Dinner
🌐 mattsbig breakfast.com

⑤⑤⑤

Vincent on Camelback
A local favorite since 1986, Vincent's offers inventive menus blending Southwestern ingredients with a Provençal flair in dishes such as duck confit with *pommes Lyonnaise* and citrus sauce.

🏛 3930 E Camelback Rd
🕙 Lunch; Sun & Mon
🌐 vincentson camelback.com

⑤⑤⑤

← The striking modern facade of the popular Arizona Science Center

EXPLORING METROPOLITAN PHOENIX

Did You Know?

Until 1884, Scottsdale was called Orangedale as it was considered the ideal place to grow citrus fruit.

In addition to its urban population of 1.6 million, Phoenix has a burgeoning number of residents in its metropolitan area, totaling more than 4.7 million. The city fills the Salt River Valley, occupying more than 2,000 sq miles (5,180 sq km) of the Sonoran Desert. Metropolitan Phoenix includes the cities of Scottsdale with its golf courses and designer stores, Tempe, which is home to Arizona State University, and Mesa with its Hohokam legacy.

⑧ Scottsdale

W experiencescottsdale.com

Fashion, art, and the Old West come together in Scottsdale. Best known for its many golf courses – there are more than 200 in and around the city – Scottsdale is also replete with luxury hotels and spas, upscale shopping, and fine dining.

In the heart of downtown, where the city was founded in the late 19th century, is Old Town Scottsdale (Main Street between Scottsdale Road and Brown Avenue). Behind its frontier-style facades you can shop for everything from souvenirs to Western wear and jewelry. Main Street ends at the Scottsdale Civic Center Mall, a welcome respite of grass, trees, and public art. Within the grounds are the **Scottsdale Historical Museum** and the acclaimed **Scottsdale Museum of Contemporary Art**, both with changing exhibitions.

West of Scottsdale Road, Main Street is the hub of the Arts District, with fine art galleries. The Scottsdale ArtWalk takes place on Thursdays (7–9pm) along Main Street and Marshall Way. Here too is **Western Spirit: Scottsdale's Museum of the West**. Its exhibitions highlight the past and present-day art and culture of the Old West.

To the north, there are more galleries as well as Native American crafts in the Fifth Avenue Shopping District. The Scottsdale Waterfront is a fashionable shopping and dining complex.

Scottsdale Historical Museum

Ⓐ ⚑ 7333 E Scottsdale Mall ⏱ Sep–May **W** scottsdalehistory.org

Scottsdale Museum of Contemporary Art

⚘ ⚘ ⚘ Ⓐ ⚑ 7374 2nd Street ⏱ 11am–5pm Tue & Wed, 11am–8pm Thu–Sat, noon–5pm Sun **W** smoca.org

Western Spirit: Scottsdale's Museum of the West

⚘ Ⓐ ⚑ 3830 N Marshall Way ⏱ 9:30am–5pm Tue–Sat, 11am–5pm Sun **W** scottsdalemuseumwest.org

Scottsdale Waterfront, with designer shops and restaurants, at dusk

⑨ (images)

Taliesin West

🏠 12345 N Taliesin Dr, Scottsdale ⏰ Times vary; check website 🚫 Easter, Thanksgiving, Dec 25 🌐 franklloydwright.org

Generally regarded as one of the greatest American architects of all time, Frank Lloyd Wright (1867–1959) established the 600-acre (240-ha) Taliesin West complex as a winter school for his students in 1937. Wright came to prominence in Chicago during the 1890s with a series of strikingly original houses designed in elegant, open-plan style. Although noted for his use of local materials such as desert rocks and earth, he also pioneered the use of precast concrete.

Taliesin West is approached along a winding desert road. The muted tones of the low-lying buildings reflect Wright's enthusiasm for the desert setting. He was careful to enhance, rather than dominate, the landscape.

Today, Taliesin West is home to the School of Architecture

DESERT SPAS

Phoenix and Scottsdale are famous for their fabulous spas. Many are situated within luxurious hotel-spa resorts, where a variety of day packages and treatments can be enjoyed. You can indulge in desert-inspired treatments that use natural Sonoran botanicals such as aloe vera; hot stone massages; red clay or creosote body wraps; and desert gemstone rituals. Native American healing treatments are a specialty at the Aji Spa at Wild Horse Pass Resort & Spa (www.wildhorsepass.com).

→

Equilibrium by Heloise Crista in the Taliesin West garden

at Taliesin and the Frank Lloyd Wright Foundation, where students live and work. There are a variety of tours that range from one to three hours. Ninety-minute tours begin every hour from 9am to 4pm. Online booking is strongly recommended.

⑩ (images)

The Cosanti Foundation

🏠 6433 E Doubletree Ranch Rd, Paradise Valley ⏰ 9am–5pm Mon–Sat, 11am–5pm Sun 🚫 Public hols 🌐 arcosanti.org

In 1947, Italian architect Paolo Soleri (1919–2013) came to study at Taliesin West. Nine years later, he set up the Cosanti Foundation to further his investigations into what he termed "arcology": a combination of architecture and ecology to create new urban habitats (p84). Today, the Cosanti site consists of simple, low structures housing studios, a gallery, and workshops. Many are built below ground level and covered with mounds of earth for natural insulation. The workers make and sell their trademark wind bells. Self-guided walking tours are available, but guided tours are by reservation only.

⑪ (images)

Mystery Castle

🏠 800 E Mineral Rd ⏰ Oct–May: 11am–3:30pm Thu–Sun 🌐 mymystery castle.com

Mystery Castle is possibly Phoenix's most eccentric attraction. In 1927, Boyce Luther Gulley came to Phoenix from Seattle hoping that the warm climate would improve his ailing health. His daughter had loved building sand castles on the beach, and since Phoenix was so far away from the ocean, Gulley created a real-life fairy-tale sandcastle for her. He started work in 1930 and continued until his death in 1945. Discarded bricks and scrapyard junk, including old car parts, have been used to build the structure. The 18-room interior can be seen on a guided tour, which explores the quirky building and its eclectic collection of antiques and furniture.

The muted tones of the low-lying buildings reflect Wright's enthusiasm for the desert setting. He was careful to enhance, rather than dominate, the landscape.

⑫ 🛠️ 🎭 🍴 🖥️ 🛍️

MUSICAL INSTRUMENT MUSEUM

📍 4725 E Mayo Blvd ⏰ 9am–5pm daily ❌ Thanksgiving 🌐 mim.org

Since its opening in 2010, this impressive institution has become one of the top museums in the USA. Displaying more than 6,800 musical instruments from around the globe, it is the world's largest museum of its kind.

What makes this museum particularly outstanding is the audio and video technologies that accompany the exhibits, letting you hear the instruments and see them being played in their original settings. On the first floor are the delightful Mechanical Music Gallery, and the Artist Gallery, where changing exhibits feature instruments played by Elvis Presley, Johnny Cash, and other music legends from around the world. Don't miss the hands-on Experience Gallery, where you can play some unusual instruments. On the second floor, the galleries are organized geographically, highlighting beautiful and often intriguing instruments from some 200 countries. They are often paired with traditional clothing and artifacts. As you listen through your headphones, you are transported on a musical journey around the world.

> 💬 INSIDER TIP
> **Visiting**
>
> Galleries are often busiest on weekday mornings due to school trips. Music lovers should consider buying a two-day pass, valid for seven days, to cover everything at a leisurely pace.

THE THEREMIN

One of the museum's most unusual musical instruments is the truly eerie-sounding Theremin, which is played without any physical contact. Two metal antennas sense the performer's hands, which control the frequency with one hand and volume with the other. You can try it out for yourself in the Experience Gallery.

→ Musical instruments adorning MIM's galleries

音乐是心灵之声
Music is the language of the soul

1 The 12-ft- (3.7-m-) tall octobasse in the Orientation Gallery is one of only a handful in existence.

2 The museum's architecture evokes musical themes through raised stonework reminiscent of musical notes.

3 At the Thumb Piano display in the Africa Gallery visitors can dance to music.

Sonoran desert
cactus flowers in
Papago Park

←

movement controlled
by banks and canals
rather than fences.

⑬ Papago Park

🏠 625 N Galvin Parkway &
Van Buren St ⓦ phoenix.
gov/parks/trails/locations/
papago-park

Papago Park is a popular place
to unwind, with several hiking
and cycling trails, picnic areas,
and fishing lakes. Within the
park, the Desert Botanical
Garden is a 145-acre (59-ha)
area devoted to more than
20,000 cacti and protected
desert flora from around the
world. Guided tours explain
the extraordinary life cycles of
the desert plants. The rolling
hills and lakes of the Phoenix
Zoo also occupy a large area
of the park. The zoo reproduces
a series of habitats, including
the Arizona-Sonora Desert
and a tropical rainforest. It
provides a home for more
than 1,400 animals, their

⑭ Camelback Mountain

Named for its humped shape,
Camelback Mountain rises
high above its suburban
surroundings 7 miles (11 km)
northeast of downtown
Phoenix. One of the city's
most distinctive landmarks,
the mountain is a granite and
sandstone outcrop formed by
prehistoric volcanic forces.
Camelback Mountain is best
approached from the north
via the marked turn off
McDonald Drive near the
junction of Tatum Boulevard.
From the parking lot, a well-
marked path leads to the
summit, a steep climb that

covers 1,300 ft (390 m) in the
space of a mile. Camelback
Mountain adjoins the Echo
Canyon Recreation Area, a
lovely enclave with a choice
of shady picnic sites.

⑮ Tempe

ⓦ tempetourism.com

As home to the main campus
of Arizona State University
(ASU), Tempe has a younger
vibe than most places in
metropolitan Phoenix. That
makes for a lively nightlife
scene downtown, especially
along its Mill Avenue hub.
Don't miss the striking Tempe
City Hall, an inverted pyramid
made of bronzed glass and
steel, with a flower-filled
sunken courtyard. Walking
around, you'll see lots of public
art; students are encouraged
to display their work, and even
utility boxes are brightened
up with quirky designs.
Contemporary art is on display
at the **ASU Art Museum**. The
campus also has the beautiful

> One of the city's most distinctive
> landmarks, Camelback Mountain is a
> granite and sandstone outcrop formed
> by prehistoric volcanic forces.

← Papago Park, which has a variety of cycling and hiking trails

Frank Lloyd Wright-designed **ASU Gammage Auditorium**, one of the biggest venues for Broadway shows in the USA.

When the heat builds up you can cool off at the **Big Surf Water Park** or the **Tempe History Museum**.

ASU Art Museum

🕙🅿 🏠 51 E 10th St 🕐 11am-5pm Tue-Sat (to 8pm Thu during term time) 🌐 asuart museum.asu.edu

ASU Gammage Auditorium

🅿 🏠 1200 South Forest Ave 🌐 asugammage.com

Big Surf Water Park

🕙🅿🅿 🏠 1500 N McClintock Dr 🕐 10am-6pm Mon-Sat, 11am-6pm Sun 🌐 bigsurffun.com

Tempe History Museum

🕙 🏠 809 E Southern Ave 🕐 10am-5pm Tue-Sat, 1-5pm Sun 🌐 tempe.gov

---

⑯

Mesa

Arizona's third-largest city after Phoenix and Tucson, Mesa was settled by the Hohokam

people over 2,000 years ago. They built hundreds of miles of canals to irrigate the desert, many of which are still in use today and make for cooling walks in the desert heat. You can learn more at the **Park of the Canals**. The city's other main historical site, the **Mesa Grande Cultural Park**, is a five-minute drive away. Here you can see Hohokam buildings from 1100 to 1400 BC.

Among the more modern attractions are the the **i.d.e.a. Museum**, which is aimed at keeping younger kids entertained and educated, and the **Mesa Contemporary Arts Museum**. Foodies will want to head out to **Queen Creek Olive Mill**, in neighboring Queen Creek, where you can tour the olive oil factory and taste and buy the products.

Park of the Canals

🏠 1710 N Horne 🕐 6am-10pm daily 🌐 parkofthecanals.org

Mesa Grande Cultural Park

🕙🕙 🏠 1000 N Date 🕐 Oct-May: 10am-2pm Wed-Fri, 10am-4pm Sat & Sun 🌐 arizonamuseumof naturalhistory.org

i.d.e.a. Museum

🕙🕙🕙 🏠 150 W Pepper Pl 🕐 9am-4pm Tue-Thu & Sat, 9am-6pm Fri, noon-4pm Sun 🌐 ideamuseum.org

Mesa Contemporary Arts Museum

🕙 🏠 1 E Main St 🕐 10am-5pm Tue, Wed, Fri & Sat, 10am-8pm Thu, noon-5pm Sun 🌐 mesaartscenter.com

Queen Creek Olive Mill

🕙🕙🕙🕙 🏠 25062 S Meridian Rd, Queen Creek 🕐 8am-5pm Sun-Thu, 8am-9pm Fri & Sat 🌐 queencreek olivemill.com

---

⑰

Pueblo Grande Museum and Archaeological Park

🏠 4619 E. Washington St 🕐 9am-4:45pm Tue-Sat, 1-4:45pm Sun 🕐 Public hols 🌐 pueblogrande.com

Located 5 miles (8 km) east of downtown Phoenix, this museum displays an ancient Hohokam ruin, as well as many artifacts, including cooking utensils and pottery. Many pieces come from the adjacent Archaeological Park, the site of a Hohokam settlement from the 8th to the 14th centuries. The site, originally excavated in 1887, has ruins and signs indicating the many irrigation canals once used by the Hohokam to water crops.

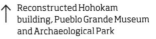

↑ Reconstructed Hohokam building, Pueblo Grande Museum and Archaeological Park

❷

TUCSON

🅰 C6 ✈ 10 miles (16 km) S of downtown 🚆 Amtrak, 400 E Toole Ave 🚌 Greyhound Lines, 471 W Congress
ℹ 100 S Church Ave; www.visittucson.org

Arizona's second-largest city after Phoenix, Tucson is located on the northern boundary of the Sonoran Desert in Southern Arizona, in a basin surrounded by five mountain ranges. The city was officially founded by Irish explorer Hugh O'Connor in 1775. Tucson's pride in its history is reflected in the careful preservation of its 19th-century downtown buildings.

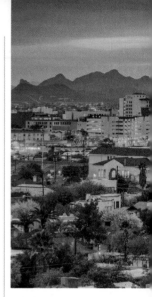

① 🏛

El Presidio Historic District

This is believed to be one of the oldest inhabited sites in the US – archaeological excavations have found artifacts from the prehistoric Hohokam people, who lived on this spot from around AD 700 to 900. The original Spanish fortress (presidio), San Agustin del Tucson, was established in 1775 by Irishman Hugo O'Connor, who worked for the Spanish crown. The reconstructed presidio is now a museum. More than 70 of the houses here were constructed during the Territorial period, before Arizona became a state in 1912. The oldest are built of adobe in Spanish-Mexican style, while the later Anglo-American dwellings are Victorian brick buildings separated by gardens. Today the buildings are largely occupied by shops, art galleries, and restaurants.

Tours of El Presidio Historic District are run by the Tucson Museum of Art.

② 🎨🏛🍴🛍

Tucson Museum of Art and Historic Block

🏛 140 N Main Ave 🕙 10am-5pm Tue-Sun, 10am-8pm first Thu of month
🌐 tucsonmuseumofart.org

Opened in 1975, the Tucson Museum of Art is located in

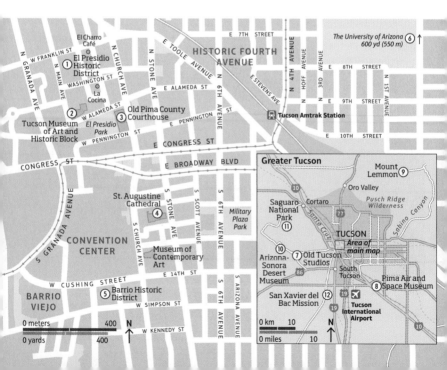

El Charro Café
① El Presidio Historic District
La Cocina
② Tucson Museum of Art and Historic Block
El Presidio Park
③ Old Pima County Courthouse
Tucson Amtrak Station
④ St. Augustine Cathedral
Military Plaza Park
CONVENTION CENTER
Museum of Contemporary Art
BARRIO VIEJO
⑤ Barrio Historic District

W FRANKLIN ST · W GRANADA AVE · N MAIN AVE · N CHURCH AVE · WASHINGTON ST · W ALAMEDA ST · N STONE AVE · E TOOLE AVENUE · E 7TH STREET · HISTORIC FOURTH AVENUE · E ALAMEDA ST · E PENNINGTON ST · E CONGRESS ST · CONGRESS ST · E BROADWAY BLVD · S GRANADA AVENUE · S STONE AVE · S SCOTT AVENUE · S 6TH AVENUE · S CHURCH AVENUE · E 14TH ST · W CUSHING STREET · W SIMPSON ST · S 6TH AVENUE · S ARIZONA AVENUE · W KENNEDY ST · E STEVENS AVE · N 4TH AVENUE · HOFF AVENUE · 3RD AVENUE · N 1ST AVENUE · 8TH STREET · 9TH STREET · 10TH STREET

The University of Arizona ⑥ 600 yd (550 m)

0 meters 400
0 yards 400
N

Greater Tucson

Saguaro National Park ⑪ · Cortaro · Oro Valley · Mount Lemmon ⑨ · Pusch Ridge Wilderness · Sabino Canyon · Santa Cruz · TUCSON · Area of main map · ⑩ Arizona-Sonora Desert Museum · ⑦ Old Tucson Studios · South Tucson · Pima Air and Space Museum ⑧ · San Xavier del Bac Mission ⑫ · Tucson International Airport

0 km 10
0 miles 10
N

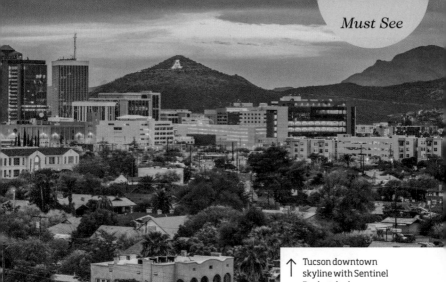

↑ Tucson downtown skyline with Sentinel Peak at dusk

El Presidio Historic District. The museum encompasses five of the presidio's oldest dwellings – all of which are more than 100 years old. These historic buildings house some of the museum's extensive collection. The sculpture gardens and courtyards also form part of the Historic Block complex.

The art museum's collections include American art, Asian art, modern and contemporary works, Latin American art, European art, and folk art. It also has Pre-Columbian artifacts, some of which are 2,000 years old, displayed in the second-floor gallery. The Spanish Colonial collection features stunning pieces of religious art. The 1850s Casa Cordova houses *El Nacimiento*, a large Nativity scene with more than 300 earthenware figurines created in the 1970s by Maria Luisa Tena. The J. Knox Corbett House, built in 1907, has Arts and Crafts pieces (1880–1930), including a William Morris chair. The Goodman Pavilion of Western Art (also called Edward Nye Fish House), built in 1868, displays art of the American West and hosts changing exhibitions. Romero House is home to the Romero potters ceramics studio, while the Stevens/Duffield House houses the museum's restaurant.

Both guided and self-guided walking tours of the Historic Block are run by the museum.

INSIDER TIP
Downtown Shopping

Opposite the Tucson Museum of Art, the Old Town Artisans complex is a warren of small shops selling Southwestern art, ranging from textiles to pottery and paintings.

③

Old Pima County Courthouse

🏠 115 N Church Ave
🕙 10am–5pm daily 🌐 visit southernarizona.com

The former main county courthouse with its pretty tiled dome is a downtown landmark. It was built in 1927, and now houses the Southern Arizona Heritage and Visitor Center. The position of the original presidio wall is marked out in the court-yard, and a section of the wall, 3 ft (1 m) thick and 12 ft (4 m) high, can still be seen inside.

←

The elegant Old Pima County Courthouse, in the Mission architectural style

←

The ornate Spanish Colonial facade of St. Augustine Cathedral

believe that if their candles burn for a whole night, their wishes will come true.

⑥
The University of Arizona

🏠 811 N Euclid Ave
🕐 9am–5pm Mon–Fri (Sep–Apr: also 9am–4pm Sat & Sun) 🌐 arizona.edu

Several museums are located on or near the University of Arizona campus, about a mile (1.5 km) east of downtown. The Arizona Historical Society Museum traces Arizona's history from the arrival of the Spanish in 1540 to modern times. The University of Arizona Museum of Art focuses on European and American fine art, from the Renaissance to contemporary pieces. Opposite the Museum of Art is the excellent Center for Creative Photography, which contains the work of many of the 20th century's greatest American photographers. Visitors can view the extensive archives by reserving in advance. The Flandrau Science Center features a range of child-friendly interactive exhibits.

One of the most renowned collections of artifacts, covering 2,000 years of Native American history, is displayed by the Arizona State Museum, which was founded in 1893.

EAT

El Charro Café
Opened in 1922, this is one of the oldest family-owned restaurants in the US and features innovative Tucson-style Mexican food. Savor the legendary *carne seca* (shredded sun-dried Angus beef) marinated in garlic and lime juice.

🏠 311 N Court Ave
🌐 elcharrocafe.com

$$$

La Cocina
Dine in the shaded courtyard or the colorful cantina filled with artwork at this casual café serving an eclectic mix of Mexican, Southwestern, and international dishes. There's regular live music too.

🏠 201 N Court Ave
🕐 Dinner Sun & Mon
🌐 lacocinatucson.com

$$$

④
St. Augustine Cathedral

🏠 192 S Stone Ave
🌐 cathedral-staugustine.org

Begun in 1896, St. Augustine Cathedral was modeled after the Spanish Colonial style of the Cathedral of Querétaro in central Mexico. This gleaming white building has an imposing sandstone facade with intricate carvings of the yucca, the saguaro, and the horned toad – three symbols of the Sonoran Desert. A bronze statue of St. Augustine, the city's patron saint, stands above the main door.

⑤
Barrio Historic District

This area was Tucson's main business district in the late 19th century. Today, its quiet streets are lined with attractive original adobe houses painted in bright colors. On nearby Main Street is the "wishing shrine" of El Tiradito, which marks the spot where a young man is said to have been killed as a result of a lovers' triangle. Local people light candles here for his soul and they still

Did You Know?

The Center for Creative Photography houses an archive of works by the great photographer Ansel Adams.

EXPLORING GREATER TUCSON

Beyond the city center, greater Tucson extends north to the Santa Catalina Mountains, whose foothills are the start of a scenic drive to the top of Mount Lemmon. To the west are the Tucson Mountains, which frame the western portion of Saguaro National Park; the park's other half lies east of the city. To the south lies the beautiful mission church of San Xavier del Bac, which stands out from the flat, desert landscape of the Tohono O'odham Indian Reservation.

Old Tucson Studios

📍 201 S Kinney Rd
🕐 Due to COVID-19
🌐 oldtucson.com

Modeled on an old Western town of the 1860s, Old Tucson Studios was built in 1939 as a set for the movie, *Arizona*. It formed the backdrop for some of Hollywood's most famous Westerns, including *Gunfight at the OK Corral* (1957), as well as for the popular TV series *Little House on the Prairie* (1977–83). For many years, it also operated as a popular theme park until its closure in 2020 due to COVID-19. Plans to reopen its iconic buildings and grounds are currently underway.

Pima Air and Space Museum

📍 6000 E Valencia Rd
🕐 9am–5pm daily (last adm 3pm) 🚫 Thanksgiving, Dec 25 🌐 pimaair.org

The Pima Air and Space Museum contains one of the largest collections of aircraft in the world. Visitors are met with the astonishing sight of more than 300 vintage aircraft set out in ranks across the desert. The VC-118 "Air Force 1" planes used by presidents Kennedy and Johnson are on display here alongside a replica of the Wright brothers' famous 1903 aircraft and bombers from World War II. Exhibits in five aircraft hangars show military and aviation memorabilia, including a

HIDDEN GEM
Cold War Secrets

Situated 25 miles (40 km) from Pima Air and Space Museum, the Titan Missile Museum tells the story of the Titan II nuclear missile that was on alert from 1963 to 1987 in the context of the Cold War (*www.titan missilemuseum.org*).

replica World War II barracks. The adjacent Davis-Monthan Air Force Base displays more than 2,000 planes, including B-29s and supersonic bombers.

Mount Lemmon

🌐 visitmountlemon.com

At 9,157 ft (2,790 m), Mount Lemmon is the highest peak in the Santa Catalina Mountains and a popular summer destination. A one-hour scenic drive, beginning in the Tucson city limits and connecting to the Mount Lemmon Highway, takes you to the summit. There are 150 miles (240 km) of hiking trails here, while a side road leads to the resort village of Summerhaven. At the top, the Mount Lemmon Ski Valley lift operates most of the year.

View of surrounding mountains from the top of Mount Lemmon

ARIZONA-SONORA DESERT MUSEUM

🏠 2021 N Kinney Rd, Tucson ⏰ Mar–Sep: 7:30am–5pm daily; Oct–Feb: 8:30am–5pm daily
🌐 desertmuseum.org

There's no place more enjoyable for learning about the plants and wildlife of Southern Arizona than this impressive natural history park. Within a desert setting, it encompasses a botanical garden, a variety of animal habitats, and a museum.

A 2-mile (3-km) walkway winds through the grounds, passing more than 1,200 native plant species. Take the half-mile- (800-m) Desert Loop Trail to see coyotes and javelinas in wide, natural enclosures. Head for the Mountain Woodland section to see a mountain lion, a black bear, and endangered Mexican gray wolves. Other exhibits give you close-up views of creatures ranging from comical prairie dogs to scary snakes. Docents are stationed along the trail to answer questions and give hands-on demonstrations of interesting facets of desert life. You can also attend informative presentations in the lecture theater.

> 💬 INSIDER TIP
> **Visiting**
>
> Plan to stay a minimum of two hours here, but to see everything at a leisurely pace you could easily spend half a day or more. There is little shade on the Desert Loop, so sun protection is a must. You'll enjoy your visit more if you take it slow and allow rest breaks from the desert heat.

↑ Visitors strolling along the walkway through the museum grounds

Did You Know?

Although it looks like a small boar, the javelina (a type of peccary), is of a different species than the domesticated pig.

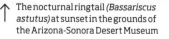

↑ The nocturnal ringtail *(Bassariscus astutus)* at sunset in the grounds of the Arizona-Sonora Desert Museum

Raptor Free-Flight Show

▶ Don't miss this awesome program, held twice a day in winter, when trainers work with hawks, owls, and other birds of prey to demonstrate their power, intelligence and beauty in flight. After the show, visitors can take photos of the birds.

Hummingbird Aviary

◀ Arizona is home to many species of native and migrating hummingbirds. Dozens of these colorful little birds hover and dart across your path as you walk through this delightful enclosure. You may even see a tiny nest.

Cat Canyon

▶ It's rare to see these elusive desert predators in the wild. Cat Canyon provides a rocky habitat where you can get a look at bobcats, ocelots, and others.

Riparian Corridor

◀ Rivers and streams provide a shady oasis in the desert heat. Here you'll find playful river otters, shy coatis, and nimble bighorn sheep clambering over their rocky home.

Cactus Garden

▶ Along the trail are beautiful native cacti and succulents, from fat blooming barrels to prickly pears to fuzzy teddy bear chollas and towering saguaros.

Saguaro cactus forest viewed from the Saguaro Cactus Drive ↑

⑪ 🌀 Ⓜ 🏠

SAGUARO NATIONAL PARK

📍 3693 S Old Spanish Trail 🕐 Tucson Mountain District (west): sunrise–sunset daily; Rincon Mountain District (east): 7am–sunset daily 🚫 Thanksgiving, Dec 25 🌐 nps.gov/sagu

Perhaps the most famous symbol of the American Southwest, the saguaro (pronounced sa-wah-ro) cactus grows only in the Sonoran Desert. The park, which was set up in 1994 to protect this unique species, comprises two tracts of land on the eastern and western flanks of Tucson. Together they cover more than 142 sq miles (368 sq km).

Both sections of the park are equally rewarding. In the western side, the 9-mile (14.5-km) Bajada Loop Drive runs deep into the park on a dirt road, past hiking trails and picnic areas. The Signal Hill Trail leads to ancient Hohokam petroglyphs carved into the volcanic rock. The eastern park has the oldest saguaros, which can be seen along the 8-mile (13-km) Cactus Forest Drive. There are also more than 100 miles (160 km) of hiking trails here. You'll see an intriguing array of other cacti and desert plants; watch for desert wildlife, including javelinas, coyotes, roadrunners, and Gambel's quail.

↑ White flowers blooming at the top of an arm of a Saguaro cactus in spring

↑ Ancient Hohokam petroglyphs carved into rock in western Saguaro National Park

THE MIGHTY SAGUARO

The largest species of cactus in the US, the saguaro has a life span of up to 200 years. Those that survive into old age may grow up to 50 ft (15 m) tall and weigh over 8 tons (7,250 kg). Saguaros grow very slowly; the first arms only appear when the plant is 75–100 years old. In late April to May, white flowers appear, which are pollinated by hummingbirds, bees, and bats. In June, mature saguaros produce red fruit, which is harvested by Native Americans and made into jellies and a ceremonial fermented drink.

SAN XAVIER DEL BAC MISSION

▣ 1950 W San Xavier Rd, 10 miles (16 km) S of Tucson on I-19
🕐 7am–5pm daily   🌐 sanxaviermission.org

The oldest and best-preserved mission church in the Southwest, San Xavier del Bac rises out of the stark, flat landscape of the Tohono O'odham Reservation, its white walls dazzling in the desert sun.

A mission was first established here by the Jesuit priest Father Eusebio Kino in 1700. The complex seen today was built by O'odham laborers *(p47)* under the direction of Franciscan missionaries and was completed in 1797. Built of adobe brick, the mission is considered to be the finest example of Spanish Colonial architecture in the US. The church also incorporates other styles, including several Baroque flourishes. In the 1990s its interior was extensively renovated, and five *retablos* (altarpieces) were restored to their original glory. On entering the church, visitors are struck by the dome's ceiling with its paintings of religious figures. Vivid pigments of vermilion and blue were used to contrast with the stark white stone background.

The bell tower's elegant white dome reflects the Moorish styles that are incorporated into San Xavier's Spanish Colonial architecture.

→
Layout of San Xavier del Bac Mission

The mortuary chapel contains a statue of the Virgin Mary surrounded by candles.

The carved statues to the left of the entrance represent St. Agatha of Catania and St. Agnes of Rome.

←
The ornate facade of San Xavier del Bac Mission, decorated with carved figures of saints

EXPERIENCE Phoenix and Southern Arizona

Did You Know?

San Xavier del Bac Mission is popularly called "the white dove of the desert".

The altar dome and high transepts are filled with painted wooden statuary and covered with murals depicting scenes from the Gospels.

↑ The spectacular gold-and-red main altar, decorated in Mexican Baroque style

This statue of the Virgin in the Chapel of Our Lady is one of the church's three sculptures of Mary. Here she is shown as La Dolorosa or Sorrowing Mother.

The patio is closed to the public but can be seen from the museum.

The museum includes a sheepskin psalter and photographs of other historic missions on the Tohono O'odham Reservation.

EXPERIENCE MORE

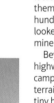

3

The Apache Trail

🅰C5 🚌 ℹ️125 N 2nd St, Phoenix; www.visit phoenix.com

Heading east from Phoenix, Highway 60 cuts straight across the desert to the suburb of Apache Junction at the start of Highway 88. The road then winds up into the Superstition Mountains. Called the Apache Trail for the Native Americans who once lived here, this stretch of Highway 88 is a scenic 40-mile (64-km) route up to Theodore Roosevelt Lake.

Highway 88 begins by climbing up into the hills, and after 5 miles (8 km) reaches the Lost Dutchman State Park, named for the gold mine quarried here by Jacob Waltz and Jacob Weiser in the 1870s. These two miners found huge gold nuggets but kept the location of the mine to themselves. After their deaths, hundreds of prospectors looked for the famed gold mine but without success.

Beyond the state park, the highway passes by several campsites and through rugged terrain before reaching the tiny hamlet of Tortilla Flat. This settlement is at the east end of slender Canyon Lake,

the first of several Salt River reservoirs created to provide Phoenix with water. The lake has a marina and cruises are offered on *Dolly Steamboat*. As the road climbs higher into the Superstition Mountains it becomes more difficult to negotiate, before reaching the 280-ft- (85-m-) high Theodore Roosevelt Dam, where there is good fishing and water sports.

Three miles (5 km) east of the dam, the **Tonto National Monument** comprises two large sets of ruined cliff dwellings. The Salado people, who created some of the pottery on display at the Heard Museum *(p94)*, built these pueblos of rock and mud in the early 1300s. A short trail leads up to the 19-room Lower Cliff Dwelling, but the 40-room Upper Cliff Dwelling can be visited only with a ranger.

Tonto National Monument
⊘ 🅰Hwy 188 ⏲8am–5pm daily; Upper Cliff Dwelling: Nov–Apr: Fri–Mon 🚫Dec 25 🌐nps.gov/tont

---

INSIDER TIP
Apache Trail Lakes

With marinas where you can rent all manner of boats and get out onto the water, Apache, Canyon, Saguaro, and Roosevelt lakes are great scenic spots to beat the summer heat.

4

Globe

🅰C5 🚌 ℹ️Globe Chamber of Commerce, 1360 N Broad St; www.globe miamichamber.com

The mining town of Globe lies about 100 miles (160 km) east of Phoenix in the wooded Dripping Spring and Pinal Mountains. In 1875, prospectors struck silver near here, and Globe was founded as a mining town and supply center. It was named for a large silver nugget, shaped like a globe, unearthed in the hills nearby. The silver was quickly exhausted, but copper mining thrived until 1931. Today, Globe has an attractive historic district with several notable late 19th- and early 20th-century buildings. The **Gila County Historical Museum** outlines its history.

Gila County Historical Museum

⊛ ⊛ 🏠 1330 N Broad St 📞 (928) 425-7385 ⏰ 10am–4pm Tue–Fri, 11am–3pm Sat 🚫 Jan 1, Dec 25

---

5 ⊛

Casa Grande Ruins National Monument

🅰 C5 ⏰ 9am–5pm daily (May–Sep: to 4pm) 🚫 Jul 4, Thanksgiving, Dec 25 🌐 nps.gov/cagr

From around 200 BC until the mid-1400s, the Hohokam people farmed the Gila River Valley to the southeast of Phoenix. The distinctive structure that makes up the Casa Grande National Monument was built in the

┌─────────────────────────────┐
│ **ASTRONOMY IN SOUTHERN ARIZONA**

Southern Arizona's dark, clear nights have made it an international center for astronomy. Prestigious observatories such as Kitt Peak National Observatory (tel 520 318-8720) and the Fred Lawrence Whipple Observatory (tel 520 879-4407) can be toured (reserve in advance). However, even without high-powered equipment, anyone can enjoy the constellations in the night skies.

└─────────────────────────────┘

early 14th century and named the "Big House" by a passing Jesuit missionary in 1694. This sturdy four-story structure has walls up to 4 ft (1.2 m) thick and is made from locally quarried caliche, a hard-setting subsoil. The visitor center has some interesting exhibits on Hohokam history and culture.

Casa Grande sits 15 miles (24 km) east of Interstate Highway 10 (I-10) on the out-skirts of the town of Coolidge.

---

6 ⊛ Ⓜ 🖵

Biosphere 2 Center

🅰 C6 ⏰ 5 miles (8 km) NE of junction of Hwys 77 & 79 ⏰ 9am–4pm daily 🚫 Thanksgiving, Dec 25 🌐 b2science.org

Biosphere 2 is a unique research facility that was set up in 1991. Eight people were sealed within a futuristic structure of glass and white steel furnished with five of the Earth's habitats: rainforest, desert, savanna, marsh, and an ocean with a living coral reef. Over a period of two years the effect of the people

on the environment, as well as the effect on them of isolation in this "world," were studied.

Today there are no people living in the Biosphere, which is being used as an earth science research facility.

7

Yuma

🅰 A6 🚆 Amtrak, 281 S Gila St 🚌 Greyhound, 1245 S Castle Dome Ave 🚩 Yuma Convention and Visitors' Bureau, 201 N 4th Ave; www.visityuma.com

In a strategic position at the confluence of the Colorado and Gila rivers, Yuma rose to prominence in the 1850s, when the river crossing became the gateway to California for thousands of gold seekers. Fort Yuma, built in 1849, also boosted steamboat traffic along the Colorado River.

Today, Yuma's hot and sunny winter climate makes it a popular winter destination. Two state historic parks highlight its rich history: Yuma Quartermaster Depot, along the Colorado, looks at river transportation and army life in the late 1800s; Yuma Territorial Prison re-creates conditions at this former prison facility from 1876 to 1909.

←

The majestic Superstition Mountains, accessed via the scenic Apache Trail

↑ Sunrise over the blooming desert landscape of Organ Pipe Cactus National Monument

8

Organ Pipe Cactus National Monument

⚑ B6 ☐ Off Hwy 85, S of Why ⓦ nps.gov/orpi

The organ pipe is a Sonoran desert species of cactus, which is a cousin to the saguaro (p109) but with multiple arms branching up from the base. The organ pipe is rare in the United States, growing almost exclusively in this large and remote area along the Mexican border in southwest Arizona. Many other plant and animal species flourish in this unspoiled desert wilderness, although a lot of animals, such as snakes, jackrabbits, and kangaroo rats, emerge only in

the cool of the night. Other cacti such as the saguaro, the Engelmann prickly pear, and the teddybear cholla are best seen in early summer for their glorious displays of floral color.

There are two popular scenic routes through the park: the 21-mile (34-km) Ajo Mountain Drive takes two hours and winds through startling desert landscapes in the foothills of the mountains. The 37-mile (60-km) Puerto Blanco Drive leads to a half-hour trail into Red Tanks Tinaja, a natural water pocket, and the picnic area near Pinkley Peak. Hiking trails in the park range in difficulty from paved, wheelchair-accessible paths to wilderness walks. A visitor

center offers exhibits on the park's flora and fauna, as well as maps and camping permits, and there are guided walks available in winter.

Be aware that the park is a good two-and-a-half- to three-hour drive from Tucson. If you want to explore this area in any detail, plan to camp overnight. Ajo, 34 miles (55 km) to the north, has motels and services.

9

Tumacácori National Historical Park

⚑ C7 ☐ 1891 E I-19 Frontage Rd, Tumacácori ◷ 9am–5pm daily ☒ Thanksgiving, Dec 25 ⓦ nps.gov/tuma

Just 3 miles (5 km) south of Tubac lies Tumacácori National Historical Park, with the beautiful ruined Mission San José de Tumacácori. The present church was built around 1800 on the ruins of the original 1691 mission established by a Jesuit priest,

→

Mission San José de Tumacácori in Tumacácori National Historical Park

---

> ### BIRDWATCHING IN THE CANYONS OF SOUTHERN ARIZONA
>
> Although seemingly dry, Southern Arizona gets about 11 inches (280 mm) of rain annually. This enables a range of vegetation to flourish, from cacti to colorful wildflowers in spring. In turn, this attracts an amazing variety of birds. The canyons between Tucson and the Mexican border offer the best birdwatching. Just off I-19, Madera Canyon plays host to some 400 bird species, from hummingbirds and warblers, to rare species such as the brown-crested flycatcher. Ramsey Canyon, in the Huachuca Mountains, is the country's hummingbird capital, with 14 varieties of these tiny, delicate creatures.

Father Eusebio Kino. The mission was abandoned in 1848, and today its weather-beaten ocher facade, arched entry, and carved wooden door are evocative reminders of former times. The cavernous interior has large patches of exposed adobe brick and faded murals. You can also explore the orchard, cemetery, storehouse, and other ruins on the extensive grounds, where there are occasional craft demonstrations October through April.

A small museum provides an excellent background on both the mission builders and Pima people. La Fiesta de Tumacácori (p55) is held on the mission grounds the first weekend in December, with folk dances, music, and food.

---

⑩

Nogales

Ⓐ C7 🚌 ℹ️ 123 W Kino Park; www.thenogales chamber.org

Nogales is really two towns that straddle the US border with Mexico, at the end of Mexico's Pacific Highway. Arizona's largest international border community, it is a busy port of entry, handling huge amounts of freight, including many of

the winter fruit and vegetables sold in North America. The town attracts large numbers of visitors in search of bargains – decorative blankets, furniture, and crafts are good value. People used to shop on both sides of the border, but the US government has issued warnings over crossing into Mexico, as ongoing drug wars have made border towns potentially dangerous, and visitors are at risk of theft.

If you cross over into Mexico, you are advised to leave your car on the US side, where attendants mind the parking lots, and to walk across the border. Not only is parking extremely difficult, but cars with US license plates are likely targets for thieves. It can also take two to three hours to go through customs by car. Visas are required only for those traveling farther south than the town and for stays of more than 72 hours. US and Canadian citizens should always carry a passport for identification, as drivers' licenses may not be sufficient proof of citizenship. Foreign nationals should make sure their visa status enables them to re-enter the US; those on the Visa Waiver Program (p272) should not encounter any problems.

↑ Colorful ceramic planter crafted in the artists' colony of Tubac

⑪

Tubac

Ⓐ C6 🌐 tubacaz.com

The Royal Presidio (fortress) of San Ignacio de Tubac was built in 1752 to protect the Spanish-owned ranches and mines, as well as the nearby missions of Tumacácori and San Xavier del Bac, from attacks by the indigenous Pima people. Tubac was also the first stopover on the overland expedition to colonize the San Francisco Bay area in 1776. The trek was led by the fort's captain, Juan Bautista de Anza. Following his return, the garrison moved north to Tucson, and, for the next hundred years, Tubac declined. Today, the town is a small but thriving art colony, with attractive shops, galleries, and restaurants lining the streets around the plaza.

Tubac's historical remains are displayed at the **Tubac Presidio State Historic Park**, which encompasses the foundations of the original presidio in an underground display, as well as several historic buildings. Also here, the Presidio Museum contains artifacts covering over 100 years of Tubac's history, including painted altarpieces and colonial furniture.

Tubac Presidio State Historic Park
🚻♿ Ⓐ 1 Burruel St
🕐 9am–5pm daily 🚫 Dec 25
🌐 azstateparks.com/tubac

12

Tombstone

⚑D6 **ℹ**109 S 4th St; www.tombstonechamber.com

The site of the 1881 gunfight at the **OK Corral** between the Earp brothers, Doc Holliday, and the Clanton gang, Tombstone was founded by Ed Schieffelin, who went prospecting on Apache land in 1877 despite a warning that "all you'll find out there is your tombstone." He found a silver mountain instead, and his sardonically named shanty town boomed with the ensuing silver rush. One of the wildest towns in the West, Tombstone was soon full of prospectors, gamblers, cowboys, and lawmen. In its heyday, it was larger than San Francisco.

In 1962 "the town too tough to die" became a National Historic Landmark. Allen Street, with its wooden boardwalks, shops, and restaurants, is the town's main thoroughfare.

↑ An old Wild West stagecoach on the dusty streets of Tombstone, a National Historic Landmark

The OK Corral is preserved as a museum, and regular re-enactments of the infamous gunfight are staged daily at 11am, noon, 2pm, and 3:30pm.

Tombstone Courthouse, the seat of justice for the county from 1882 to 1929, is now a State Historic Site. It contains a museum featuring the restored courtroom and historical artifacts, including photographs of some of the town's famous characters.

Those who perished in Tombstone, peacefully or otherwise, are buried in the famous Boothill Cemetery, just north of town.

$37 million

The worth of the silver that was extracted from the mines in Tombstone between 1880 and 1887.

Queen Hotel dominate the historic town center, while clusters of houses cling to the surrounding mountainsides.

Visitors can tour the mines that once flourished here, such as the deep underground Queen Mine. Exhibits at the Bisbee Mining and Historical Museum illustrate the realities of mining and frontier life here.

STAY

Tombstone Monument Ranch

Designed to resemble an Old West town, this ranch with rooms has a saloon with swing doors.

⚑D6 **⌂**895 W Monument Rd, Tombstone **ⓦ**tombstonemonumentranch.com

$(\$)(\$)(\$)$

Tombstone Bordello Bed & Breakfast

A former bordello with tasteful rooms.

⚑C6 **⌂**107 W Allen St, Tombstone **ⓦ**tombstonebordello.com

$(\$)(\$)(\$)$

OK Corral

⊛ **⌂**326 E Allen St **⊙**9am–5pm daily **⊗**Thanksgiving, Dec 25 **ⓦ**ok-corral.com

Tombstone Courthouse

⊛⊕ **⌂**223 Toughnut St **⊙**9am–5pm daily **⊗**Dec 25 **ⓦ**azstateparks.com

---

13

Bisbee

⚑D7 **🚍** **ℹ**478 Dart Rd; www.discoverbisbee.com

The discovery of copper here in the 1880s sparked a mining rush, and by the turn of the 20th century Bisbee was the largest city between St. Louis and San Francisco. Victorian buildings such as the Copper

14 ⊛ Ⓜ ⬚ 🖐

Kartchner Caverns State Park

⚑D6 **⊙**9am–5pm daily (mid-Dec–May: 8am–6pm); tours 9am–4pm (by reservation) **⊗**Dec 25 **ⓦ**azstateparks.com/kartchner

Located in the Whetstone Mountains, the Kartchner

→

Unusual rock formations dotting Chiricahua National Monument

Caverns were discovered in 1974, when two cavers crawled through a sinkhole into 7 acres (3 ha) of caverns filled with colorful formations. They kept their discovery a secret for 14 years, as they explored these cave formations made of layers of calcite deposited by dripping or flowing water over millions of years. In 1988 the land was bought by the state.

Visitors are not permitted to touch the features, as skin oils stop their growth. Along with stalactites and stalagmites, there are other types of formation such as the 21-ft (6-m) soda straw, the turnip shields, and popcorn.

Chiricahua National Monument

AD6 **A**Off Hwy 181 **B**Dec 25 **W**nps.gov/chir

The Chiricahua Mountains were once the homeland of a band of Apache people. This 19-sq-mile (49-sq-km) area now preserves stunning rock formations, which were created by a series of volcanic eruptions around 27 million years ago. Massive rocks balanced on small pedestals, soaring rock spires, and enormous stone columns make up the bizarre landscape.

Amerind Foundation

AD6 **i**2100 N Amerind Rd, Dragoon **O**10am–4pm Tue-Sun **B**Public hols **W**amerind.org

The name Amerind is a contraction of "American Indian." This private archaeological and ethnological museum contains tens of thousands of artifacts from different Native American cultures. All aspects of Native American life are shown here, with displays covering Inuit masks, Cree tools, and sculpted effigy figures from Mexico's Casas Grandes.

The adjacent Fulton-Hayden Memorial Art Gallery has works by Western artists such as William Robinson Leigh (1866–1955) and Frederic Remington (1861–1909).

Willcox

AD6 **i**1500 N Circle I Rd; www.willcoxchamber.com

Once known as the "Cattle Capital of the West," the small town of Willcox is surrounded by the grasslands of Arizona's ranching country. Its heritage is on show in the frontier-era buildings of downtown and the old railroad depot. The

Rex Allen Cowboy Museum pays tribute to this local lad and singing cowboy of old Hollywood Westerns. There are excellent displays on Geronimo and the Chiricahua Apache at the **Chiricahua Regional Museum**.

Willcox grows the majority of Arizona's wine grapes. You can taste a variety of local wines at Willcox Commercial Store, the oldest retail shop in the state.

Rex Allen Cowboy Museum

A150 N Railroad Ave **O**10am–1pm Mon, 11am–3pm Tue-Sat **W**rexallenmuseum.org

Chiricahua Regional Museum

A127 E Maley St **C**(520) 384-3971 **O**10am–5pm Mon-Sat

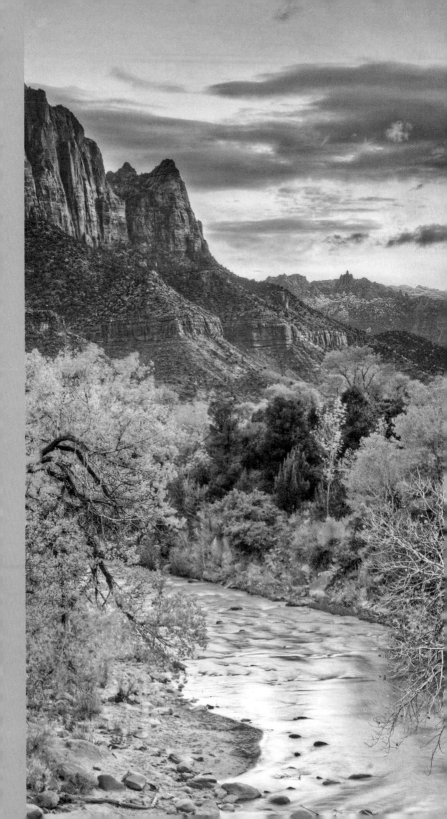

SOUTHERN UTAH

The first people to live in this region were Paleoamericans 12,000 years ago. Later, the Ancestral Puebloans thrived in southeastern Utah, building cliff dwellings along the San Juan River. The Mormons arrived in 1847, successfully establishing settlements in this harsh land.

The five national parks in this region are favorite destinations, so much so that each is inundated with up to four million visitors a year. Today, most people come to the area to enjoy the outdoors. Hiking, mountain biking, and four-wheel driving are all popular activities, as well as riverfloat trips and whitewater adventures. St. George and Cedar City are the biggest towns in Southern Utah. A number of smaller communities, however, such as Springdale, Torrey, and Bluff, have good motels and restaurants. Moab meanwhile offers outdoor activities by day and entertainment by night.

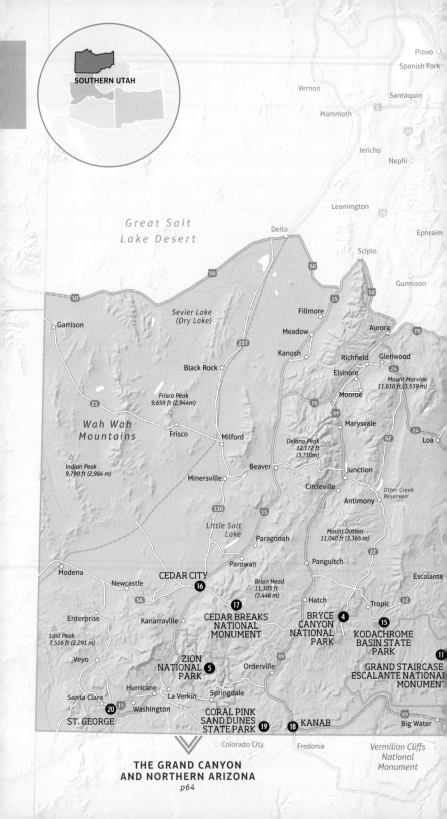

Provo
Spanish Fork
Santaquin

Vernon
Mammoth

Jericho
Nephi

Leamington

Great Salt
Lake Desert

Delta
Ephraim

Scipio

Gunnison

Fillmore

Sevier Lake
(Dry Lake)

Meadow
Aurora

Kanosh
Richfield   Glenwood

Elsinore
Mount Marvine
11,610 ft (3,539 m)

Black Rock
Monroe

Frisco Peak
9,659 ft (2,944 m)
Marysvale

Wah Wah
Mountains
Loa

Frisco
Milford
Delano Peak
12,172 ft
(3,710 m)

Indian Peak
9,790 ft (2,984 m)
Beaver

Minersville
Junction

Circleville
Otter Creek
Reservoir

Antimony

Mount Dutton
11,040 ft (3,365 m)

Little Salt
Lake

Paragonah
Panguitch

Escalante

Modena
Parowan

Newcastle
CEDAR CITY
16

Brian Head
11,305 ft
(3,446 m)

17
Hatch
BRYCE
CANYON
NATIONAL
PARK **4**
Tropic

15

Enterprise
Kanarraville
CEDAR BREAKS
NATIONAL
MONUMENT
KODACHROME
BASIN STATE
PARK

Lost Peak
7,516 ft (2,291 m)

11

Veyo
ZION
NATIONAL
PARK **5**
Orderville
GRAND STAIRCASE
ESCALANTE NATIONAL
MONUMENT

Santa Clara
Hurricane
La Verkin
Springdale

20 **15**
ST. GEORGE
Washington

CORAL PINK
SAND DUNES
STATE PARK **19**
18
KANAB
Big Water

Colorado City
Fredonia
Vermilion Cliffs
National
Monument

**THE GRAND CANYON
AND NORTHERN ARIZONA**
p64

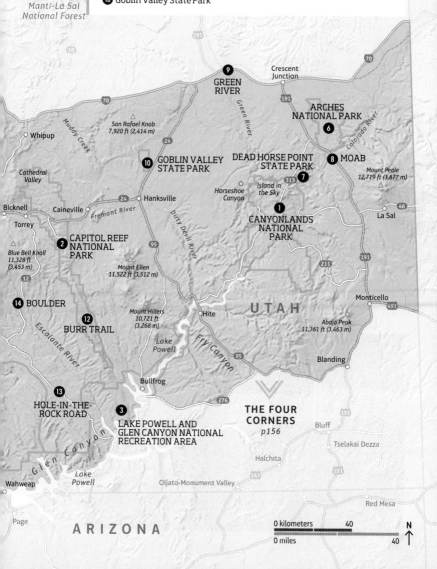

SOUTHERN UTAH

Must Sees
1. Canyonlands National Park
2. Capitol Reef National Park
3. Lake Powell and Glen Canyon National Recreation Area
4. Bryce Canyon National Park
5. Zion National Park
6. Arches National Park

Experience More
7. Dead Horse Point State Park
8. Moab
9. Green River
10. Goblin Valley State Park
11. Grand Staircase-Escalante National Monument
12. Burr Trail
13. Hole-in-the-Rock Road
14. Boulder
15. Kodachrome Basin State Park
16. Cedar City
17. Cedar Breaks National Monument
18. Kanab
19. Coral Pink Sand Dunes State Park
20. St. George

❶ 🏃 🏕

CANYONLANDS NATIONAL PARK

🅐D2 🅦nps.gov/cany

Millions of years ago, the Colorado and Green Rivers cut winding paths deep into rock, creating a labyrinth of rocky canyons, mesas, buttes, and spires that form the heart of this stunning wilderness. With fantastic hiking trails and plenty of breathtaking photo opportunities, this park promises an unforgettable experience.

The confluence of the rivers as the center of the park divides its 527 sq miles (1,365 sq km) into three districts: the Needles, the Maze, and the grassy plateau of the Island in the Sky. The rivers themselves constitute a fourth district. Because of its remote nature, Canyonlands is generally less crowded than southern Utah's other national parks. The districts have their own distinct character and are two to six hours' drive apart. No roads link them, so most visitors only visit one section at a time.

Island in the Sky is the most popular due to its easy access by car. A 12-mile (19-km) scenic road runs from the visitor center to Grand View Point, with its panoramic view over the rivers and canyons. The Needles, named for its colorful sandstone spires, is primarily a backcountry district with over 60 miles (97 km) of interconnecting hiking trails. The Maze is rugged and remote, best suited to experienced hikers. Horseshoe Canyon is a big draw here.

←

Hiking in the Needles District of Canyonlands National Park

HORSESHOE CANYON

It's a long drive on dirt roads to reach the Horseshoe Canyon trailhead, then a minimum five-hour round-trip hike into the canyon, at the northern end of the Maze district. It's definitely worth the effort to see some of the most significant rock art in North America. The panel in the Great Gallery depicts well-preserved intricate, life-size human figures and hunting scenes, painted in the Barrier Canyon style by hunter-gatherers during the Late Archaic period (2000–1000 BC).

←

Mesa Arch in the Island of the Sky district at sunrise, with a keyhole view of the landscape

Did You Know?

Spring through fall, park rangers present geology talks at the Grand View Point.

Picturesque view above Grand View Point in the Island of the Sky district ↑

Admiring the view from one of the park's many overlooks ↑

EXPLORING CANYONLANDS NATIONAL PARK

The park has many good hiking trails. At Island in the Sky, Mesa Arch is reached by a short, easy trail that starts halfway along the main road. The views through the arch make it a great spot for photos, especially at sunrise. At Grand View Point, you can walk a mile along the edge of the canyon to a second awesome overlook at the end of the mesa. In the Needles, easy to moderate hikes include the Cave Springs trail, which leads to a historic cowboy camp and prehistoric petroglyphs, and the Pothole Point trail. Both districts contain more strenuous and overnight hikes. The Maze area is best tackled by hardy backcountry veterans. You'll need a permit to visit the more remote areas; check the website for permit info.

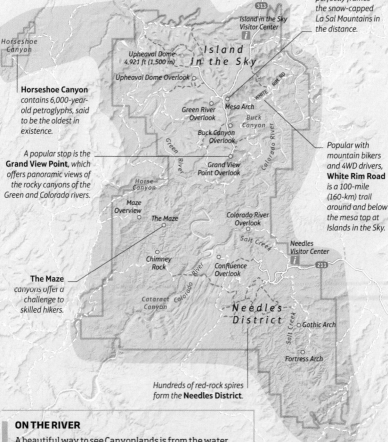

An easy and rewarding 500-yard (457-km) trail leads to **Mesa Arch**, which perfectly frames the snow-capped La Sal Mountains in the distance.

Horseshoe Canyon contains 6,000-year-old petroglyphs, said to be the oldest in existence.

A popular stop is the **Grand View Point**, which offers panoramic views of the rocky canyons of the Green and Colorado rivers.

Popular with mountain bikers and 4WD drivers, **White Rim Road** is a 100-mile (160-km) trail around and below the mesa top at Islands in the Sky.

The Maze canyons offer a challenge to skilled hikers.

Hundreds of red-rock spires form the **Needles District**.

ON THE RIVER

A beautiful way to see Canyonlands is from the water. Above the confluence, both the Colorado and Green rivers have miles of calm water that make for relaxing trips by kayak, canoe, or other shallow-water craft. Below the confluence, the rivers surge through Cataract Canyon on a thrilling, 14-mile (23-km) stretch of white water. The park website lists local companies that run river trips.

0 km 5
0 miles 5

N

2 〈icons〉

CAPITOL REEF NATIONAL PARK

🅰C2 📍Hwy 24, 10 miles (16 km) E of Torrey 🌐nps.gov/care

Located in the heart of red-rock country in south-central Utah, Capitol Reef National Park is filled with colorful cliffs, deep canyons, enormous domes, and hidden arches. A scenic drive runs past the main highlights, while hundreds of miles of trails lead into the backcountry of desert rock.

Around the turn of the 20th century, prospectors coming across the desert were forced to stop at the Waterpocket Fold, a vast 100-mile- (160-km-) long wall of rock that runs north–south through the desert. They likened it to an ocean reef and thought its round white domes resembled the nation's Capitol Building, hence the park's name. As the light changes through the day, the multicolored cliffs, buttes, and rock formations do indeed resemble a tropical reef. Among the sandstone landmarks that can be seen from Highway 24 that cuts across the park are the sculpted red tower of Chimney Rock and the massive white bulk of Capitol Dome. An 8-mile (13-km) scenic drive runs south from the visitor center to the towering cliffs of Capitol Gorge. Hiking trails in the Waterpocket District have fantastic views of Waterpocket Fold. Cathedral Valley, the rugged northern

↑ Fremont petroglyph figures carved into sandstone

FRUITA HISTORIC DISTRICT

In the 1880s, Mormon settlers moved into the isolated Fremont River valley. They planted thousands of apple, peach, plum, pear, and apricot trees, and also grew grapes, walnuts, and almonds, and consequently founded a village called Fruita. Today you can see the historic remains of the Fruita school-house, blacksmith shop, the Gifford House Store and Museum, and more than 22 orchards which are still thriving.

section of the park, holds numerous impressive desert landscapes and rock formations.

The park has a long record of human habitation, dating to the Fremont Culture. Named after the river, these people lived in the Capitol Reef area from around AD 300 to 1300. Their rock art can be seen along Highway 24, at Capitol Gorge, and in backcountry areas. The homestead of Mormon settlers who moved here in the late 19th century is now a museum.

↑ Sun setting over the red rocks of Capitol Reef National Park

EXPLORING CAPITOL REEF NATIONAL PARK

Start by exploring the pioneer buildings of the Fruita Historic District, just beyond the visitor center. Past the Fruita Schoolhouse on Highway 24, a short trail leads to a wonderful group of Fremont petroglyphs carved into the rocks. The petroglyphs depict human figures often decorated with headdresses and jewelry, animal figures, and abstract designs. Nearby, the Hickman Bridge Trail leads past the ruins of a Fremont pit house and granary.

In Capitol Gorge, at the end of the Scenic Drive, a short walk brings you to the Pioneer Register, where early travelers marked their passage by carving their names and dates on the canyon walls. The Cathedral Valley Scenic Backway is an adventurous, off-road loop 58 miles (93 km) long, popular with mountain bikers and four-wheelers.

Cathedral Valley

Upper South Desert Overlook

C a p i t o l

Lower South Desert Overlook

Fremont River

R e e f

24

Hickman Bridge

Fremont Petroglyphs

Gifford Farmhouse

Capitol Gorge

24

N a t i o n a l

Strike Valley

P a r k

Muley Canyon

Waterpocket Fold

Suprise Canyon

Norton-Bullfrog Road

Halls Creek Overlook

The vast rock monoliths that tower over the desert in **Cathedral Valley** give the valley its name.

The **Fremont petroglyphs** were created between 700 and 1250 and can be seen on a rock wall in the Fremont Canyon.

Visitors can tour the 1908 **Gifford Farmhouse**, now a museum dedicated to the 1880s Mormon settlement that once flourished here.

Capitol Gorge *can be reached from the scenic route that extends about 10 miles (16 km) into the heart of the park.*

Waterpocket Fold *was formed 65 million years ago as the Earth's crust buckled upward. The multicolored ripples of rock that run the length of the park continue to be shaped by erosion.*

Notom-Bullfrog Road *is an adventurous drive for 70 miles (113 km) south to Lake Powell, along a partly unpaved road. Cars can negotiate the road in dry weather, but extra gas and water are essential.*

← Waterpocket Fold, the main geologic feature in the park, viewed from the air

0 kilometers   10

0 miles   10

N ↑

Did You Know?

The Hickman Bridge
Trail is an easy
2-mile (3-km)
round-trip hike.

↑ A hiker standing below
Hickman Bridge, a large
natural arch

3 🛠️ 🎿 🍴 ☕ 🛍️

LAKE POWELL AND GLEN CANYON NATIONAL RECREATION AREA

🅰️ C3 📍 2 miles (3 km) N of Page on Hwy 98, off Hwy 160 🌐 nps.gov/glca

Established in 1972, the Glen Canyon National Recreation Area (NRA) covers more than 1,560 sq miles (4,040 sq km) of dramatic desert and canyon country around the 185-mile- (298-km-) long Lake Powell. On summer weekends, the lake is a busy place as powerboats, waterskiers, houseboat parties, jet skis, and catamarans explore its myriad sandstone side canyons.

📷 PICTURE PERFECT
Glen Canyon Dam Overlook

For a great shot of the Colorado River flowing out from beneath the massive face of the dam, climb the short trail south of the Carl Hayden Visitor Center to the Glen Canyon Dam Overlook.

The second-largest man-made lake in the country after Lake Mead (p268), Lake Powell was created by damming the Colorado River. The recreation area is Y-shaped, running from Lee's Ferry in Arizona, following the San Juan River east almost to the town of Mexican Hat in Utah, and heading northeast to the Orange Cliffs west of Canyonlands National Park (p122).

The lake is a mecca for watersports enthusiasts. The recreation area has several marinas, where you can rent motorboats, jet skis, or kayaks to explore the lake's clear blue waters and 96 side canyons. Houseboat rentals are especially popular, with residents cruising the salmon-pink cliffs and coves by day, and partying on the beaches at night. Glen Canyon is also one of the most popular hiking, biking, and 4WD destinations in the US.

↑ The blue waters of Lake Powell surrounding the cliffs and boulders of the flooded canyon

1 Kayaking on Lake Powell is a popular activity. Kayaks can be rented from the Waheap and Bullfrog marinas.

2 Boat tours departing from Waheap Marina take visitors around Lake Powell past Rocky Mountain scenery.

3 Rainbow Bridge National Monument, within Glen Canyon National Recreation Area, is the world's largest known natural bridge and can be reached by tour boat.

EXPLORING LAKE POWELL AND GLEN CANYON NRA

The Glen Canyon Dam lies south of the Utah border at Page, Arizona. You can sign up for 45-minute tours of this facility at the Carl Hayden Visitor Center. In Page, drop in at the museum (p147) dedicated to the lake's namesake, John Wesley Powell. The museum is also the town's visitor center, where rafting trips, boat tours, and other activities can be booked. South of Page is a stunning over-look set above the Colorado River at Horseshoe Bend, while north of the town is the Antelope Canyon, which lies on Navajo land and can only be visited on guided tours. There are a variety of day hikes you can take thoughout the Glen Canyon NRA.

🔍 HIDDEN GEM
Hanging Garden

Near the Glen Canyon Dam, an easy 1-mile (0.6-km) trail leads to the Hanging Garden, where water seeping through the rocks has created a green oasis of lush plants growing in the alcoves of the colorful, striated cliffs.

← Bands of curving sandstone at Antelope Canyon, a famous slot canyon

Rising 309 ft (94 m) above Lake Powell, **Rainbow Bridge** is the largest known natural bridge in the world, accessible by boat from Wahweap or Bullfrog marinas.

Antelope Canyon is a famously deep slot canyon.

Glen Canyon Dam rises 710 ft (216 m) above the bedrock of the Colorado River.

Lees Ferry was a Mormon settlement in the 19th century. Today, this outpost offers tourist facilities, including a ranger station and campground.

Escalante River

Waterpocket Fold

Stevens Arch

Coyote Natural Bridge

330

Hole in the Rock

Last Chance Bay

Dangle Rope Marina

Big Water

Warm Creek Bay

Lake Powell

Rainbow Bridge National Monument

89

Wahweap

Wahweap Marina

Antelope Island

West Canyon

Glen Canyon Dam

Antelope Canyon

Rainbow Plateau

Navajo Canyon

i Page

Lees Ferry

Horseshoe Bend

98

89

Marble Canyon

0 km   10
0 miles   10

N ↑

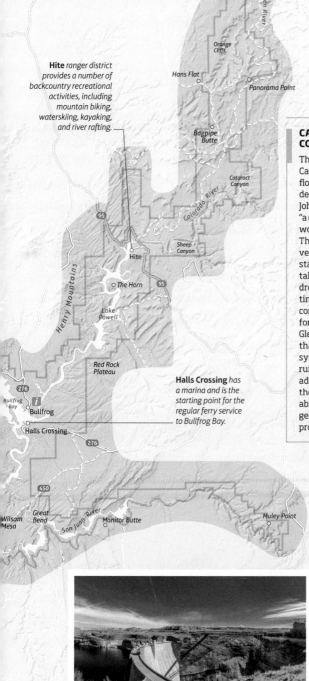

Hite *ranger district provides a number of backcountry recreational activities, including mountain biking, waterskiing, kayaking, and river rafting.*

Halls Crossing *has a marina and is the starting point for the regular ferry service to Bullfrog Bay.*

CANYON CONTROVERSY

The completion of Glen Canyon dam in 1963 flooded the area described by explorer John Wesley Powell as "a curious ensemble of wonderful features." The project was controversial right from the start as environmentalists deplored the drowning of the pristine canyon, and many continue to campaign for the restoration of Glen Canyon, believing that ancient ecosystems are being ruined. Pro-dam advocates point out the value of the dam's ability to store water, generate power, and provide recreation.

← Glen Canyon Dam and Bridge, achievements of engineering

4 🏂 🚵 🍴 🛍️

BRYCE CANYON NATIONAL PARK

🅰️ C2 📍 Hwy 63, off Hwy 12 🌐 nps.gov/brca

Despite its name, this spectacular landmark is not a solitary canyon, but a series of deep, natural amphitheaters. The largest of these, Bryce Amphitheater, is filled with flame-colored pinnacle rock formations called hoodoos, the hallmark of this national park. Bryce Canyon contains more hoodoos than any other place on earth.

The Paiutes, once hunters here, described these vast, mesmerising fields of irregular pink, orange, and red spires as "red rocks standing like men in a bowl-shaped recess."

Bryce is high in altitude, reaching elevations of around 8,000–9,000 ft (2,400–2,700 m). A scenic road runs for 18 miles (29 km) along the rim of Paunsaugunt Plateau, from the park's only entrance in the north to its highest elevation in the south. From April to October, a free shuttle bus operates from the Visitor Center to the four main viewpoints at Sunrise, Sunset, Bryce, and Inspiration Points. There is also a free three-and-a-half-hour bus tour that stops at many more viewpoints and goes all the way to the end at Rainbow Point. From Bryce Point and Sunset Point you can look down over the tight maze of hoodoos and fins known as the Silent City. Nearby is the historic Bryce Canyon Lodge, built in 1923.

GREAT VIEW
Pretty Peaks

Bryce Canyon is famous for its clear skies. Most days, you can see Navajo Mountain, 80 miles (129 km) south on the Utah-Arizona border. On very clear days you can see across the Grand Canyon to Humphrey's Peak, which is 150 miles (242 km) away.

1 The Utah prairie dog is a threatened species. One of the largest groups lives in the park.

2 Hoodoos are formed as rain, wind, and ice erode "fins" of harder rock that become columns. These further erode into strangely shaped hoodoos.

3 Most of the many trails in the park start along the canyon rim.

↑ The hoodoos of Bryce Amphitheater viewed from Inspiration Point at dawn

EXPLORING BRYCE CANYON NATIONAL PARK

The canyon's maze of pillars and channels is best appreciated on foot. Numerous hiking trails take you down into the bowls where you can walk among the hoodoos and other formations. They include easy day hikes, like the short Queens Garden trail and longer Rim Trail, the moderate Navajo Loop trail through a slot canyon, and the challenging Fairyland and Peek-A-Boo loop trails. Many trails are interconnected. Others share the route with horseback and mule treks to the canyon floor.

Bryce Canyon is breathtakingly beautiful in winter, when snow dusts the colorful pinnacles. After a deep snowfall, snowshoeing, cross-country skiing, and winter hiking are possible in the park. And there are ranger-guided Full Moon Snowshoe Hikes from November to March. Stargazing is spectacular under the park's natural dark skies – on a clear night, you can see 2.2 million light years to the Andromeda Galaxy. Astronomy programs are offered throughout the year; check the schedule at the visitor center.

← The graceful Natural Bridge, framing a picturesque view of the distant valley far below

The **Natural Bridge** is located a few yards from the park's scenic highway. Officially, it is a natural arch and not a bridge, as it was formed not by a river but by the same natural forces (of wind, rain, and ice) that created the park's hoodoos.

The **Agua Canyon** overlook features some of the most delicate and beautiful of the park's formations, as well as a good view of the layered pink sandstone cliffs typical of the Paunsaugunt Plateau.

The 1.4-mile (2-km) round-trip **Navajo Loop** trail zig zags sharply down the cliff face for 500 ft (150 m) to finish in a slow meander among slot canyons and rock stands. The climb back up the trail is particularly strenuous.

Swamp Canyon Butte
Mud Canyon
Noon Canyon Butte
Noon Canyon
Natural Bridge
Bridge Canyon
Agua Canyon
Ponderosa Canyon
Rainbow Point
Yovimpa Point
Yovimpa Spring
NAVAJO LOOP
Pink Cliffs
Riggs Spring

Bryce Canyon Airport

Shakespear Point
7,842 ft (2,390 m)

63

12

Bryce Canyon City

Mossy Cave

Fairyland Point

Visitor Center

FAIRYLAND LOOP TRAIL

12

Bryce Canyon Lodge

Sunrise Point

Sunset Point

Inspiration Point

Thor's Hammer

63

Bryce Point

Bryce Amphitheater

Paria View

Pink Cliffs

From the **Sunrise Point** *lookout it is easy to see why early settler Ebenezer Bryce, after whom the park is named, called it "a helluva place to lose a cow".*

Sunset Point *is one of the major lookouts in Bryce Canyon. In spite of its name, it faces east, so while sunrises can be spectacular here, sunsets can be a little anticlimactic.*

Eroded sandstone hoodoos, such as **Thor's Hammer**, *are carved into the pink cliffs of the highest "step" of the Grand Staircase.*

In both winter and summer the **Bryce Amphitheater** *is best seen from Inspiration Point. The panoramic vista of snow-covered rock spires is among the most popular views of the park.*

| 0 kilometers | 3 |
| 0 miles | 3 |

N ↑

BIRD-WATCHING

Bryce Canyon provides shelter for 175 bird species, including migratory birds. Violet-green swallows are frequently seen along the Rim Trail. Two osprey nests are located along the scenic drive. You may also be lucky enough to see peregrine falcons, eagles, and even the rare California condor, which has been spotted from Bryce Point.

↑ The towering Thor's Hammer, one of the more distinctive hoodoos in Bryce Canyon

The Virgin River winding through Zion Canyon, bordered by lush foliage ↑

5 ⬤ 🏞 👣 🍽

ZION
NATIONAL PARK

🅰B3 📍Hwy 9, near Springdale 🌐nps.gov/zion

One of the most popular of all of Utah's natural wonders, Zion Canyon was carved by the Virgin River and then widened and sculpted by wind, rain, and ice. The canyon walls rise up to 2,000 ft (600 m) on both sides, and are shaped into jagged peaks and formations in shades of red, pink, and white.

Mormon settlers moved to the canyon in the 1860s and named it Zion, after an ancient Hebrew word meaning "sanctuary" or "refuge". Many of the rock formations, such as the Three Patriarchs and the Altar of Sacrifice, have biblical references. Farming continued on the canyon floor until 1909, when it was declared a national monument. It became Utah's first national park in 1919.

The lower reaches of the Virgin River meander through the banks of cottonwood oak and willow trees that grow beneath the gradually sloping walls at the start of the canyon. The river seems gentle, but the force of its current is responsible for forming the canyon. Luxuriant foliage along the river banks provides shade for the area's abundant wildlife, including birds, mule deer, and bobcats. In spring the wild meadows bordering the river banks sport a profusion of wild flowers. However, sudden summer rainstorms may cause floods and areas of the park near the river to be closed.

↑ The pink-red hues of the Altar of Sacrifice rock formation at sunrise

↑ Hikers on the narrow Angels Landing trail, a popular scenic hike with sheer drop-offs and stunning viewpoints

PARK SHUTTLE

From mid-March to late November the only way to explore the inner core of Zion Canyon is via the park's frequent shuttle buses. Parking is limited the rest of the year, so visitors are advised to take the free Springdale Shuttle, which ferries people from various stops in town to the park's entrance. The shuttle inside the park runs from the Visitor Center, making nine stops along Zion Canyon Scenic Drive.

Exploring Zion National Park

Inside the park, the 6-mile (10-km) Zion Canyon Scenic Drive follows the Virgin River into the ever-narrowing canyon. From the visitor center, board the park's free shuttle, which stops at nine locations on the Zion Canyon Scenic Drive, forming a loop. Shortly beyond the southern entrance to the park, stop at the Zion Human History Museum for a fascinating look at the park through the ages. Other stops along the Scenic Drive give access to such geological highlights as the Court of the Patriarchs, the Great White Throne, Weeping Rock, and Angels Landing.

There are a variety of hiking trails along the route; some lead to nearby waterfalls and alcoves, while others, like the demanding East and West Rim trails, climb right out of the canyon. At the end of the the Zion Canyon Scenic Drive lies the park's most popular trail. Involving no climbing, the 1.3-mile (2-km) paved River Walk follows the Virgin River to where the canyon walls rise to over 2,000 ft (600 m). The trail offers beautiful views of the river as it winds between red sandstone walls. There is a separate entrance to Kolob Canyons, another great area for hiking, in the remote

↑ Visitors at Weeping Rock, with water "seeping" out of the rock

northwestern region of the park. Other popular activities in the park include horseback riding, swimming in the Virgin River, and cycling. Bike rentals are available at many rental companies throughout the Springdale area.

INSIDER TIP
Park Programs

There are many free, ranger-led activities in the park. These include hikes and bird walks, Ride with a Ranger shuttle tours, nature center youth programs, and evening talks on stargazing and wildlife.

> Look up to see the park's unusual hanging gardens of mosses, ferns, and wildflowers on tall cliffs, fed by water seeping out of sandstone.

Flora and Fauna

The Colorado Plateau, the Great Basin, and the Mojave Desert converge in the park, creating a habitat for a diverse range of plants and animals. Mule deer, desert bighorn sheep, golden eagles, and other raptors are often spotted. The riparian area of the Virgin River is surprisingly lush with huge cottonwood trees and nearby wetlands. Look up to see the park's unusual hanging gardens of mosses, ferns, and wildflowers on tall cliffs, fed by water seeping out of sandstone.

Weeping Rock

An easy, self-guided trail leads to Weeping Rock, an eroded, bowl-shaped cliff face where water oozes out from between two different sandstone strata. This creates a year-round spring that nourishes hanging gardens of moss, ferns, grass, as well as wildflowers in spring.

The Narrows

Rock walls tower 1,000 ft (305 m) high along the slenderest stretch of Zion Canyon. The only trail through this awesome gorge is right in the Virgin River itself. Explore it on a short splash upstream, make the strenuous, all-day hike to Big Spring and back (10 miles/16 km round-trip), or get a permit for the adventurous downstream hike (16 miles/26 km) from Chamberlain's Ranch.

Kolob Canyons

Towering peaks of Navajo sandstone surround this wilderness area in Zion National Park, 40 miles (64 km) north of the crowded Zion Canyon. There are viewpoints along a 5-mile (8-km) scenic drive, while hiking trails lead to waterfalls, old homestead cabins, and rock formations such as Double Arch Alcove, West Temple, and the Kolob Arch.

↑ Hiking in the Virgin River through the Narrows, and the Subway pool *(inset)*, part of a slot canyon in North Creek

6 🤿 Ⓜ 🛍️

ARCHES
NATIONAL PARK

🅐 D2 🏠 Hwy 191, 5 miles (1.5 km) N of Moab 🌐 nps.gov/arch

The highest number of natural stone arches found anywhere in the world are in Arches National Park, one of the most popular national parks in the region. There are more than 2,000 of these red rock wonders; along with pinnacles, towers, and balanced rocks, they make a stunning sight against the deep-blue desert sky.

The arches are formed through a process that takes millions of years; today's arches continue to slowly erode and will eventually collapse. The Arches Visitor Center provides an excellent introduction to the geology of this beautiful but fragile land, which continues to be chiseled away by the forces of nature. Many of the landmark arches can be seen from the main road through the park, and a wealth of hiking trails lead deeper into this amazing landscape. One of the best descriptions of the park's pristine beauty is by author and environmentalist Edward Abbey, who worked here as a park ranger in 1956–7, and wrote about the landscape in his classic memoir *Desert Solitaire*.

> **The arches are formed through a process that takes millions of years; today's arches continue to slowly erode.**

📷 PICTURE PERFECT
Light and Shade

Late afternoon and early evening are the best times for photography at the Arches National Park. The red arches glow in the setting sun, and there's a beautiful play of light and shadow. The warm light of early morning is another good time to capture colorful hues.

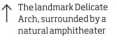

↑ The landmark Delicate Arch, surrounded by a natural amphitheater

1 The Fiery Furnace is one of the most dramatic areas of the park for hiking, with a maze of canyons, fins, and spires.

2 Ute petroglyphs portraying bighorn sheep and men on horseback can be seen near Wolfe Ranch on the Delicate Arch Trail.

3 In the Windows Section, the dramatic Double Arch is a formation of two arches that share the same stone for their foundation.

Exploring Arches National Park

Arches National Park becomes extremely busy from March through October, especially around holiday weekends. Parking at popular trailheads is limited and full most of the day. To avoid congestion at the entrance gate and parking areas, arrive early in the morning or late in the afternoon.

The park's highlights can be seen from the many viewpoints dotted along the Arches Scenic Drive. It starts at the visitor center at the park's south end, just off Highway 191. If you spend ten minutes at each viewpoint, it takes about a total of three hours to drive the entire park road. Several easy trails start from parking lots at the road's viewpoints. The loop at Balanced Rock is a short trail suitable for children; part of it is paved and accessible to wheelchairs. Delicate Arch Viewpoint is a similarly gentle hike. The short Windows loop is an easy trail suitable for families, its first 100

↑ Kayaking up the Colorado River below the cliffs of Arches National Park

yards are wheelchair-accessible. Following the bottom of a canyon, the Park Avenue Trail leads past huge rock monoliths, including the Courthouse Towers and Nefertiti.

In addition to hiking, biking is a popular activity in and around the park. Bikes are only allowed on the park's designated roads, paved and unpaved. Several outfitters in Moab (p146) offer tours on a range of mountain bike trails. Most are difficult and are suitable only for experienced climbers. Local companies around Moab offer jeep tours, horseback riding, and rafting or kayaking trips on the Colorado and Green rivers.

> **Following the bottom of a canyon, the Park Avenue Trail leads past huge rock monoliths, including the the Courthouse Towers and Nefertiti.**

NATURE'S SCULPTOR

The Arches National Park "floats" on a salt bed, which was created about 300 million years ago. Over millions of years, this salt layer liquefied under the pressure exerted by the rock above it, and eventually bulged upward, cracking the sandstone above. Over time the cracks eroded, leaving long fins of rock. As these fins in turn eroded from the ground up, the remaining sections of rock formed arches, which range today from the solid-looking Turret Arch to the graceful Delicate and Land-scape arches.

Petrified Dunes

▷ Covering several acres, these unusual formations lie between Courthouse Towers and the Windows areas. They were created when ancient sand dunes hardened into stone beneath layers of heavier sediment that later eroded away. Watch for the scenic overlook off the main park road.

Fiery Furnace

▽ Discover hidden arches on ranger-led walks in this spectacular maze of narrow passages, sculpted rocks, and canyons, which takes its name from its fiery glow at sunset. There are morning and evening walks; sign up in advance at the visitor center. This is a challenging hike, and permits are required if not entering the area on a guided walk.

The Windows Section

In this section, a one-mile (1.6 km) loop trail leads to Turret Arch, then the North and South Windows arches, situated side by side. With excellent viewing spots available, many visitors photograph North and South arches, framed by the sandstone Turner Arch.

Wolfe Ranch

The park was once home to John Wesley Wolfe, a Civil War veteran who built a small ranch in the late 1800s. The rustic wood cabin he shared with his family still stands and is listed on the National Register of Historic Places.

Balanced Rock

▷ This formation, consisting of a precariously balanced boulder on top of a sandstone spire, reaches a height of 128 ft (39 m) and is one of the park's most famous icons. Good views of it are available from the trail as well as the scenic road route. Don't miss this awesome spectacle, as eventually the gravity-defying boulder will topple down as the rocky landscape continues to erode.

↑ Turret Arch seen through the South Window in the scenic Windows Section

EXPERIENCE MORE

7

Dead Horse Point State Park

D2 **Hwy 313** **6am–10pm daily** **stateparks.utah.gov**

The high mesa of Dead Horse Point lies just outside the entry to the Island in the Sky of Canyonlands National Park. Unforgettable views of the Colorado River and the maze of deep canyons , formed by millions of years of geologic activity, are a high point here.

According to legend, this park owes its name to the fact that it was once used as a natural corral for wild mustangs. A group of horses not chosen for taming were once left in this dry site for some unknown reason, eventually dying of thirst within sight of the Colorado River far below. The park also features several short hiking trails that follow the cliff edge, including a paved trail, offering variations on the truly amazing view.

The drama of this place has not been lost on Hollywood. Famous as the spot where Thelma and Louise drove off the edge in the 1991 film of the same name, these cliffs were scaled by Tom Cruise at the beginning of *Mission: Impossible 2* (2000).

8

Moab

D2 **25 E Center St; www.discovermoab.com**

In 1952 a local prospector discovered the first of several major uranium deposits outside Moab. Overnight, the town became one of the wealthiest communities in America. When the uranium market declined in the 1970s, Moab was saved by tourism and its proximity to Arches and Canyonlands national parks.

Today, Moab is one of the top destinations for lovers of the outdoors. Mountain bikers come here to experience the famous Slick Rock Trail and the challenging ride to Moab Rim, a strenuous trail of about 10 miles (16 km). There is also a vast choice of hiking and 4WD routes taking in some of this region's fabulous landscapes.

Matheson Wetlands Preserve off Kane Creek Boulevard has 2 miles (3 km) of hiking trails along a riverside wetland that is home to birds and wildlife.

White water rafting, paddleboarding, and kayaking on the Colorado River are other popular activities here.

With its mild, pleasant climate and Wild West feel, the town is popular with second-home owners and has a good selection of shops, restaurants, and galleries.

Matheson Wetlands Preserve

Off Kane Creek Blvd **(435) 259-4629** **Dawn–dusk daily**

Did You Know?

The name "Moab" comes from an ancient biblical kingdom.

A hiker enjoying the view from an overlook in Dead Horse Point State Park ↑

←

Tackling the rapids of the notoriously wild Green River in a rowboat

10

Goblin Valley State Park

🅰C2 🅰Off Hwy 24 🕒6am–10pm daily 🌐stateparks.utah.gov

The "goblins" of Goblin Valley State Park are a group of mushroom-shaped rocks, or hoodoos, intricately carved by erosion. Visitors are free to wander among these rocks, which are up to 10 ft (3 m) in height. Two paved and several unpaved trails lead down to the valley floor.

💬 **INSIDER TIP**
State Park Fees and Passes

Like the national parks, most state parks charge a day-entry fee. If you are planning to visit several parks, check to see if they offer passes for unlimited admission. Camping fees are extra.

9

Green River

🅰D2 ℹ460 E Main St; (435) 564-3448

Located in a broad, bowl-shaped valley, the town of Green River grew around a ford of the wild river of the same name in the 19th and early 20th centuries. Primarily a service town, it is also a launching spot for those braving the white water of the Green and Colorado rivers.

It was from here that the explorer and ethnologist John Wesley Powell began his intrepid exploration of the Colorado River and Grand Canyon in 1871. The expedition resulted in the creation of the first maps of the area. The **John Wesley Powell River History Museum** has about 20,000 sq ft (1,860 sq m) of displays tracing the history of the area's exploration and also includes a film about Powell's expedition.

John Wesley Powell River History Museum

🎨🎫 🅰1765 E Main St 🕒Apr–Oct: 9am–7pm Mon–Sat, noon–5pm Sun; Nov–Mar: 9am–5pm Tue–Sat 🚫Public hols 🌐johnwesleypowell.com

The striking sandstone formations of Goblin Valley State Park

⓫ Grand Staircase-Escalante National Monument

🅐 C3 🛈 755 W Main St, Escalante; www.blm.gov

Established by President Clinton in 1996, the Grand Staircase-Escalante National Monument encompasses 1,570 sq miles (4,066 sq km) of rock canyons, mountains, and high desert plateaus. It was named for the four cliff faces called Vermilion, Grey, White, and Pink, raised 12 million years ago, that build in tiered steps from Bryce Canyon to Grand Canyon across the Colorado Plateau.

The Bureau of Land Management intends to preserve the area's wild state. It has declated that no new roads, facilities, or campgrounds will be built here.

The spectacular beauty of the monument is best explored on scenic drives combined with day-long hikes. Highway 89 follows the park's southern boundary, in places hugging the base of the towering Vermilion cliffs.

⓬ Burr Trail

🅐 C2 🛈 755 W Main St, Escalante 🖥 nps.gov/glca/planyourvisit/driving-the-burr-trail.htm

Partly paved, the Burr Trail is one of the world's most famous hairpinned roads. It winds through the Grand Staircase-Escalante National Monument past some of Utah's most dramatic and beautiful scenery. A 40-mile (65-km) stretch follows Deer Creek, rising through the winding red-rock maze of Long Canyon. At the canyon's end, the view opens out to reveal the pristine valleys of the Circle Cliffs and Capitol Reef. The trail crosses Capitol Reef as an unpaved road before reaching Bullfrog Marina at Lake Powell (p130) and is passable only by 4WD, high-clearance vehicles in dry weather.

> Partly paved, the Burr Trail is one of the world's most famous hairpinned roads. It winds through the Grand Staircase-Escalante National Monument.

HIDDEN GEM
Lower Calf Creek Falls

This waterfall, a 126-ft (38-m) plume that drops past lush gardens into an emerald-green pool, can be accessed via a trail that begins at Calf Creek Campground, off Hwy 12 near Boulder.

⓭ Hole-in-the-Rock Road

🅐 C3 🛈 755 W Main St, Escalante 🖥 nps.gov/glca

In 1879 a group of 230 Mormon settlers headed out from Panguitch, hoping to create a new settlement in southeastern Utah. They were brought to a halt by the yawning 2,000-ft- (610-m-) deep abyss of Glen Canyon. Undeterred, they dynamited a narrow hole through a wall of rock and constructed a primitive road down the sheer sides of the canyon. Lowering their wagons and cattle down the path by ropes they finally reached the bottom, only to repeat the whole process in

←

Jacob Hamblin Arch in the
Grand Staircase-Escalante
National Monument

of rock with steep drops on
either side. Beyond Boulder,
Highway 12 climbs to the
9,400-ft- (2,865-m) summit
of Boulder Mountain.

15

Kodachrome Basin State Park

🅐C3 🏠2905 S Kodachrome
State Park Rd 🕕6am-
10pm daily 🌐 stateparks.
utah.gov

A few miles east of Bryce
Canyon and 9 miles (14 km)
south of Highway 12,
Kodachrome Basin State Park
features 67 freestanding sand
pipes, or rock chimneys. They
formed as geyser vents
millions of years ago, when
the area is said to have
resembled the geothermal
terrain of Yellowstone
National Park. The park was
christened in 1948, when a
National Geographic photo-
graphic expedition named
it for the film they used to
capture its multicolored
monoliths set against the
bright blue sky. Hiking trails
of varying difficulties lead
to outstanding vistas.

reverse to ascend the far side.
They finally founded the town
of Bluff in 1880 *(p182)*.

Their original route, Hole-
in-the-Rock Road, offers a trip
through the wild interior of
the Grand Staircase-Escalante
National Monument. The
road is rough in places, but
passable. Intrepid hikers can
explore Peekaboo and Spooky
slot canyons, two slot canyons
barely one foot (30 cm) wide
in places. A 4WD vehicle is
needed to cross the last
6 miles (10 km) to the
pioneers' "Hole in the Rock,"
a 50-ft (15-m) slit that offers
views of Lake Powell.

14

Boulder

🅐C2 ℹ460 Hwy 12

The tiny town of Boulder is
home to the Anasazi State
Park, which offers restored
ruins and a museum detailing
the history of the Ancestral
Puebloans, who lived here
between AD 1050 and 1200.
Before Highway 12 was built,
Boulder was virtually isolated
and was the last town in
America to receive its mail by

pack mule. Today, it makes
a welcome rest stop along
Highway 12, which connects
Highway 89 and Capitol Reef
National Park. This road has
some of the most spectcular
and diverse landscapes found
along any road in the USA.

Between Escalante and
Boulder, Highway 12 winds
through a landscape of vividly
colored, towering rock
formations and twisting
canyons. Just before Boulder,
the road offers white-knuckle
excitement as it traverses the
Hogsback, a knife-edge ridge

SLOT CANYONS

The Southwest is famous
for its slot canyons.
These deep gorges, just a
few inches wide in spots,
are formed when water
etches its way through
soft rock, carving out
slender passageways.
To Native Americans,
slot canyons were
spiritual places. They
make amazing hiking
routes, but the threat
of flash flooding also
makes them dangerous
if rain is forecast.

> In Cedar City, the Frontier Homestead State Park Museum pays tribute to the indomitable and pioneering spirit of the early Mormons.

16 Cedar City

B2 **🚗🚌** **i** 581 N Main St; www.visitcedarcity.com

Founded in 1851 by Mormons (*p154*), this town developed as a center for mining and smelting iron in the latter part of the 19th century. Today, it offers hotels and restaurants within an hour's drive of Zion National Park (*p138*).

In town, the **Frontier Homestead State Park Museum** pays tribute to the indomitable and pioneering spirit of the early Mormons. It features an extensive collection of more than 300 wagons and early vehicles, including an original Wells Fargo overland stagecoach.

Cedar City's Shakespeare Festival, which runs annually from late June to mid-October, is staged in a replica of London's neo-Elizabethan Globe Theatre and attracts large audiences from the area.

Frontier Homestead State Park Museum

⊗ 🏠 635 N Main St
📞 (435) 586-9290 ⏰ Jun-Aug: 9am–6pm daily; Sep-May: 9am–5pm Mon-Sat
🚫 Jan 1, Thanksgiving, Dec 25

17 Cedar Breaks National Monument

A2 **Off Hwy 14**
w nps.gov/cebr

Around 20 miles (32 km) east of Cedar City, along Highway

14, Cedar Breaks National Monument features a spectacular geologic amphitheater of vibrant pink and orange limestone cliffs, topped by deep green forest. Carved by erosion, sculpted columns rise in ranks of color, and resemble a smaller, less-visited version of Bryce Canyon (*p134*). The area remains open to crosscountry skiers in winter. In summer, Cedar Breaks is covered with a stunning display of colorful wildflowers. An annual wildflower festival is held in July.

18 Kanab

B2 **i** 745 E Hwy 89; www.visitsouthern utah.com

This small town was named for Fort Kanab, established in 1864 but abandoned only two years later following frequent Native American attacks. Mormon settlers founded the town in 1874. Its main purpose today is to offer reasonably priced food and accommodations to vacationers traveling between Grand Canyon, Zion, and Bryce Canyon national parks.

Often referred to as the "gateway to Lake Powell," Kanab is also known as Utah's "Little Hollywood," a reference to the hundreds of movies and TV shows that have been filmed in and around the town, from *Butch Cassidy and the Sundance Kid* (1969) and *The Outlaw Josey Wales* (1976) to *Planet of the Apes* (1968 and 2001) and *Mission: Impossible 2* (2000). Details of film sets open to the public may be obtained from the visitor center.

Did You Know?

Cedar Breaks' Paiute name, "u-map-wich," means "place where rocks slide down constantly."

→
Sunset over snow-covered cliffs at Cedar Breaks National Monument

⓲ ⊘

Coral Pink Sand Dunes State Park

🅰B4 🕒Dawn-dusk daily
🌐stateparks.utah.gov

About 10 miles (16 km) west of Kanab, the Coral Pink Sand Dunes State Park is a sea of ever-shifting pink dunes that cover more than 5.8 sq miles (15 sq km). This harsh desert landscape was created when wind eroded the rich red sandstone cliffs surrounding the site, slowly depositing sand in the valley below. Interpretive signs relate the story of the dunes' geological formation. A path leads out into the dunes, where you can enjoy the thrill of sliding down them. The park is a popular with riders of ATVs (all-terrain vehicles) and dune buggies.

⓴

St. George

🅰B3 🚆🚌 🛈20 N Main St;
www.greaterzion.com

Established in 1861 by Mormons (p154), the town of St. George has since

↑ Brigham Young Winter Home Historic Site, the former Mormon leader's residence in St. George

experienced a population boom as retirees from all over the US discovered its mild climate and tranquil atmosphere. The towering gold spire that can be seen over the town belongs to Utah's first Mormon Temple, finished in 1877. A beloved project of Mormon leader and visionary Brigham Young (1801–77), it remains a key site. Although only Mormons are allowed inside the temple,

the visitor center, which relates its history, is open to all visitors.

St. George's association with Brigham Young began when he built a winter home here in 1871. While he and his family lived here he continued his work of directing the affairs of the Church of Jesus Christ of Latter-Day Saints. The elegant and spacious **Brigham Young Winter Home Historic Site** is now a museum and has preserved much of its first owner's original furnishings.

Brigham Young Winter Home Historic Site

⊘🕒 🏠67 West 200 North St
📞(435) 673-2517 🕒Apr-Sep:
9am-7pm Mon-Fri, 1-7pm
Sun; Oct-Mar: 9am-5pm
Mon-Fri, 1-5pm Sun

💬 INSIDER TIP
Cycling to Snow Canyon

Snow Canyon State Park lies 5 miles (8 km) northwest of St. George on Highway 18. It offers hiking trails that lead to volcanic caves and million-year-old lava flows. A paved bike path leads through the park and back to town.

THE MORMONS

The Church of Jesus Christ of Latter Day Saints was founded by Joseph Smith (1805–44), a farm worker from New York State. In 1820 Smith claimed to have had visions of the Angel Moroni. The angel led him to a set of golden tablets, which he translated and later published as the Book of Mormon, leading to the founding of the Mormon church. This new faith grew rapidly but attracted hostility because of its political and economic beliefs, and because it practiced polygamy. Seeking refuge, the Mormons moved to Illinois in 1839.

THE TREK WEST

After Smith was killed by an angry mob in 1844 leadership passed to Brigham Young. In 1846, Brigham Young led a band of Mormons west from Illinois in the hope of escaping persecution and founding a safe haven in Salt Lake Valley. Young wished to find "a place on Earth that nobody wants." The pioneers traveled across bleak prairies and over mountains in primitive wagons, braving the fierce winter and summer weather. Pilgrims rode or walked for a year, arriving in Utah in July, 1847.

Salt Lake City was painstakingly laid out in a grid system over the unpromising, and previously unsettled, landscape of Utah's Salt Lake Basin. The grid ensured wide streets, decent-sized houses, and enough land that each family

↑ A Mormon pioneer family in front of their log cabin in the Great Salt Lake Valley in the late 19th century. Today, about 55 percent of Utah's citizens are Mormons.

Did You Know?

Mormonism's most controversial practice, polygamy, was outlawed in 1890.

↑ The St. George Utah Temple, completed in 1877, after the migration west

could be self-sufficient. After they had established themselves in Salt Lake Valley, church members fanned out across the west. By 1900, many agricultural colonies and more than 300 towns had been founded. One of these colonies was in Las Vegas (p268), where 30 Mormons, sent by Brigham Young, built a mission and a small fort.

The St. George (p153) Utah Temple was constructed under the aegis of Brigham Young. For the 15 million Mormons worldwide, it is a potent symbol of a faith based on work, sobriety, and cooperation, with the emphasis on humanitarian service. Mormon missionaries preach their faith throughout the world and church membership continues to grow.

BRIGHAM YOUNG

Born in Vermont in 1801 of a Protestant family, Brigham Young, carpenter, painter, and glazier, joined the Mormons in Ohio in 1832. He took charge of the great migration west in 1846, arriving in Salt Lake City in 1847. In 1849 he established the territory of Deseret, which encompassed present-day Utah. The Mormon settlers turned the desert into fruitful farmland. Despite being removed from political office in 1857, Young was head of the Mormon church until his death in 1877.

↑ Pilgrims on the migration from Illinois to Utah between 1846 and 1847

THE FOUR CORNERS

Although it receives less than 10 inches (25 cm) of rainfall per year, this arid land has supported life since the first Paleoamericans arrived perhaps 12,000 years ago. The people now known as the Ancestral Puebloans lived here from about AD 500 until the end of the 13th century. They were responsible for the many evocative ruins, including those at Mesa Verde, Chaco Canyon, and Hovenweep National Monument. Their descendants include the Hopi, whose pueblos are said to be the oldest continually occupied towns in North America. The Navajo arrived here in the 15th century, and their spiritual center is Canyon de Chelly with its 1,000-ft (330-m) red rock walls. Monument Valley's impressive land-scape has been used as a backdrop for countless movies and TV shows. The region is popular for hiking, fishing, and white water rafting.

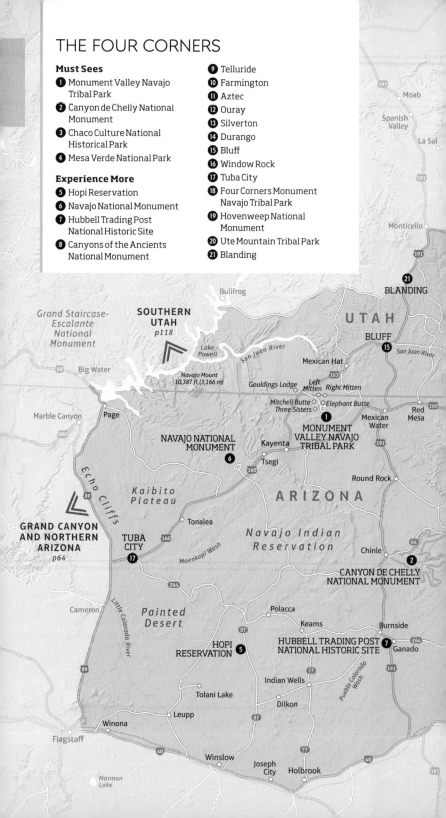

THE FOUR CORNERS

Must Sees

1 Monument Valley Navajo Tribal Park

2 Canyon de Chelly National Monument

3 Chaco Culture National Historical Park

4 Mesa Verde National Park

Experience More

5 Hopi Reservation

6 Navajo National Monument

7 Hubbell Trading Post National Historic Site

8 Canyons of the Ancients National Monument

9 Telluride

10 Farmington

11 Aztec

12 Ouray

13 Silverton

14 Durango

15 Bluff

16 Window Rock

17 Tuba City

18 Four Corners Monument Navajo Tribal Park

19 Hovenweep National Monument

20 Ute Mountain Tribal Park

21 Blanding

MONUMENT VALLEY NAVAJO TRIBAL PARK

D3 **Hwy 163** **navajonationparks.org/tribal-parks/monument-valley**

Located within the Navajo Reservation on the border of Arizona and Utah, Monument Valley is full of awe-inspiring sandstone buttes and mesas that soar upward from a seemingly boundless desert.

These ancient, towering rocks have come to symbolize the American West, largely because Hollywood has used these breathtaking vistas as a backdrop for hundreds of movies, TV shows, and commercials since the 1920s.

Centuries ago, Monument Valley was a lowland basin. Over time, eroded material from the Rocky Mountains built up layers of sediment, and pressure from below the surface uplifted the basin into a high plateau. Forces of erosion then chiseled through the layers of hard and soft rock, creating the spectacular formations that rise up to 1,000 feet (305 m) above the valley floor. The Three Sisters are among the most distinctive pinnacle rock formations at Monument Valley. Others include the Totem Pole and the "fingers" of the Mittens. The park is spectacular at night too, with dark skies that reveal billions of stars and the timeless wonder of the landscape.

The valley was home to the Ancestral Puebloans until AD 1300. Over 100 sites and ruins have been found dating from these ancient people, including petroglyphs.

Today, these lands are sacred to the Navajo. Apart from a designated scenic drive and hiking trail, other areas within the tribal park are only accessible with a licensed guide.

↑ The Three Sisters and other formations reflected in a car mirror

↑ The Milky Way sparkling over the alien-looking terrain of Monument Valley

HOLLYWOOD IN MONUMENT VALLEY

Director George B. Seitz first used the area's spectacular buttes as a backdrop in his 1924 film, *The Vanishing American*. A young John Wayne - and the Western movie genre itself - shot to stardom with John Ford's first film here, *Stagecoach* (1939). Ford shot nine more movies in Monument Valley, including *The Searchers* (1956), hailed as one of the finest Westerns ever made. Sergio Leone paid homage to Ford with his 1968 film, *Once Upon a Time in the West*. Monument Valley has also starred in such classics as *2001: A Space Odyssey* (1968), *Easy Rider* (1969), *Thelma and Louise* (1991), and *Forrest Gump* (1994).

The iconic Left Mitten, Right Mitten, and Merrick Butte in the glow of the sunset

↑ A Navajo guide on horseback heading into the park

Exploring Monument Valley

The 17-mile (27-km) Valley Scenic Drive is a self-guided route within Monument Valley Navajo Tribal Park, which offers 11 scenic viewpoints. Fees are collected at the visitor center. The drive is along a well-marked dirt and gravel road with rough surfaces and a steep incline. High-clearance vehicles are recommended. It is unsuitable for some passenger cars and motorcycles. The most popular stop along the route is John Ford's Point, which is said to have been the film director's favorite view of the valley. The closest view of the Three Sisters, one of the most photographed sights in the park, can be seen from here. Various stalls at this stop offer a range of Navajo handicrafts. A

nearby hogan (Navajo dwelling) serves as a gift shop, where Navajo weavers demonstrate their craft. Navajo weavers are usually considered to be the finest in the Southwest; one rug can take them months to complete and sells for thousands of dollars.

To get off the beaten path, you can hire Navajo guides for hiking, horseback, or 4WD tours to fascinating and less-visited parts of the valley. The guides share stories of Native American myths and history along the way. There are a variety of tours, and you can sign up in advance or on the day at the visitor center or at Goulding's Lodge, a former trading post and now a museum of the valley's cinematic history, which also offers accommodations. Petroglyphs, such as those of bighorn sheep, can be seen on Navajo-guided tours of rock art sites, which are dotted around the valley's ancient ruins.

The Wildcat Trail is the only self-guided hiking trail within the park. This moderate, 4-mile (6.4-km) loop takes you to some of the most scenic spots, where you'll be surrounded by landmark formations such as Merrick Butte and the Mitten Buttes.

> **The closest view of the Three Sisters, one of the most photographed sights in the park, can be seen from John Ford's Point.**

The distinctive Gossips and towering Totem Pole red-rock spires at sunrise ↑

① A Navajo woman in a hogan prepares wool for weaving a rug.

② The North Window Overlook provides some of the best views of key formations, such as Merrick Butte and the Mittens.

③ The beautiful Teardrop Arch near Gouldings Lodge is located on a scenic lookout from where there are sweeping views of the major monuments in the valley.

Spider Rock, rising high from the canyon floor – one of the park's most distinctive geologic features ↑

❷ Ⓜ Ⓨ

CANYON DE CHELLY NATIONAL MONUMENT

📍 D3 🏠 2 miles (3.5 km) east of Chinle and Hwy 191 🌐 nps.gov/cach

Few places in North American have a longer or more eventful history of human habitation than Canyon de Chelly. Four periods of Native American culture have been unearthed here. The sandstone cliffs of the canyon reach as high as 1,000 ft (300 m), towering above the neighboring meadows and desert landscape in the distance. The canyon floor is fringed with cottonwood bushes, watered by the Chinle Wash.

The earliest remains found in the canyon are of the Basketmaker people dating to around AD 300, followed by the Ancestral Puebloans, who created the cliff dwellings in the 12th century. They were succeeded by the Hopi, who lived here seasonally for around 300 years, taking advantage of the canyon's fertile soil. In the 1700s, the Hopi left the area and moved to the mesas, returning to the canyon to farm during the summer months. Today, the canyon is the cultural and geographic heart of the Navajo Nation. Pronounced "de Shay," de Chelly is a Spanish corruption of the Navajo word *Tsegi*, meaning Rock Canyon.

Canyon de Chelly is very different from the sparse desert landscape that spreads from its rim. Weathered red rock walls, just 30-ft- (9-m-) high at the canyon mouth, rise to more than 1,000-ft- (300-m-) high within the canyon, creating a sheltered world. About 40 Navajo families live in the park. Navajo hogans dot the canyon floor; Navajo women tend herds of sheep and weave rugs at outdoor looms. Everywhere Ancestral Puebloan ruins dot the canyon. The White House Ruins, a group of rooms occupied by Ancestral Puebloans between 1060 and 1275, seem barely touched by time and are among the most striking ruins in the park. The trail leading up to them offers superb views. Navajo-led 4WD tours along the scenic North and South rims are a popular way to view the sites in the park.

↑ Navajo Fortress rock tower, the site of a siege in 1864 after Navajos climbed to the summit to escape Kit Carson's army

MASSACRE CAVE

The canyon's darkest hour was in 1805, when a Spanish force under Antonio Narbona entered the area to subdue the Navajo, claiming they were raiding their settlements. While some Navajo fled, others took refuge in a cave high in the cliffs. The Spanish fired into the cave, and Narbona boasted that he had killed 115 Navajo, including 90 warriors. Navajo accounts are different, claiming that most of the warriors were absent (probably hunting), and those killed were mostly women, children, and the elderly.

← The steep 2.5-mile (5-km) round-trip trail leading to the ancient White House Ruins

Cliff dwellings of the White House Ruins, tucked into a tiny hollow in the cliff ↑

Exploring Canyon de Chelly

The White House Ruins Trail is the only site within the valley of the canyon that can be explored without a Navajo guide. Aside from this, you can take scenic drives along the rims without joining a guided tour. The South Rim Drive is a 37-mile (60-km) round-trip offering stops at the White House, Sliding House, and Junction ruins, taking in Spider Rock, and views of the de Chelly and Monument canyons, Defiance Plateau and the Chuska Mountains. The North Rim Drive is a 34-mile (55-km) round-trip with stops at cliff dwellings, including Antelope House, Mummy Cave, and Yucca and views of de Chelly and del Muerte canyons.

↑ A Navajo riding on horseback on the sandy floor of Canyon de Chelly National Monument

> INSIDER TIP
> **Canyon Guided Tours**
>
> A list of authorized companies offering hiking, horseback, and vehicle guided tours is on the park's website. Reservations are recommended from March to October. Ranger-led hikes can be booked at the visitor center.

Antelope House Ruin

▶ Named for a pictograph of an antelope painted by Navajo artists in the 1830s, Antelope House has ruins dating from AD 700. They can be seen from the Antelope House Overlook along the North Rim Drive.

Tsegi Overlook

▼ This high curve along the South Rim Drive offers general panoramic views of the farm-studded canyon floor with green vegetation and the surrounding landscape. The distinctive feature that can be seen is Blade Rock – a long curving fin that projects from the North Rim cliffs right to the edge of the Chinle wash. There are several stalls here where Navajo vendors sell jewelry, pottery, and various other crafts.

Spider Rock

▶ Rising more than 800 ft (245 m) from the canyon floor, Spider Rock was, according to Navajo legends, where Spider Woman lived in the crack between the two rocks and taught her people the art of weaving.

Hogan Interior

Made of horizontal logs, the hogan is the traditional dwelling of the Navajo and the center of Navajo family life. A smoke hole in the center provides a link with the sky, while the dirt floor gives contact with the earth. A door faces east to greet the rising sun.

Canyon Vegetation

▶ Within the canyon, cottonwood, oak, and olive trees line the river washes; the land itself is a fertile oasis of lush meadows, alfalfa and corn fields, and fruit orchards.

KIT CARSON AND THE "LONG WALK"

In 1863, the US government sent Kit Carson (p204) under the command of General James A. Carlton to the Four Corners to settle the problem of Navajo raids. In January 1864 Carson entered Canyon de Chelly, capturing the Navajo hiding there. In 1864, they were among 9,000 Navajo who were driven on the "Long Walk," a forced march of 370 miles (595 km) from Fort Defiance to Bosque Redondo in New Mexico. There, in a pitiful reservation, more than 3,000 Navajo died before the US government accepted the resettlement as a failure and allowed them to return to the Four Corners.

3 🏛 🏔

CHACO CULTURE NATIONAL HISTORICAL PARK

🅰 E4 🚗 25 miles (40 km) SE of Nageezi off US 550 🕖 7am–4pm daily
🚫 Jan 1, Thanksgiving, Dec 25 🌐 nps.gov/chcu

One of the most impressive cultural sites in the Southwest, Chaco Canyon has well-preserved ruins comprising the largest and most complex pre-Columbian buildings in North America. A UNESCO World Heritage Site, these ruins are considered sacred by the Hopi and Pueblo peoples.

The ruins in Chaco Canyon reflect the sophisticated architectural and organizational skills of the Ancestral Puebloan civilization that existed here between AD 850 and 1250. With its 16 "great houses" (pueblos containing hundreds of rooms) and many lesser sites, the canyon was the political, religious, and cultural center for settlements that covered much of the Four Corners.

At its peak during the 11th century, Chaco was one of the most important pre-Columbian cities in North America. Despite the site's size, it is thought that Chaco's population was small because the land could not have supported a large community. Archaeologists believe that the city was mainly used as a ceremonial gathering place, with a year-round population of less than 3,000. Probably the social elite, the inhabitants supported themselves largely by trading. A turquoise-processing and bead-making industry flourished in the canyon. The many kivas (round, ceremonial chambers) also suggest its nature as a gathering place.

The largest "great house" was Pueblo Bonito, with more than 600 rooms. Other ruins include Chetro Ketl, with more than 500 rooms, and Casa Rinconada, a great kiva, which was the largest religious chamber at Chaco.

PETROGLYPHS

Intriguing petroglyphs (carvings) and a number of pictographs (painted rock art) can be seen along several hiking trails. Some show figures of the sun and moon in alignment, suggesting that the Chacoans practiced archaeoastronomy. Others show human, animal, and supernatural figures. An easy place to see them is along the Petroglyph Trail, which runs along the cliff face between Pueblo Bonito and Chetro Ketl, or along the trail to Una Vida.

←

Pueblo Bonito, the largest and most famous "great house" in Chaco

① Fajada Butte, one of the park's iconic features, rises 135 meters (443 ft) above the canyon floor.

② Ancestral Puebloan petroglyphs near Una Vida pueblo show animal and mythical figures.

③ Guided tours of the massive Pueblo Bonito complex take place regularly from May through October.

Exploring Chaco Culture National Historical Park

The site is accessed via a 13-mile (21-km) dirt road that is affected by flash floods in wet weather. Inside the park, you can follow the 9-mile (15-km) paved Canyon Loop Drive that passes several of Chaco's highlights. There is parking at all major sites. From the visitor center, a trail leads to Una Vida and the petroglyphs. Pueblo Bonito is the must-see site in the canyon; buy a trail guide which points out key features of Chacoan great house architecture. There are four hiking trails, ranging from 3 miles (5 km) to 8 miles (13 km) for a round trip. They take you through the backcountry to more remote Chacoan sites, with wonderful views of the mesa landscape along the way. Be sure to get a free backcountry hiking permit from the visitor center. Biking the Canyon Loop Drive is another great way to visit the sites.

INSIDER TIP
Tours

Guided tours of the "great house" sites take place May through October, and sometimes in April. Ask at the visitor center. Night Sky programs run Friday and Saturday evenings April through October.

The many kivas were probably used by visitors for religious ceremonies.

Did You Know?

An International Dark Sky Park, Chaco is one of the best places in the US for star gazing.

← The ruins of Pueblo Bonito as they are today

Chaco's skilled builders had only stone tools to create finely wrought stonework.

↑ Detail of a doorway inside the Pueblo Bonito

The Pueblo Bonito was four stories high.

The building had a unique D-shaped structure.

Hundreds of rooms within Pueblo Bonito show little sign of use and are thought to have been kept for storage or for guests arriving to take part in ceremonial events.

↑ Reconstruction of the Pueblo Bonito, showing how it might have looked

4

MESA VERDE NATIONAL PARK

🅰E3 🅰Hwy 160, about 35 miles (56 km) W of Durango
🆆nps.gov/meve

The high, forested mesa overlooking the Montezuma Valley was home to the Ancestral Puebloans for more than 700 years. Within the canyons that cut through the mesa are some of the best-preserved and most elaborate cliff dwellings built by Native Americans.

Mesa Verde, meaning "Green Table," was a name given to the area by the Spanish in the 1700s. The ruins were discovered by local ranchers in the late 19th century, and the national park was created in 1906 to protect this amazing human legacy.

Nearly 5,000 archaeological sites have been found in the park, including 600 cliff dwellings. They provide a fascinating record of the people who lived here, from the 1st century AD Basketmaker period to the complex Ancestral Puebloan society that built the many-roomed cliff dwellings between 1100 and 1250. Living in large family groups, they hunted, foraged, and farmed on the fertile mesa.

Pueblo buildings beneath the overhanging cliffs ranged from single storage rooms to villages of more than 150 rooms, with round ceremonial kivas and lookout towers. Built of hard sandstone blocks, held together with adobe

> 💬 INSIDER TIP
> **Twilight Tour**
>
> An intimate experience, the Cliff Palace Twilight Tour is limited to just 15 people. When the crowds have gone, you can sense the ancient atmosphere of these dwellings, while the light and shadow from the setting sun creates dramatic photographs.

↑ Visitors on a viewing platform at the cliff dwellings in Mesa Verde National Park

mortar, these dwellings filled every available space in the alcoves. With 150 rooms and 23 kivas, Cliff Palace is the largest cliff dwelling and is the site that most visitors focus on. The location and symmetry suggest that architecture was important to the builders. Other key sites that can be visited include Square Tower House, Long House, Step House, and Balcony House, where access is by climbing three ladders, high above the canyon floor, then crawling through a tunnel.

By around 1300, these impressive cliff homes had been abandoned and the people had moved south to New Mexico and Arizona, where they merged with the ancestors of today's Pueblo communities. They may have left because of drought, crop failures, warfare, or better opportunities; their disappearance is one of the great mysteries of Mesa Verde.

↑ Cliff Palace, the largest Ancestral Puebloan cliff dwelling found anywhere

Timeline

Must See

c 550 AD
First pit houses appear during the Basketmaker period.

c 700
First small villages are built at Mesa Verde.

1100–1300
Extensive pueblo complexes are built by Ancestral Puebloans, including 600 cliff dwellings.

1300
Ancestral Puebloans migrate from Mesa Verde; nobody knows for sure why.

1888
Cowboys looking for stray cattle discover Cliff Palace dwelling, sparking the start of exploration of other ruins in Mesa Verde.

1906
Mesa Verde is designated a national park.

1908
Archaeological excavation and preservation starts, continuing to this day.

1910s
Tourists start visiting in increasing numbers.

1976
Lands are added to the National Park with new wilderness designations.

1978
Mesa Verde is designated a World Heritage Site, one of the first World Heritage sites in the US.

The ruins of Spruce Tree House, nestled in the cliffs of Chapin Mesa ↑

GUIDED TOURS

Many sites can be seen on self-guided tours. To visit Cliff Palace, Balcony House, and Long House, you must take a ranger-guided tour. The tours are strenuous, and involve climbing ladders, hiking, and crawling through a tunnel. You can buy tickets up to two days in advance.

Exploring Mesa Verde National Park

Start at the Visitor and Research Center, and then continue to Chapin Mesa, which holds the highest concentration of sites open to the public. It is reached along the Mesa Top Loop Road, a 6-mile (10-km) scenic route with cliff dwelling overlooks and short, paved trails. Branch off along the Cliff Palace Loop Road for more great views overlooking key sites. Wetherill Mesa, on the western side of the park, is less visited and contains Long House, Kodak House, Step House, and the Badger House Community. There's a more relaxed experience here, with most sites reached along walking trails.

To protect the park's archaeological treasures, outdoor activities are largely restricted to hiking on designated trails. The park offers special backcountry tours and hike-and-bike adventure treks in season. In winter, park trails are open for crosscountry skiing and snowshoeing, a magical experience.

Museum Artifacts

Some three million objects, from pottery to baskets to stone tools, have been found at Mesa Verde. Displays at the Visitor and Research Center and the Chapin Mesa Museum provide fascinating insights into this ancient world.

Petroglyph Point Trail

This 2.4-mile (4-km) loop trail passes a large petroglyph panel. The trail is narrow and rocky, with several steep drop-offs along the canyon wall on the way to the petroglyph panel. The trailhead is located near the Chapin Mesa Archeological Museum.

1 A large petroglyph panel, depicting hand prints, animals, humans, and spirals, can be seen along the Petroglyph Point Trail.

2 Visitors can climb up a ladder to reach Long House on Wetherill Mesa.

3 Balcony House has 40 well-preserved rooms and several kivas. It is the cliff dwelling with the most difficult access.

GREAT VIEW
Overlooks

From Park Point, the highest elevation on the mesa, you'll have panoramic views. Other great viewpoints include Kodak House Overlook and the Soda Canyon Overlook, which has a splendid view of Balcony House.

THE ANCESTRAL PUEBLOANS

The hauntingly beautiful and elaborate ruins left behind by the ancient Ancestral Puebloans have captured the public imagination. Also known as Anasazi, a name coined by the Navajo meaning "Ancient Enemy Ancestor," they are seen as the ancestors of today's Pueblo peoples. The first Ancestral Puebloans are thought to have settled at Mesa Verde in around AD 500, where they lived in pithouses. By AD 800 they had developed masonry skills and began building housing complexes using sandstone. From 1100 to 1300 AD, impressive levels of craftsmanship were reached in weaving, pottery, jewelry, and tool-making.

THE PUEBLO PEOPLE

By 1300 AD the Ancestral Puebloans had abandoned many of their long-established settlements and migrated to areas where new centers emerged. Theories on why this occurred include a 50-year drought; the strain that a larger population placed on the desert's limited resources; and a lengthy period of social upheaval, perhaps stimulated by increasing trade with tribes as far away as central Mexico. Archaeologists agree that the Ancestral Puebloans did not disappear but live on today in Puebloan descendants who trace their origins to Mesa Verde, Chaco, and other sacred sites.

Still used by modern Puebloans today, the kiva was the religious and ceremonial center of Ancestral Puebloan life. Kivas often had no windows and were accessed through a hole in the roof. Small kivas were used by a single family unit, while large ones accommodated the whole community.

← Intricately decorated Ancestral Puebloan ceramic jar (c 1100-1125)

TOP 4 ANCESTRAL PUEBLOAN RUINS

Canyon de Chelly National Monument
See the remains of 5,000 years of habitation (p164).

Chaco Culture National Historical Park
Large, well-preserved cliff dwellings have been preserved (p168).

Mesa Verde National Park
There are 600 cliff dwellings on this mesa (p172).

Aztec Ruins National Monument
Enter a fascinating reconstructed Great Kiva at this site (p181).

The huge Pueblo Bonito at Chaco Canyon, which had more than 400 rooms and 40 kivas ↑

↑ Reconstructed interior of the Great Kiva at the Aztec Ruins National Monument

↑ Landscape of striped red-rock boulders in the Hopi Reservation

EXPERIENCE MORE

5 (🚗) (🍴) (🛍️)

Hopi Reservation

⚠ D4 🏠 Hopi Cultural Center, Hwy 264, Second Mesa; www.hopicultural center.com

The Hopi, Arizona's only Pueblo community, are the direct descendants of the Ancestral Puebloans, whom they call the Hisatsinom. The Hopi Reservation is surrounded by the lands of the Navajo. The landscape is harsh and barren, yet the Hopi have cultivated the land here for a thousand years. They worship, through the kachina, the living spirits of plants and animals, believed to arrive each year to stay with the tribe during the growing season (December to July). Most of the Hopi villages are on or near one of three mesas (flat-topped elevations), named First, Second, and Third Mesa. A guided tour is the best way to experience the mesas. Tours and how to book are listed on the Experience Hopi website (www.experiencehopi.com).

The most visited site is Walpi, the ancient pueblo on First Mesa, which was first inhabited in the 12th century. To reach Walpi, visitors drive up to the mesa from the Pollaca settlement to the village of Sichomovi. Nearby, the Ponsi Visitor Center is the departure point for the one-hour Walpi tours. Walpi was constructed to be easily defended, and straddles a dramatic knife edge of rock extending from the tip of First Mesa. In places Walpi is less than 100 ft (33 m) wide, with a drop of several hundred feet on both sides. The Walpi tour includes several stops where visitors can purchase *kachina* figurines and distinctive handcrafted pottery, or sample the Hopi *piki* bread. Those wishing to shop further can continue on to Second Mesa, where several galleries and stores offer an array of Hopi arts and crafts. The Hopi Cultural Center on Second Mesa is home to a restaurant, the only hotel for miles around, and a museum that has a collection of photographs depicting scenes of Hopi life.

On narrow, rocky Third Mesa, Old Oraibi pueblo, thought to have been founded in the 12th century, is claimed to be the oldest continuously occupied human settlement in North America.

ARTISANS OF THE INDIAN RESERVATION

The artisans on each Hopi mesa specialize in a particular craft. On First Mesa, this is carved figures (representing the kachina spirits) and painted pottery; on Second Mesa, it is silver jewelry and coiled baskets; and on Third Mesa, wicker baskets and woven rugs. You can purchase crafts directly from the artists, or from shops on the reservation.

Did You Know?

The Hopi believe in Animism – that all animals, trees, rocks, and plants have a spirit and a soul.

6

Navajo National Monument

C3 ⏱ 8am-5:30pm daily (mid-Sep-May: 9am-5pm) 🚫 Jan 1, Thanksgiving, Dec 25 🌐 nps.gov/nava

Although named after its location on the Navajo Reservation, this monument is actually known for its Ancestral Puebloan ruins. The most accessible ruin here is the beautifully preserved, 135-room pueblo of Betatakin, which fills a vast, curved niche in the cliffs of Tsegi Canyon. An easy one-mile (1.6-km) trail from the visitor center leads to an overlook where Betatakin is clearly visible on the far side, near the canyon floor.

A much more demanding 17-mile (27-km) round-trip hike leads to Keet Seel, a larger and more successful community than Betatakin. Construction began in about 1250, but the site is thought to have been abandoned by 1300. Only a limited number of permits to visit the ruin are issued each day and the hike requires overnight camping at a basic camp site.

7

Hubbell Trading Post National Historic Site

D4 🛣 AZ264, near Ganado ⏱ 8am-6pm daily (Oct-Mar: to 5pm) 🌐 nps.gov/hutr

At the heart of the Navajo reservation in the small town of Ganado, the Hubbell Trading Post was established in the 1870s by trader John Lorenzo Hubbell and is the oldest continuously operating trading post in the Navajo Nation. The Navajo traded wool, blankets, turquoise, and other items in exchange for tools, household goods, and food. The trading posts were also a resource during times of need. When a smallpox epidemic struck in 1886, Hubbell used his house as a hospital.

Today, the post still hums with trading activities. One room is a working general store, its rafters hung with frying pans and hardware, and its shelves stacked with cloth, medicines, and food. Another room is filled with Navajo baskets, Hopi kachina dolls, and handwoven rugs, while another has a long row of glass cases with impressive silver and turquoise jewelry.

Visitors can tour Hubbell's restored home and view the significant collection of Southwestern art. At the visitor center, Navajo women demonstrate rug-weaving.

---

8 🏛

Canyons of the Ancients National Monument

D3 🛣 9651 Rd N, Cortez ⏱ 10am-4pm daily 🌐 blm.gov

This vast site protects the nation's greatest density of indigenous archaeological remains, encompassing 10,000 years of Northern

↑ Pottery at the Anasazi Heritage Center, in the Canyons of the Ancients

Ancestral Puebloan culture. More than 6,000 ancient sites, including cliff dwellings, kivas (religious chambers), petroglyphs, and shrines, have been recorded here. Among the highlights are the Great Kiva at Lowry Pueblo and the Painted Hand Pueblo. It can be hard to find the sites without a map, so first stop by the Anasazi Heritage Center, which doubles as the monument's visitor center. The museum here has displays and interactive exhibits on the ancient Pueblo cultures of the region. Hiking trails of varying degrees of difficulty cross this rugged landscape. Bring plenty of water and food as none is available within the park.

↑ Handwoven Navajo rugs for sale at Hubbell Trading Post National Historic Site

↑ Main Street in Telluride, with a mountain backdrop; a skier tackling the local slopes *(inset)*

9

Telluride

🅰 E2 🚲🚌 🛈 236 W Colorado Ave; www.telluride.com

Once a mining town, Telluride is now a popular ski resort with upscale boutiques and restaurants. The exclusive Mountain Village lies across a mountain ridge reached by a free 12-minute gondola ride.

In summer there are walks and riding trails, and fishing in the lakes and rivers. The town also hosts an annual international film festival, as well as several music festivals.

10

Farmington

🅰 E3 🚲🚌 🛈 3041 E Main St; www.farmingtonnm.org

This dusty ranch town, a good base for exploring the nearby monuments, is home to the rather unusual **Bolack Museum of Fish and Wildlife**, which houses the world's largest collection of mounted game animals. The **Farmington Museum** focuses on local history and geology and features a children's gallery with interactive exhibits.

About 25 miles (40 km) west of Farmington is Shiprock, named for the 1,500-ft (457-m) rock peak that thrusts up from the valley floor. To the Navajo, this rock is sacred. Note that visitors can only observe the peak from the roadsides of Highways 64 or 33.

Eight miles (12 km) south are the **Salmon Ruins**, once an outlying Chaco settlement. These ruins were protected from gravediggers by the Salmon family, who homesteaded here in the 1870s. As a result, a century later archaeologists recovered many artifacts, which are on display in the excellent on-site museum. Outside the museum trails lead to the ruins, which show the superb level of skill of the ancient stonemasons.

Bolack Museum of Fish and Wildlife

♿ 🕐 🏠 3901 Bloomfield Hwy 🕐 9am–3pm Mon–Sat 🚫 Public hols 🌐 bolack museums.com

Farmington Museum

♿ 🏠 3041 E Main St 🕐 8am–5pm Mon–Sat 🌐 farmingtonmuseum.org

Salmon Ruins

♿🕐 🏠 6131 Hwy 64 🕐 8am–5pm Mon–Fri, 9am–5pm Sat & Sun (Nov–Apr: noon–5pm Sun) 🚫 Jan 1, Easter, Jul 4, Thanksgiving, Dec 25 🌐 salmonruins.com

300

The number of people estimated to have inhabited Salmon Ruins.

11

Aztec

🅰 E3 🛈 110 North Ash St; www.aztecnm.com

The small town of Aztec was named for its ruins, which are Ancestral Puebloan, and not Aztec as early settlers believed. Preserved as the **Aztec Ruins National Monument**, the site's 500-room pueblo flourished in the late 1200s. Visitors can look inside a rebuilt kiva (religious chamber).

Aztec Ruins National Monument

♿ 🚫 🚗 North of Hwy 516 on Ruins Rd 🕐 8am–6pm daily (9am–4pm in winter) 🚫 Jan 1, Thanksgiving, Dec 25 🌐 nps.gov/azru

---

12

Ouray

🅰 E2 🚹 1230 North Main St; www.ouraycolorado.com

The wonderfully preserved old mining town of Ouray, 23 miles (37 km) north of Silverton on Highway 550, is a popular base for hikers and 4WD enthusiasts. To the south of town, a loop road leads to Box Canyon Falls Park.

EAT

Chop House Restaurant

This eatery uses only organic fowl, non-threatened fish species, and local ingredients.

🅰 E2 🚗 233 W Colorado Ave, Telluride 🌐 newsheridan.com

$$$

221 South Oak

Candlelight and white linen create an elegant ambience at this fine restaurant with an eclectic menu.

🅰 E2 🚗 221 South Oak St, Telluride 🕐 Lunch 🌐 221southoak.com

$$$

13

Silverton

🅰 E2 🚹 414 Greene St; www.silvertoncolorado.com

This well-preserved mining town is a registered National Historic Landmark. The facades along Blair Street have altered little since the days of the 1880s silver-mining boom that gave the town its name. On Greene Street is the 1902 County Jail, which houses the **San Juan County Historical Museum**. Greene Street East leads 13 miles (21 km) north to the ghost town of Animas Forks, which was abandoned after the mines ran out of silver.

San Juan County Historical Museum

♿ 🚗 1557 Greene St 🕐 Late May–mid-Oct: 10am–5pm daily (Oct 1–mid-Oct: to 3pm) 🌐 sanjuancountyhistoricalsociety.org

---

14

Durango

🅰 E3 🚆 🚌 🚹 802 Main Ave; www.durango.org

Durango is a lovely town with shady tree-lined streets and splendid Victorian architecture. Its attractive setting, on the banks of the Animas River,

💬 INSIDER TIP
Autumn Color

A good time to make the trip on the Durango and Silverton Narrow Gauge Railroad is September, when fall colors cover the mountainsides. Booking ahead is recommended.

draws increasing numbers of residents, making the town the largest community in this part of Colorado. It is famous as the starting point of the **Durango and Silverton Narrow Gauge Railroad**, perhaps the most scenic train ride in the US. A 1920s coal-fired steam train ferries more than 200,000 visitors each year on a leisurely journey along the Animas River valley, up steep gradients through canyons and mountain scenery, to Silverton. Passengers may choose to ride in either Victorian or open-sided "gondola" cars that offer great views. Several stops along the way allow hikers and anglers access to the pristine backcountry of the beautiful, vast San Juan National Forest.

Durango and Silverton Narrow Gauge Railroad

♿ 🚗 479 Main Ave 🕐 Times vary, check website 🌐 durangotrain.com

↑ The Animas River just north of Durango, winding through a beautiful forested landscape

The Durango and Silverton Narrow Gauge Railroad traveling through the Animas River Valley

15

Bluff

🅐D3 🆆bluffutah.org

This charming town, settled in 1880 by the Mormons of "Hole-in-the-Rock-Road" fame (p148), is a good base for exploring Utah's southeast corner. Trips along the gentle San Juan River can be taken, which include stops at Ancestral Pueblo ruins that can be reached only by boat.

About 12 miles (20 km) south of Bluff, a marked turn leads onto the 17-mile (27-km) dirt road through the Valley of the Gods. Like a smaller version of Monument Valley (p160), this place features high rock spires, buttes, and mesas, but none of the crowds.

16

Window Rock

🅐D4 🚌 🆆discover navajo.com

The capital of the Navajo Nation, Window Rock is named for the natural arch found in the sandstone cliffs located about a mile north of the main strip on Highway 12.

The **Navajo Nation Museum**, one of the largest Native American museums in the US, houses displays that cover the history of the Ancestral Puebloans and the Navajo.

Navajo Nation Museum

⊘ 🄰 Hwy 264 & Post Office Loop Rd 🄲 (928) 871-7941 🄾 8am–5pm Mon–Fri, 9am–5pm Sat

> About 12 miles (20 km) south of Bluff, a marked turn leads onto the 17-mile (27-km) dirt road through the atmospheric Valley of the Gods.

17

Tuba City

🅐C4 🄸 Tuba City Trading Post, 10 N Main St; (928) 283-5441

Named for Tuuvi, a Hopi who converted to the Mormon faith, Tuba City is best known for the 65-million-year-old dinosaur tracks found just off the main highway, 5 miles (8 km) southwest of the town. This is the largest community in the western section on the Navajo Reservation and a good spot from which to explore the Navajo National Monument (p179) and the Hopi Reservation (p178).

18

Four Corners Monument Navajo Tribal Park

🅐D3 🄰 Junction of Hwys 160 and 41 🆆discover navajo.com

There is something compelling about being able to put one foot and hand in each of four states. The Four Corners Monument is the only place in the US where four states (Utah, Arizona, Colorado, and New Mexico) meet at one point.

19

Hovenweep National Monument

🅐D3 🄰East of Hwy 191 🆆nps.gov/hove

One of the most mysterious Ancestral Puebloan sites in the Southwest, the ruins at Hovenweep lie along the rims of shallow canyons on a remote high plateau in the southwest corner of Colorado. The culture here reached its peak between 1200 and 1275. The ruins consist of six prehistoric Puebloan-era villages built between 1200 and 1300 spread over a 20-mile (32-km) expanse of canyons and mesas. The well-preserved ruins include unique round, square, and D-shaped towers, and look much as they did when W. D. Huntington, leader of a Mormon expedition, first came upon the site in 1854. The site was named later, in 1874, after an Ute word meaning "Deserted Valley." Very little is known of these people beyond the clues found in the pottery and tools that they left behind.

The Hovenweep towers might have been defensive fortifications, astronomical observatories, storage silos, or religious structures.

Self-guided hiking trails explore each of Hovenweep's six separate sets of ruins, which lie a few miles apart.

Ruins in Ute Mountain Tribal Park; pictographs within the park *(inset)*

20 ⊕ ⊛ 🖰

Ute Mountain Tribal Park

⚑D3 🛈Junction of Hwys 160 and 491; www.utemountain tribalpark.info

The Ute Mountain Tribal Park ruins are one of the Southwest's better kept secrets. The Ancestral Puebloans first arrived in this region in about AD 400. They closely followed the Mesa Verde *(p172)* development pattern, eventually creating numerous fine cliff dwellings, including the 80-room Lion House. These ruins have few visitors because of their inaccessibility. Visitors

Ancestral Puebloan towers at Hovenweep National Monument

can use their own vehicles and join the dusty tours led by local Ute guides (at 9am daily; make sure to book ahead), or pay an extra charge to be driven.

21

Blanding

⚑D3 🛈12 N Grayson Parkway; www.utah.com/ blanding

A tidy Mormon town at the base of the Abajo Mountains, Blanding is home to the **Edge of the Cedars State Park Museum**. The park contains modest Ancestral Puebloan ruins, including a small kiva, or religious chamber. The museum has well-thought-out displays on the history of these ancient people and other cultures that have inhabited the region.

Edge of the Cedars State Park Museum
⊛ ⚑660 W 400 N ⏰9am–2pm daily ⚑Jan 1, Thanksgiving, Dec 24, 25 & 31 🖰stateparks.utah.gov

A DRIVING TOUR
SAN JUAN SKYWAY

Distance 236 miles (380 km) **Stopping-off points**
Ridgeway State Park on Hwy 550 offers great views of
the San Juan Mountains

The San Juan Skyway is a 236-mile (380-km) loop through
some of America's finest scenery. The route travels three
highways (550, 145, and 160) over the San Juan Mountains,
past 19th-century mining towns and through forests and
canyons. There are 14 peaks above 14,000 ft (4,200 m).
Between Silverton and Ouray the road is also known as the
Million Dollar Highway, having either been named for the gold-
rich gravel used in the road's construction or, according to
another theory, because the road was expensive to build.

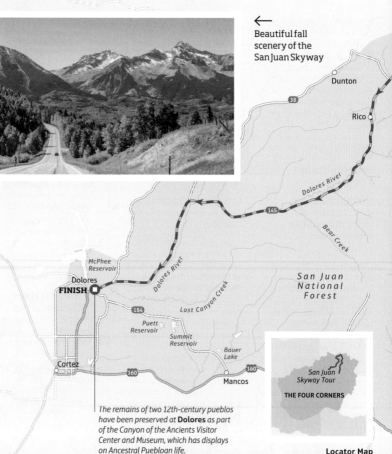

← Beautiful fall
scenery of the
San Juan Skyway

Placerville

Sawpit

Leopard Creek

38

Dunton

Rico

Dolores River

145

Bear Creek

McPhee Reservoir

Dolores River

Dolores
FINISH

Lost Canyon Creek

San Juan
National
Forest

184

Puett Reservoir

Summit Reservoir

Bauer Lake

160

Cortez

160

Mancos

*The remains of two 12th-century pueblos
have been preserved at **Dolores** as part
of the Canyon of the Ancients Visitor
Center and Museum, which has displays
on Ancestral Puebloan life.*

San Juan
Skyway Tour

THE FOUR CORNERS

Locator Map
For more detail see p158

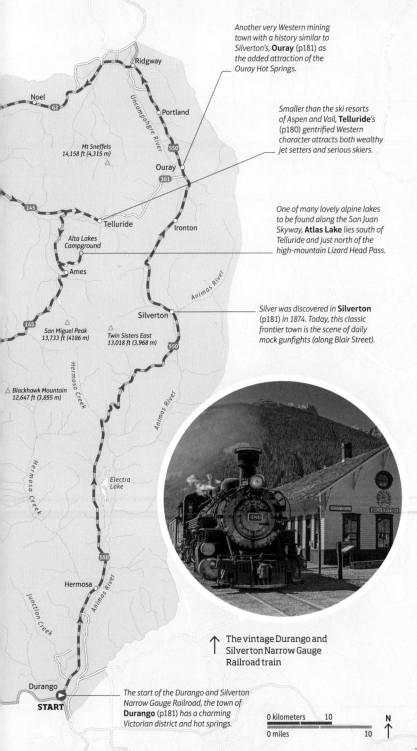

Another very Western mining town with a history similar to Silverton's, **Ouray** (p181) as the added attraction of the Ouray Hot Springs.

Smaller than the ski resorts of Aspen and Vail, **Telluride**'s (p180) gentrified Western character attracts both wealthy jet setters and serious skiers.

One of many lovely alpine lakes to be found along the San Juan Skyway, **Atlas Lake** lies south of Telluride and just north of the high-mountain Lizard Head Pass.

Silver was discovered in **Silverton** (p181) in 1874. Today, this classic frontier town is the scene of daily mock gunfights (along Blair Street).

Ridgway

Noel

62

Portland

*Mt Sneffels
14,158 ft (4,315 m)*

Ouray

361

550

Uncompahgre River

145

Telluride

Ironton

*Alta Lakes
Campground*

Ames

Animas River

Silverton

145

*San Miguel Peak
13,733 ft (4186 m)*

*Twin Sisters East
13,018 ft (3,968 m)*

550

Hermosa Creek

△ *Blackhawk Mountain
12,647 ft (3,855 m)*

Animas River

Hermosa Creek

*Electra
Lake*

550

Hermosa

Animas River

Junction Creek

↑ The vintage Durango and Silverton Narrow Gauge Railroad train

Durango

START

The start of the Durango and Silverton Narrow Gauge Railroad, the town of **Durango** (p181) has a charming Victorian district and hot springs.

0 kilometers   10
0 miles   10

N
↑

SANTA FE AND NORTHERN NEW MEXICO

It was probably the fertile landscape of the Rio Grande valley that attracted the Ancestral Puebloans in the 1100s to this region. Their descendants still live today in pueblo villages and are famous for producing distinctive crafts and pottery. Taos Pueblo is the largest of the pueblos, its fame due both to its adobe architecture and its ceremonial dances performed on feast days.

Upon arrival of the Spanish in the first half of the 16th century, Catholic priests tried to convert the Pueblo people to Christianity. Decades of oppression by Spanish colonials led to Pueblo unrest. In 1680 a Pueblo rebellion succeeded in expelling the Spanish from the Upper Rio Grande, destroying churches and burning many buildings in Santa Fe. However, the colonists returned to take possession of the region 12 years later. By the 1750s the number of Pueblo villages had shrunk by half. New Mexico was firmly under Spanish rule until 1821, when Mexico gained its independence from Spain. Two years after the start of the Mexican–American War in 1846, New Mexico was ceded to the United States.

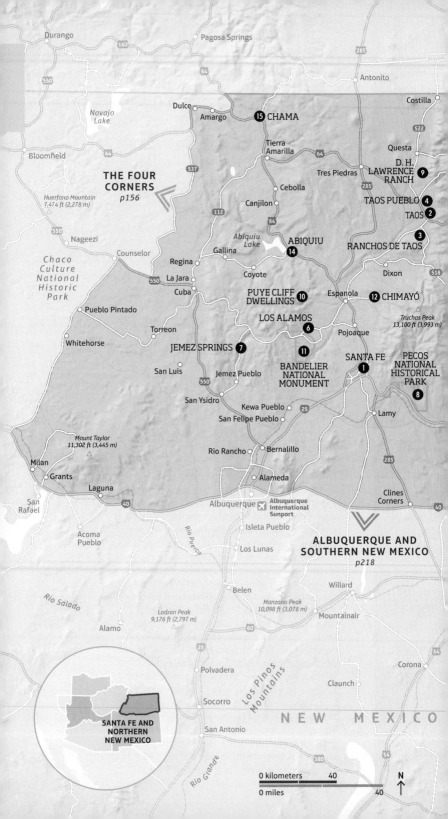

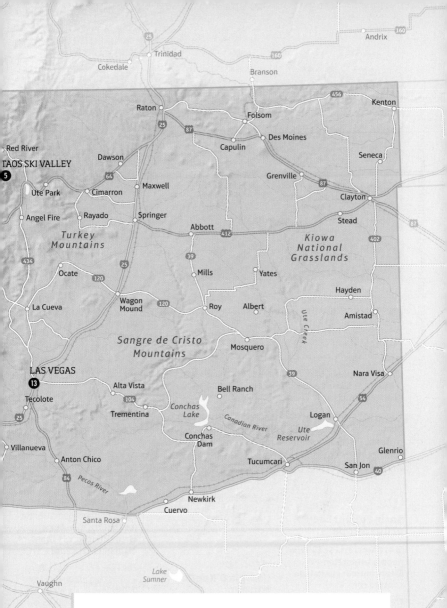

Andrix
Trinidad
Cokedale
Branson
160
160
Raton
Folsom
Kenton
456
25
87
Capulin
Des Moines
Seneca
Red River
Dawson
TAOS SKI VALLEY
Grenville
5
64
Clayton
Ute Park
Maxwell
Cimarron
87
Angel Fire
Rayado
Springer
Stead
Turkey
Abbott
Kiowa
Mountains
612
National
Grasslands
402
434
Ocate
Mills
Yates
120
Hayden
La Cueva
Wagon
25
Mound
120
Roy
Albert
Amistad
Sangre de Cristo
Mountains
Mosquero
LAS VEGAS
Nara Visa
13
39
54
Alta Vista
Bell Ranch
Tecolote
104
Conchas
Logan
25
Lake
Ute
Trementina
Canadian River
Reservoir
Villanueva
Conchas
Glenrio
Dam
Anton Chico
Tucumcari
84
San Jon
Pecos River
40
Newkirk
Cuervo
Santa Rosa
Lake
Sumner
Vaughn
Ute Creek

SANTA FE AND NORTHERN NEW MEXICO

Must Sees

1 Santa Fe
2 Taos

Experience More

3 Ranchos de Taos
4 Taos Pueblo
5 Taos Ski Valley
6 Los Alamos
7 Jemez Springs

8 Pecos National Historical Park
9 D. H. Lawrence Ranch
10 Puye Cliff Dwellings
11 Bandelier National Monument
12 Chimayó
13 Las Vegas
14 Abiquiu
15 Chama

Lincoln
National
Forest

↑ The Pueblo Revival-style architecture of historic downtown Santa Fe

❶

SANTA FE

🏔F4 ✈10 miles (16 km) SW of Santa Fe 🚌Lamy, 18 miles (29 km) S of Santa Fe 🚉Santa Fe Depot 🛈Plaza Galeria, 66 E San Francisco St; www.santafe.org

The artist colony of Santa Fe has a rich history and beautiful architecture. The blending of three distinct cultures – Hispanic, Native American, and Anglo – contribute to its vibrancy. About one in six residents works in the arts and the artistic legacy is everywhere.

①
Shrine of Our Lady of Guadalupe

🏠417 Agua Fria St 🕙9am-noon & 1-4pm Mon-Fri 🌐santuariodeguadalupe santafe.com

This 1795 adobe church of Santuario de Guadalupe is dedicated to the Virgin of Guadalupe, patron saint of both the Mexican and Pueblo peoples. The church marked the end of the old Camino Real (Royal Road), the main trade route from Mexico. A painted altarpiece of the Virgin graces the interior.

② 🖌🏛
Georgia O'Keeffe Museum

🏠217 Johnson St 🕙10am-5pm daily (to 7pm Fri) 🚫Easter, Thanksgiving, Dec 25, Jan 1 🌐okeeffe museum.org

This museum is dedicated to New Mexico's most famous resident artist, Georgia O'Keeffe (*p213*). Some of her best-loved paintings are on display here, including *Purple Hills II* and *Ghost Ranch, New Mexico* (1934), as well as her sculptures and lesser-known works, such as paintings inspired by Lake George and New York City.

③ 🖌🎨🏛
Palace of the Governors

🏠Palace Ave, Santa Fe Plaza 🕙10am-5pm Tue-Sun (to 7pm Fri; May-Oct: also Mon) 🚫Public hols 🌐palace ofthegovernors.org

The Palace of the Governors is the oldest public building in continuous use in America. Built in 1610, it was the seat

> **INSIDER TIP**
> **Native American Crafts Market**
>
> Buy beautiful jewelry, fine pottery, and other lovely Native American crafts directly from the artists, who spread their wares daily under the portal of the Palace of the Governors.

The Palace of the Governors is the oldest public building in continuous use in America. Built in 1610, it was the seat of regional government for 300 years.

Timeline

1598
▽ Juan de Oñate founds the New Mexico colony and establishes the city of Santa Fe.

1610
Santa Fe becomes the capital under Governor Don Pedro de Peralta.

1848
New Mexico is ceded to the United States.

1680
Settlers flee the colony following the Pueblo Revolt.

1821
▲ Mexico gains independence from Spain.

1912
New Mexico becomes the 47th US state, with Santa Fe as the capital.

of regional government for 300 years. Exhibits here trace the history and culture of New Mexico from 1540 to 1912. Among the highlights are rare Native American hide paintings and a stagecoach, but the real star is the building itself. Free daily tours bring to life all that happened here. Downtown walking tours (for an additional fee) are also offered April to October.

④ 🗺️ 🎫 🛍️
New Mexico History Museum

🏛️ 113 Lincoln Ave 🕙 10am-5pm daily 🚫 Nov-Apr: Mon; public hols 🌐 nmhistory museum.org

Adjacent to the Palace of the Governors, the New Mexico History Museum presents fascinating stories of the American West. Using striking displays and interactive exhibits, each gallery highlights a different chapter of the state's rich past, from early Native American tribes to modern times.

⑤ 🗺️ 🛍️
IAIA Museum of Contemporary Native Arts

🏛️ 108 Cathedral Pl 🕙 10am-5pm Mon & Wed-Sat, noon-5pm Sun 🚫 Public hols 🌐 iaia.edu

Housed in a Pueblo Revival-style building, this museum contains the National Collection of Contemporary Native American Art. Traditional pottery, textiles, and beadwork are displayed alongside modern paintings and "mixed-media works.

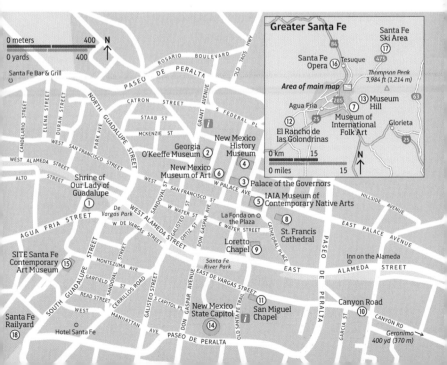

The facade of the ↑
New Mexico Museum
of Art, built in 1917

of folk art from all over the world, including toys, miniature theaters, dolls, and paintings, as well as religious and traditional art.

The eastern gallery holds the awe-inspiring Girard Wing, the largest collection of cross-cultural works in existence. More than 100,000 objects – including icons, paintings, puppets, dolls, and small clay, wood, paper, and cloth figures from more than 100 countries – are displayed at various heights; many artifacts even hang from the ceiling. The highlights include ceramic figures arranged in attractive scenes, ranging from a Polish Christmas to a Mexican baptism.

The Hispanic Heritage Wing contains Spanish Colonial and Latino decorative art, such as rare hide paintings, while the East Bartlett Wing displays rugs, blankets, textiles and costumes from Africa, Asia, and South America. It is easy to see the depth of craft and detail in each piece.

(6) 🏛 🛍

New Mexico Museum of Art

🏠 107 W Palace Ave
🕙 10am–5pm Tue–Sun (to 7pm first Fri of month) 🚫 Public hols
🌐 nmartmuseum.org

Built to showcase New Mexico's growing art scene, this building is one of the earliest examples of modern Pueblo Revival-style architecture – a blend of Spanish Colonial and Native American styles. The design owes much to the nearby Pueblo mission churches. The collection comprises over 20,000 pieces of Southwestern art from the 19th century onward.

→
Masks and other objects on display at the Museum of International Folk Art

(7) 🏛 🎭 🛍

Museum of International Folk Art

🏠 706 Camino Lejo
🕙 10am–5pm daily
🚫 Public hols 🌐 winter nationalfolkart.org

This charming museum houses a stunning collection

Did You Know?

Wealthy Chicagoan Florence Dibell Bartlett founded the Museum of International Folk Art in 1953.

New Mexico Culture Pass

The New Mexico Culture Pass covers admission to four top Santa Fe museums as well as 11 other attractions across the state. It is valid for one year, and can be purchased at any state museum or historic site.

⑧

St. Francis Cathedral

📍 131 Cathedral Pl
🕐 Times vary, check website 🌐 cbsfa.org

The cathedral's French Romanesque-style facade is an anomaly in the heart of this adobe city, yet its honey-colored stone, glowing in the afternoon light, makes it one of its loveliest landmarks. It was built in 1869 under Santa Fe's first archbishop, Jean Baptiste Lamy, and designed by Antoine Mouly. The building replaced most of an earlier adobe church called La Parroquia, except for the side chapel of Our Lady of the Rosary. This houses the oldest statue of the Virgin Mary in North America, known as *La Conquistadora*. Carved out of wood in Mexico in 1625, the figure was brought to Santa Fe where it gained mythical status, as settlers fleeing the Pueblo Revolt in 1680 (*p58*) claimed to have been saved by the Virgin's protection.

⑨ 🛍️

Loretto Chapel

📍 207 Old Santa Fe Trail
🕐 9am–4:30pm Mon–Sat, 10:30am–4:30pm Sun
🌐 lorettochapel.com

This Neo-Gothic chapel, now used as a museum and a wedding chapel, was fashioned after Sainte-Chapelle in Paris by the architect of Santa Fe's St. Francis Cathedral. It is most famous for its staircase, a dramatically curved spiral that winds upward for 21 ft (6 m) with 33 steps that make two complete 360-degree turns. The spiral has no nails or center support – only its perfect craftsmanship keeps it aloft. When the chapel was built, it lacked access to the choir loft. Legend has it that a mysterious carpenter appeared, built the staircase, and vanished without payment. Research suggests that the highly skilled craftsman was the Frenchman François Jean Rochas.

← Stone statue of the Virgin Mary holding rosary beads outside St. Francis Cathedral

STAY

Hotel Santa Fe
Owned by the Picuris Pueblo, this welcoming hotel is stylishly decorated, making full use of striking Native American arts and crafts in public places and in guest bedrooms. The restaurant serves fine food using locally sourced ingredients.

📍 1501 Paseo de Peralta
🌐 hotelsantafe.com

$⑤$$⑤$⑤

La Fonda on the Plaza
On the site of a 1610 adobe inn on the historic Plaza, this luxurious grande dame is full of original artworks by local artists, including fantastic hand-carved and hand-painted furnishings. There is even a seasonal outdoor cocktail bar.

📍 100 E San Francisco St
🌐 lafondasantafe.com

$⑤$$⑤$$⑤$

Inn on the Alameda
This delightful pueblo-style boutique hotel has a social hour late every afternoon when guests can mingle over complimentary wine and cheese. Rooms are decorated in colorful Southwestern style, and it's close to the Canyon Road art district.

📍 303 East Alameda St
🌐 innonthealameda.com

$⑤$$⑤$$⑤$

⑩ 🍴 🏛

Canyon Road

Originally a track between the Rio Grande and Pecos pueblos, Canyon Road was later used by early settlers for hauling firewood down from the mountains on their donkeys. This upscale half-mile road is today lined with more than 100 private art galleries, artists' studios, clothing boutiques, and stores selling Native American jewelry, pottery, folk art, handmade crafts, as well as home furnishings and antiques, and gourmet restaurants, all housed in historic adobe structures. Canyon Road still attracts painters and sculptors to its studios, where the public can watch them at work.

⑪

San Miguel Chapel

🏠 401 Old Santa Fe Trail
🕐 Times vary, check website 🅦 sanmiguel chapel.org

The chapel of San Miguel is thought to have been built around 1610, making it one of the oldest churches in the US. It was built by Tlaxcala Indians, who traveled from

Mexico with the early Spanish settlers. The original dirt floor and adobe steps are still visible at the front of the altar. This simple church has great roof beams that were restored in 1692, having been burned 12 years earlier in the Pueblo Revolt. A carved wooden *reredos* (altarpiece) frames the centrally placed statue of the patron saint, San Miguel, while the side walls have paintings of religious scenes on deerskin and buffalo hide.

⑫ ✍ 🅜 🍴 🏛

El Rancho de las Golondrinas

🏠 334 Los Pinos Rd 🕐 Jun-Sep: 10am–4pm Wed-Sun
🅦 golondrinas.org

Established in the early 1700s, El Rancho de las Golondrinas ("Ranch of the Swallows") was a historic way point on the Camino Real, the old royal

road trading route that ran from Mexico City to Santa Fe. The 200-acre (80-ha) ranch served as a *paraje*, an official rest stop for settlers and explorers, and a chance for them to water their animals. Over the last three centuries, it has been home to many families, including the Bacas, who held it for 200 years. Now a living history museum, with restored buildings and historic features, this working farm re-creates life on a typical 18th-century Spanish ranch. Authentic historic crops such as squash and corn are grown here, and burros and horses are used to work the fertile land.

⑬

Museum Hill

Alongside the Museum of International Folk Art *(p194)*, three other important museums are found on

← A wagon and storage hut at El Rancho de las Golondrinas

Museum Hill. The **Museum of Indian Arts and Culture** is dedicated to traditional Native American arts and culture. Its main exhibit, "Here, Now & Always", tells the story of the Southwest's oldest communities in the words of the indigenous Pueblo, Navajo, and Apache people.

The **Wheelwright Museum of the American Indian**, established in 1937 by wealthy philanthropist Mary Cabot Wheelwright of Boston, was built to resemble a Navajo hogan traditional dwelling. The museum's focus is on its changing exhibitions of contemporary work by Native American artists and on the gallery devoted to Southwestern jewelry. In the basement, the excellent Case Trading Post re-creates the first trading posts established on the Navajo Reservation.

The **Museum of Spanish Colonial Art** holds an extensive collection of Spanish Colonial art, with over 3,000 objects including textiles, furniture, religious santos, and ceramics. Many galleries take you back through time to paint a picture of the arrival and evolution of the Spanish Colonial arts in New Mexico.

Museum of Indian Arts and Culture
◈ ⓖ 🅰710 Camino Lejo
🕙10am–5pm Tue–Sun (May–Oct: also Mon) 🚫Public hols
🌐miaclab.org

Wheelwright Museum of the American Indian
◈ 🅰704 Camino Lejo
🕙10am–5pm daily
🚫Public hols
🌐wheelwright.org

Museum of Spanish Colonial Art
◈ 🅰750 Camino Lejo
🕙10am–5pm Tue–Sun (May–Aug: also Mon)
🌐spanishcolonial.org

EAT

Geronimo
Housed in a 1756 building with adobe walls and kiva fireplaces, this intimate restaurant serves superb Southwestern fusion dishes, such as tellicherry-rubbed elk tenderloin and mesquite-grilled Maine lobster tails.

🅰724 Canyon Rd
🍴Lunch 🌐geronimo restaurant.com

$$$

Santa Fe Bar & Grill
Succulent slow-roasted, tamarind-chipotle baby back ribs and sinful adobe mud pie are the popular dishes here. Wash them down with a tequila or margarita from an extensive drinks list. Colorful Mexican furnishings, pottery, and artworks decorate the dining area.

🅰187 Paseo de Peralta
🌐santafebargrill.com

$$$

← *Apache Mountain Spirit Dancer* sculpture by Craig Dan Goseyun, Museum of Indian Arts and Culture

⑭ Ⓜ
New Mexico State Capitol

📍 Old Santa Fe Trail & Paseo de Peralta 🕐 7am-6pm Mon-Fri (Memorial Day-Aug: also 9am-5pm Sat & public hols) 🌐 nmlegis.gov

Built to resemble the sun symbol of the Zia Pueblo people, the circular State Capitol is the house of government of New Mexico. The building houses works by New Mexican artists from the Capitol Art Collection. A highlight is Holly Hughes' sculpture *The Buffalo* (1992), which uses paintbrushes for hair.

⑮ Ⓜ Ⓟ ▣ 🛍
SITE Santa Fe Contemporary Art Museum

📍 1606 Paseo de Peralta 🕐 10am-5pm Wed-Sat; (to 7pm Fri), noon-5pm Sun 🌐 sitesantafe.org

From humble origins in an old beer warehouse in the Railyard district, this exciting art museum has expanded to become a world-class venue, lauded for its dramatic architecture as well as its cutting-edge contemporary art shows. Through changing exhibitions, which feature international artists, it aims to present the most innovative visual art of our times in new and engaging ways. It is also renowned for groundbreaking biennial exhibitions, which have highlighted international art and art of the Americas.

⑯ Ⓜ Ⓟ 🛍
Santa Fe Opera

📍 5 miles (8 km) N of Santa Fe on Hwy 84/285 🕐 Late-Jun-Aug: daily 🌐 santafe opera.org

Located just north of Santa Fe near the pueblo of Tesuque, the outdoor auditorium is the setting for one of the finest summer opera companies in the world. Running since 1957 with five operas in rotating repertory each season, the Santa Fe Opera is renowned for innovative productions of both new and established operas, including a number of impressive world premieres, which attract international stars. A state-of-the-art electronic system allows the audience to read translations of the libretti on the seats in front of them. Backstage tours are available late May through August.

Visitors are advised to come prepared for Santa Fe's changeable weather when watching the performances, with warm clothing, umbrellas, rugs, and waterproof gear.

SITE Santa Fe's Sky Terrace, and *(inset)* detail from *The Storm on the Sea of Galilee* (2015) by Kota Ezawa ↓

> A centerpiece of the Santa Fe Railyard is the open-air Farmers' Market on Saturdays, which features live music and stalls with cheeses, chiles, and fresh local produce.

↑ Santa Fe Farmers' Market in the Santa Fe Railyard district on a Saturday morning

⑰ 🛷
Santa Fe Ski Area

📍 Hwy 475 ⏰ Mid-Mar-early Apr: 9:30am-4:30pm daily, weather permitting; late Nov-mid-Mar: 9am-4pm daily 🌐 skisanta fe.com

Just a 30-minute drive from historic downtown Santa Fe, the beautiful ski area sits in a 12,000-ft- (3,660-m-) high basin of the Sangre de Cristo mountains, surrounded by forest. The resort has 79 trails to suit skiers of every ability, ranging from beginners to experts, and snowboarding runs are also open. Check the website for the latest snow report. A lodge, equipment rentals, ski school, and childcare are available, as are a variety of ski packages.

From late September to mid-October, chairlift rides (on weekends, holidays and during Balloon Fiesta Week) offer splendid views of the fall colors. The RTD Mountain Trail Shuttle from downtown Santa Fe gives easy access to the ski area.

⑱ 🍽 🛍
Santa Fe Railyard

📍 Guadalupe St ⏰ Farmers' Market: 8am-1pm Tue & Sat; Artists' Market: 10am-3pm Sun 🌐 railyardsantafe.com

Spreading out from its historic train depot, the Railyard is Santa Fe's lively arts and entertainment district. Along with contemporary art galleries, unique shops, tempting restaurants, and nightlife venues, it contains a relaxing, family-friendly park and plaza with performance space for special events and festivals. A center-piece of the Railyard is the open-air Farmers' Market on Saturdays, which features live music and stalls with cheeses, chiles, and fresh local produce. There's also an Artists' Market where you can buy fantastic art and crafts from a range of friendly and talented Northern New Mexico artisans.

The Railyard is home to impressive spaces, including El Museo Cultural, a Hispanic arts and culture center; Santa Fe Clay, a ceramics art center and gallery showcasing traditional and contemporary artists; and the highly acclaimed SITE Santa Fe Contemporary Art Museum. It is also the northern terminus for the New Mexico Rail Runner, a 100-mile (161-km) commuter train network that connects the city with Albuquerque and beyond.

> 💬 INSIDER TIP
> **Friday for Art Lovers**
>
> On the last Friday of every month, the brilliant contemporary art galleries of the Sant Fe Railyard district host the free Last Friday Art Walk, when they open from 5 to 7pm. All of the galleries are within a short walk of each other. SITE Santa Fe offers free admission all day on Fridays and on Saturdays from 10am to noon during the Santa Fe Farmers' Market.

A SHORT WALK
CENTRAL SANTA FE PLAZA

Distance 1 mile (1.5 km) **Time** 25 minutes **Nearest bus** 1

The oldest state capital in North America, Santa Fe was founded by the Spanish conquistador Don Pedro de Peralta, who created a colony here in 1610. This colony was abandoned in 1680 following the Pueblo Revolt, but settlers recaptured it in 1692. When Mexico gained independence in 1821, Santa Fe was opened up to the wider world, and traders and settlers from the US arrived via the Santa Fe Trail.

The central plaza has been the heart of Santa Fe since its founding, and there is no better place to begin exploring the city. Today, it houses a Native American market under the portal of the Palace of the Governors, and the square is lined with attractive shops, cafés, and galleries.

The **New Mexico Museum of Art** (p194) *focuses on the paintings and sculpture of Southwestern artists.*

Both the heart of the city and a National Historic Landmark, the plaza is a pretty square lined with leafy cottonwood trees. The obelisk at its center commemorates the soldiers who lost their lives in the 1862 Battle of Glorieta Pass.

LINCOLN AVENUE

SHERIDAN STREET

AVENUE

PALACE

BURRO ALLEY

W. SAN FRANCISCO STREET

DON GASPAR AVENUE

GALISTEO STREET

WATER STREET

Did You Know?

At an altitude of 7,199 ft (2,194 m), Santa Fe is the highest capital city in the US.

The historic **Original Trading Post** *sells Hispanic art, antiques, and Native American crafts.*

| 0 meters | 60 |
| 0 yards | 60 |

N

Must See

SANTA FE

Central Santa Fe
Plaza

Locator Map
See pp190–191

↑ The New Mexico Museum of Art built
in 1917 in the Pueblo Revival Style

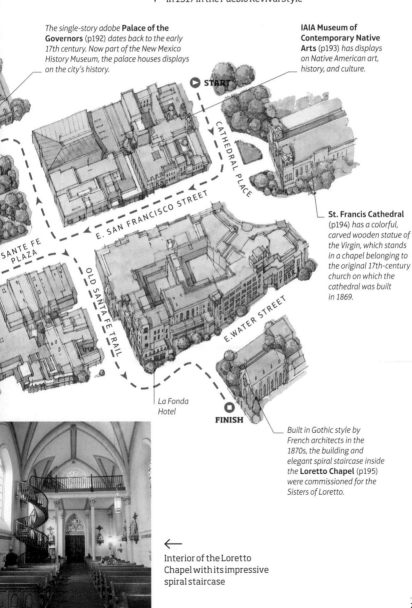

The single-story adobe **Palace of the Governors** (p192) *dates back to the early 17th century. Now part of the New Mexico History Museum, the palace houses displays on the city's history.*

IAIA Museum of Contemporary Native Arts (p193) *has displays on Native American art, history, and culture.*

● START

CATHEDRAL PLACE

E. SAN FRANCISCO STREET

SANTE FE PLAZA

OLD SANTA FE TRAIL

St. Francis Cathedral (p194) *has a colorful, carved wooden statue of the Virgin, which stands in a chapel belonging to the original 17th-century church on which the cathedral was built in 1869.*

E. WATER STREET

La Fonda Hotel

❑ **FINISH**

Built in Gothic style by French architects in the 1870s, the building and elegant spiral staircase inside the **Loretto Chapel** (p195) *were commissioned for the Sisters of Loretto.*

←
Interior of the Loretto Chapel with its impressive spiral staircase

2

TAOS

A F3 **i** 1139 Paseo del Pueblo Sur; www.taos.org

Like Santa Fe, Taos is an important center for the arts. Its plaza and the surrounding streets are lined with craft shops, cafés, and galleries, many housed in original adobe buildings. Altough Taos people have lived in the area for around 1,000 years, the town's present foundations were laid after Don Diego de Vargas resettled the area after the Pueblo Revolt in 1680.

① 🎨 🏛

Harwood Museum of Art

A 238 Ledoux St **O** 10am–5pm Wed–Fri, noon–5pm Sat & Sun **O** Jan 1, Jul 4, Thanks-giving, Dec 25 **W** harwoodmuseum.org

This museum occupies an adobe compound, built in the 19th century, that is run by the University of New Mexico. It provides a tranquil setting for paintings, sculpture, prints, drawings, and photography.

In 1898, artists Ernest Blumenschein and Bert Phillips stopped in Taos to repair a broken wagon wheel, and, entranced by the beauty of the Taos Valley, they never left. In 1915 they established the Taos Society of Artists, which existed until 1927 and helped pave the way for the growth of the tiny artistic colony of Taos into an international art center. The society mainly painted Native Americans, early Anglo settlers, and New Mexico landscapes. The Harwood Museum of Art displays work by members of the society alongside that of Modernist painters who flocked to Taos in the 1940s and 50s, and contemporary local artists. There are also collections of works by the Canadian-born American artist Agnes Martin (who spent her final years in Taos), Hispanic paintings, tin objects, and wood carvings that cover a broad range of Hispanic traditions in Northern New Mexico, and Native American paintings and sculpture.

← A courtyard in Taos, with sculptures, art galleries, and jewelry stores

adobe home with Russian-influenced woodwork that included handcrafted doors, windows, and furniture. Today his house is the Taos Art Museum, containing examples of his work as well as that of numerous members of the Taos Society of Artists.

③

Taos Plaza

Built by the Spanish and fortified after the Pueblo Revolt of 1680, Taos Plaza has been remodeled several times but remains the centerpoint of the town. Its shady trees and benches make it a relaxing spot to sit and people-watch. The copper-topped bandstand was a gift from Mabel Dodge Luhan, New Mexico's leading arts patron in the 1920s. A flag has flown continuously from the flagpole since the Civil War, when Kit Carson *(p204)* and a band of citizens raised the Union Flag to protect Taos from Confederate supporters.

MABEL DODGE LUHAN (1879-1962)

Taos' reputation as an arts colony grew in the 1920s after Mabel Dodge Luhan, a wealthy heiress from New York, moved to town. She established a literary salon and became a patron of the arts, hosting notables such as Georgia O'Keeffe and D. H. Lawrence. She married Tony Luhan, a Native American. Their home at 240 Morada Lane is a National Historic Landmark and is now an inn and conference center.

Did You Know?

Hotel La Fonda de Taos owns "forbidden" paintings by D. H. Lawrence that were banned in London in 1929.

②

Taos Art Museum at Fechin House

⌂ 227 Paseo del Pueblo Norte ⏰ May-Oct: 10am-5pm Tue-Sun; Nov-Apr: 10am-4pm Fri-Sun 🌐 taosartmuseum.org

Born in Russia in 1881, Nicolai Fechin learned woodcarving from his father. He became a talented artist, producing paintings, drawings, and sculpture. Fechin moved to Taos with his family in 1927 and set about restoring his

← Gallery dedicated to works by Agnes Martin in the Harwood Museum of Art

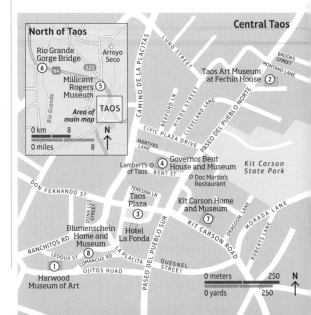

North of Taos

Rio Grande Gorge Bridge — ⑥ — Arroyo Seco

Millicent Rogers Museum ⑤

Rio Grande

Area of main map — TAOS

0 km 8
0 miles 8

N

Central Taos

LUND STREET

BROOKS STREET
MONTANO LANE

CAMINO DE LA PLACITAS

BEDFORD LN
HINDE STREET
CLEVELAND LANE

Taos Art Museum at Fechin House ②

PASEO DEL PUEBLO NORTE

CIVIC PLAZA DRIVE

MARTYRS LANE

Lambert's of Taos ④ Governor Bent House and Museum
BENT ST
Doc Martin's Restaurant

Kit Carson State Park

DON FERNANDO ST

DOÑA LUZ STREET

TERESINA LN
Taos Plaza ③

Kit Carson Home and Museum ⑦

DRAGOON LANE
MORADA LANE
ROBERTS LANE

KIT CARSON ROAD

Blumenschein Home and Museum ⑧

Hotel La Fonda

RANCHITOS RD
LEDOUX ST
COMANCHE RD
OJITOS ROAD

LA PLACITA
PASEO DEL PUEBLO SUR

QUESNEL STREET

Harwood Museum of Art ①

0 meters 250
0 yards 250

N

Governor Bent House and Museum

🏠 117 Bent St ⏰ Apr-Oct: 9am-5pm daily; Nov-Mar: 10am-4pm daily

Charles Bent became the first Anglo-American governor of New Mexico in 1846. In 1847 he was killed by Pueblo warriors who resented American rule during the Taos Revolt. The hole hacked in the adobe by his family as they attempted to flee can still be seen. Today, exhibits include guns, Native American artifacts, and animal skins.

Millicent Rogers Museum

🏠 1504 Millicent Rogers Rd ⏰ Apr-Oct: 10am-5pm daily; Nov-Mar: 10am-5pm Tue-Sun ⏰ Public hols 🌐 millicentrogers.org

Beautiful heiress and arts patron Millicent Rogers (1902–53) moved to Taos in 1947. Fascinated by the area, she created one of the country's leading museums of Southwestern arts and design. Native American silver and turquoise jewelry and Navajo weavings form the core of the exhibits, which are housed in a historic hacienda. Also featured is the pottery of the famous Puebloan artist Maria Martinez (1887–1980), with its distinctive black-on-black style.

6
Rio Grande Gorge Bridge

The dramatic Rio Grande Gorge Bridge, which opened in 1965, is the second-highest

The Rio Grande Gorge Bridge, a major landmark near Taos ↑

bridge on the US Highway System. At 650 ft (195 m) above the Rio Grande, its dizzying heights offer awesome views of the gorge and the surrounding sweeping plateau.

Kit Carson Home and Museum

🏠 113 Kit Carson Rd ⏰ 10am-5:30pm daily (Nov-Feb: to 4:30pm) ⏰ Thanksgiving, Dec 25, Jan 1 🌐 kitcarsonmuseum.org

At the age of 17, Christopher "Kit" Carson (1809–68) ran away to join a wagon train and became one of the most famous names in the West. He led a remarkable life, working as a cook and interpreter, a fur-trapping mountain man, a scout for mapping expeditions, a Native American agent, and a military officer (p166). He purchased this house in Taos in 1843 for his 14-year-old bride, Josefa Jaramillo, and lived here for the rest of his life. Carson's remarkable story, and the unpredictable nature of frontier life, are the focus of the museum exhibits, which feature antique firearms, photographs, and furniture.

Blumenschein Home and Museum

🏠 222 Ledoux St ⏰ 10am-5pm Mon-Sat, noon-5pm Sun 🌐 taoshistoric museums.org

Ernest Blumenschein (1874–1960), along with Bert Phillips and Joseph Henry Sharp, was instrumental in founding the Taos Society of Artists in 1915. The society promoted their own work and that of other

> At 650 ft (195 m) above the Rio Grande, the bridge's dizzying heights offer awesome views of the gorge and the surrounding sweeping plateau.

EAT

Doc Martin's Restaurant

Named after the county's first physician, this restaurant offers superior regional cuisine. Multicourse prix-fixe and à la carte menus are available. Try the blue corn chicken enchiladas or Doc's *chile relleno*.

🏠 125 Paseo del Pueblo Norte 🌐 taosinn.com

$ $ $

Lambert's of Taos

Lambert's serves a variety of meat, game, and seafood dishes, ranging from sumac-dusted ruby trout to lobster risotto and Harris Ranch filet mignon. It has an excellent list of international wines.

🏠 123 Bent St 🌐 lambertsoftaos.com

$ $ $

Taos artists. The museum is located in Blumenschein's former home, sections of which date from the 1790s. Paintings by Blumenschein and his family, as well as representative works produced by the Taos Society of Artists, hang in rooms decorated with fine Spanish Colonial furniture and European antiques. The splendid house, full of an impressive range of the Blumenschein family's belongings, beautifully illustrates the life of Taos artists in the first half of the 20th century as well as commemorates the Taos Society of Artists.

←

The Blumenschein Home and Museum, full of the family's possessions and art

EXPERIENCE MORE

3

Ranchos de Taos

🅰F3 ℹ1139 Paseo de Pueblo Sur, Taos; www. taos.org

Three miles (5 km) southwest of central Taos, this settlement centered around a peaceful plaza is home to the striking adobe church of **San Francisco de Asis**, built from 1710 to 1755. One of the finest examples of mission architecture in the Southwest, it has provided inspiration for many artists and was a frequent subject of the innovative American modernist artist Georgia O'Keeffe *(p213)*.

The **Hacienda Martínez** is a Spanish colonial house built in 1804 and one of very few still in existence. Its thick adobe walls and heavy zaguan (entry) gates give it a fortress-like

quality. Inside, 21 rooms surround two courtyards. The first owner, Antonio Severino Martínez, prospered through trade with Mexico and later became mayor of Taos. Examples of the merchandise he sold are displayed here.

San Francisco de Asis

🏠60 St Francis Plaza ⏰9am-4pm Mon-Sat 📅Early Jun

Hacienda Martínez

♿ 🏠708 Hacienda Way ⏰Times vary, check website 🌐taoshistoricmuseums.org

4

Taos Pueblo

🅰F3 🏠120 Veterans Hwy, Taos ⏰8am- 4:30pm Mon-Sat, 8:30am-4:30pm Sun 🌐taospueblo.com

Taos Pueblo is one of the oldest communities in the United States, having been occupied continuously for around 1,000

years. Two multistory adobe communal houses sit on opposite sides of the open central "square." Known as North House and South House, they are the largest pueblo buildings in the country and are thought to date from the early 1700s. More than 100 people live year round at Taos Pueblo as their ancestors did, with no electricity, and water supplied only from a stream. Sights include the 1850 St. Jerome Chapel, the ruins of the earlier 1619 San Geronimo Church, and the central plaza, with its drying racks for corn and chili and adobe ovens, or *hornos*. Several ground-floor dwellings are now craft shops. Guided tours are available, but visitors are asked to follow etiquette; permission must be granted prior to photographing a resident, and visitors must follow posted signs and rules. No cameras are permitted during ceremonial dances, but several festivals are open to visitors throughout the year.

←

The church of San Francisco de Asis, with a marble statue of the saint in front

---

THE RIO GRANDE

From its source in Colorado, the fifth-longest river in the US flows southeast to the Gulf of Mexico, forming the entire boundary between Texas and Mexico. It was used for irrigation by the pueblos since ancient times, and in the 16th century Spanish colonists established settlements along it. Today, crops including cotton, citrus fruits, and vegetables are grown along its fertile banks.

Skiers tackling the runs at
the Taos Ski Valley resort
beneath Wheeler Peak

5 🍴 ☕ 🛍

Taos Ski Valley

🅰 F3　🚻 10 Thunderbird Rd;
www.taosskivalley.com

During the early 1900s, Taos
Ski Valley was a bustling mining
camp. In 1955, Swiss-born skier
Ernie Blake began developing
a world-class ski resort on the
northern slopes and snow
bowls of Wheeler Peak, the
highest summit in New Mexico.
Located 19 miles (30 km) north
of Taos, it has 14 lifts and
113 runs for all abilities, but it
is particularly known for its
challenging expert terrain.
The ski season itself generally
runs from Thanksgiving to
early April, depending on the
weather. The valley also makes
a spectacular summer retreat,
popular with those seeking
relief from the summer heat.

6

Los Alamos

🅰 F4　🚻 109 Central Park Sq;
www.visitlosalamos.org

Los Alamos is famous as the
location of the Manhattan
Project (p208), the US government's top-secret research
program that developed the
atomic bomb during World
War II. Government scientists
took over this remote site in
1943, and in 1945 the first
atomic bomb was detonated
in the southern New Mexico
desert near Alamogordo (p239).

Today, the town is home
to scientists from the Los
Alamos National Laboratory,
a leading defense facility. The
Bradbury Science Museum
showcases its current and
historic research and includes
replicas of the Little Boy
and Fat Man atomic bombs
dropped on Hiroshima and
Nagasaki in 1945. The **Los
Alamos History Museum** covers the geology of the region.

Bradbury Science Museum

♿　🏠 1350 Central Ave
🕐 10am-5pm Tue-Sat, 1-5pm
Sun & Mon　🚫 Public hols
🌐 lanl.gov/museum

Los Alamos
History Museum

♿♿♿　🏠 1050 Bathtub
Row 🕐 10am-4pm daily
(9am- 4pm in summer)
🚫 Public hols　🌐 losalamos
history.org

> **The tiny town of
> Jemez Springs lies
> in San Diego Canyon,
> by the Jemez River,
> on land once
> occupied by the
> Giusewa Pueblo.**

7

Jemez Springs

🅰 E4　🚻 80 Jemez Springs
Plaza; www.jemezsprings.
org

The tiny town of Jemez Springs
lies in San Diego Canyon, by
the Jemez River, on land once
occupied by the Giusewa
Pueblo. Its ruins and those of
a 17th-century mission church
are now part of the **Jemez
Historic Site**, where you will
find fascinating remnants of
its walls and a reconstruction
of its huge main gates. A few
miles south, on Highway 4, is
the large **Jemez Pueblo**, which
is home to over 3,400 tribal
members. The main village of
Walatawa is open to visitors
only on festival days, but the
visitor center is open daily.

The region is also famous
for its hot springs. Spence Hot
Springs, 7 miles (11 km) north
of town, has several outdoor
hot pools linked by waterfalls.
There are also commercial hot
springs and spas in the town.

Jemez Historic Site

♿　🏠 Off Hwy 4　🕐 8:30am-
5pm Wed-Sun　🚫 Public hols
🌐 nmhistoricsites.org/jemez

Jemez Pueblo

🚻 Walatawa Visitor Center,
7413 Hwy 4; www.jemez
pueblo.com

THE ATOMIC AGE AND SPACE AGE

During World War II, fear that the Germans were developing an atomic bomb led the US to begin its own nuclear weapons program. In 1942 Britain and the US combined their research efforts in a program known as the Manhattan Project, based at Los Alamos. The clear skies, level ground, and sparse population made it an ideal top-secret testing area. Today, Los Alamos National Laboratory and Sandia National Laboratory in Albuquerque are the largest nuclear research facilities in the US, and remain important centers for military research and development.

ROCKET SCIENCE

Robert H. Goddard (1882-1945) is often referred to as "the father of modern rocketry", developing rocket science in his workshop in Roswell, New Mexico (p240). He launched his first liquid-fueled rocket in Massachusetts in 1926 and performed 56 flight tests in Roswell in the 1930s. By 1935 he had developed rockets that could carry cameras and record instrument readings.

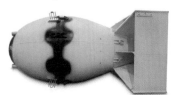

↑ Replica of Fat Man, the atomic bomb dropped on the Japanese city of Nagasaki in August 1945

THE MANHATTAN PROJECT

In 1943 an innocuous former boys' school, the Los Alamos Ranch School set high on New Mexico's remote Pajarito Plateau, was chosen as the research site for the top-secret Manhattan Project, which resulted in the world's first nuclear explosion in July 1945. Work began immediately under the direction of physicist J. Robert Oppenheimer and General Leslie R. Groves. In just over two years they had developed the first atomic bomb. It was detonated at the secluded Trinity Test Site, now the White Sands Missile Range (p239), on July 16 1945. The decision to explode the bomb in warfare was highly controversial, and some of the scientists who developed the bomb signed a petition against its use. Displays on the project can be seen at the Bradbury Science Museum in Los Alamos and the Los Alamos Historical Museum (p207).

↑ Robert H. Goddard and his assistants inspecting a Goddard rocket in his workshop in Roswell, New Mexico

SPACE FLIGHT

New Mexico is a key player in the space age as the site for NASA space missions and, more recently, Spaceport America *(p234)*.

① Ham the Astrochimp
Ham the space chimp is helped out of his capsule after becoming the first living creature to be sent into space in 1961 as part of America's space program. He returned to Earth alive.

② Astronaut Training
New Mexico's role in space, including astronaut training, is explored in the New Mexico Museum of Space History *(p239)*. Here astronauts Steven Robinson and Pedro Duque are training in a buoyancy tank, assisted by scuba divers, to simulate life in space in preparation for the 1998 Discovery shuttle mission.

③ White Sands Missile Range
A space shuttle touches down on the Northrup strip at the White Sands Missile Range on March 30, 1982. The shuttle program ended in 2011, but White Sands remains a missile testing ground.

④ Roswell
New Mexico is home to Roswell, site of the Roswell Incident, and many other UFO conspiracy theories, as illustrated by the International UFO Museum and Research Center *(p240)*.

↑ Spaceport America, New Mexico, the world's first purpose-built commercial spaceport

A kiva at Pecos Pueblo mission church; ancient pottery *(inset)*

8 Pecos National Historical Park

F4 Hwy 63 Jun-Aug: 8am-6pm daily; Sep-May: 8am-4:30pm daily Jan 1, Thanksgiving, Dec 25 nps.gov/peco

Located across Highway 63, 25 miles (40 km) southeast of Santa Fe, Pecos National Historical Park includes the ruins of the once-influential Pecos Pueblo. Situated in a pass through the Sangre de Cristo Mountains, on the Pecos River, the pueblo dominated trade routes between Plains Indians and the Pueblo peoples between 1450 and 1550.

GREAT VIEW
Glorieta Pass Battlefield Trail

The site of an 1862 battle during the American Civil War, the Glorieta Pass is a 2.3-mile (4-km) loop trail through lovely pinyon forest. Ask for the gate code and a map at the Pecos National Park Visitor Center.

Pecos Puebloans acted as a conduit for goods such as buffalo skins and meat, and Puebloan products including pottery, textiles, and turquoise. The village is thought to have been among the largest in the Southwest. It stood up to five stories high, with nearly 700 rooms housing over 2,000 people, a quarter of them warriors. When the Spanish arrived in the early 1540s, it was a strong regional power and resisted Spanish settlement for many years, burning down the mission church built there and constructing a kiva (a ceremonial chamber) in its stead in 1618. However, the Spanish returned and rebuilt the mission in 1717, and by 1821 raids, disease, and migration had taken their toll; the pueblo was almost deserted, and the 17 remaining inhabitants moved to Jemez Pueblo *(p207)*.

The pueblo site can be seen on a 1.25-mile (2-km) trail that winds past the ruins of the two Spanish mission churches and two reconstructed kivas. The visitor center has exhibits of historic artifacts and crafts, and a video covering 1,000 years of Puebloan history in the area.

9 D. H. Lawrence Ranch

F3 506 D.H. Lawrence Ranch Rd, Taos 10am-2pm Thu-Fri, 10am-4pm Sat (weather permitting) dhlawrenceranch.unm.edu

Although British writer D. H. Lawrence (1885–1939) only lived for 11 months at what was then called the Kiowa Ranch, it was a pivotal time in his life. The ranch is now a shrine to the author of *Sons and Lovers*, *Women in Love*, and other classic novels. His wife Frieda made it her home after Lawrence's death, and both are now buried in a small chapel that overlooks the buildings.

The ranch is reached after a long drive up a winding mountain road through the forest, its isolation no doubt appealing to a sensitive writer and artist like Lawrence. At the time it was a 6-mile (10-km) trip by horse and cart to the nearest town, San Cristobal.

The ranch is staffed by knowledgeable volunteers, who'll gladly walk you round the handful of simple wooden buildings and tell you all about what life was like on the ranch for Lawrence and his wife. When they weren't hiking the trails, they spent their time baking bread, chopping wood, milking their cow, and looking after their horses and chickens.

Puye Cliff Dwellings

⓾ ⟨⟩ ⟨⟩ ⟨⟩

🅰F4 **🏠Hwy 30 & Santa Clara Canyon Rd, Española** **⏱8am-6pm daily (may close earlier in winter)** **🚫Week before Easter, Jun 13, Aug 12, Dec 25** **🌐puyecliffsdwellings.com**

Home to the ancestors of today's Santa Clara Pueblo people, these impressive cliff and cave dwellings lie 7,000 ft (2,134 m) above sea level on the Pajarito Plateau. Occupied from around AD 900 to 1580, they housed up to 1,500 residents in a multistory complex built around a central plaza.

Visitors may only enter the site with a Native American guide. There are different tour options depending on budget and ability. One tour takes you to the top of the mesa, another to the cliff dwellings, which involves a steep hike to the cliff face. Both offer fascinating insights into Pueblo life and magnificent views over the valley. The restored 1930s Harvey House, built from tufa blocks and volcanic rock, has a series of exhibits and artwork on discoveries made during excavations in 1907.

→

A cliff dwelling carved into volcanic rock at Bandelier National Monument

Bandelier National Monument

⓫ ⟨⟩ ⟨⟩

🅰F4 **🏠Off Hwy 4** **🌐nps.gov/band**

Set in the rugged cliffs and canyons of the Pajarito Plateau, Bandelier National Monument has over 3,000 archaeological sites that are the remains of an Ancestral Pueblo culture. The site is thought to have been occupied by ancestors of the Puebloan peoples for around 500 years from the 12th to the 16th centuries, when successive communities grew crops of corn and squash. The earliest occupants are thought to have carved the soft volcanic rock of the towering cliffs to make cave dwellings; some time later, people built houses and pueblos from rock debris.

One of the most fascinating sights here is the ruin of the 400-room Tyuonyi pueblo. The settlement is laid out in semicircular lines of houses on the floor of Frijoles Canyon.

From the visitor center, the 1.3-mile (0.3-km) Main Loop Trail leads past the Tyuonyi village to some of the cave dwellings and the Long House – multistoried dwellings built into an 800-ft (240-m) stretch of the cliff. Petroglyphs can be spotted above the holes that once held the roof beams. Another short trail leads to the Alcove House, perched 150 ft (46 m) up in the rocks and reached by four wooden ladders and some stone stairs.

Did You Know?

With ranches covering over 60 percent of the state, New Mexico has more cows than human beings.

12

Chimayó

F4

This small town lies 25 miles (40 km) north of Santa Fe on the eastern flanks of the Rio Grande valley. Chimayó was settled by Spanish colonists in the 1700s on the site of an Native American pueblo famous for its healing natural spring. The site of the spring is now occupied by the **Santuario de Chimayó**, built by a local landowner in 1813–16 after he experienced a vision telling him to dig the foundations in earth blessed with healing powers. While digging here he uncovered a cross that once belonged to two martyred priests, and the church became a place of pilgrimage. The chapel has a beautiful *reredos* surrounding the crucifix and a side room with a pit of "holy dirt," from which you may take a sample.

Chimayó is also known for its woven blankets and rugs, which have been produced by the Ortega family for several generations. Their workshop is just off the junction with Hwy 76, while farther along, the villages of Cordova and Truchas are also known for their fine craftwork.

Santuario de Chimayó

15 Santuario Dr 9am–5pm daily (May–Sep: to 6pm) elsantuariodechimayo.us

13

Las Vegas

F4 500 Railroad Ave; www.visitlasvegasnm.com

Not to be confused with its Nevada cousin (p244), Las Vegas, New Mexico, has its own high-rolling past. The word *vegas* means "meadows" in Spanish, and the town's old Plaza was established along the lush riverfront by Spanish settlers in 1835. A lucrative trade stop on the Santa Fe Trail, Las Vegas soon

Adobe gateway to Santuario de Chimayó; its interior (inset) ↓

1881

The year that Billy the Kid was killed. His index finger was sent to the local newspaper *Las Vegas Optic.*

became a wild frontier town. The coming of the railroad in 1879 brought even greater prosperity, and new building took place around the station. Along with its newfound affluence came a wave of outlaws and other disreputable characters, including Jesse James, Wyatt Earp, and Billy the Kid. Doc Holliday moved here in 1879 and briefly owned a saloon. Before long, he found himself in hot water having shot a man dead after an argument, and had to leave town.

Grand Victorian architecture still prevails, and self-guided tours are available from the visitor center. The City of Las Vegas Museum and Rough Rider Memorial Collection showcases artifacts and photographs from throughout Las Vegas history, including Native American pottery, costumes, furniture, and farming equipment.

> The country around Abiquiu, with its red rocks, mesas, and corrugated slopes, is known as O'Keeffe Country because it inspired so many of her abstract paintings.

↑ A Cumbres and Toltec steam train in the San Juan National Forest

⑭
Abiquiu

🅰 F3

This small adobe village with sunlit dusty streets was the home of the Southwest's most famous and beloved artist, Georgia O'Keeffe, from 1946 until her death in 1986. Her village home and studio are open to visitors by reservation, and bookings must be made in advance with the Georgia O'Keeffe Museum in Santa Fe *(p192)*. The country around Abiquiu, with its red rocks, mesas, and corrugated slopes, is known as O'Keeffe Country because it inspired so many of her abstract paintings.

A few miles north of town, is the fascinating **Ghost Ranch**, a retreat and education center established and now run by Presbyterians, which was one of O'Keeffe's favorite places to paint. It features two museums, of local archaeology and palaeontology; the ranch is known for its collection of fossils. Several hiking trails also start from here.

Ghost Ranch

⊗⊗ 🄰 280 Private Dr, Hwy 84 ⊙ Welcome Center: 8am–6pm daily 🆆 ghostranch.org

⑮
Chama

🅰 E3 🅸 2372 Hwy 17; www.chamavalley.com

Founded during the 1880s silver-mining boom, Chama's highlights today include the **Cumbres and Toltec Scenic Railroad**. This narrow-gauge steam train makes a truly spectacular 64-mile (103-km) daily trip over the Cumbres Pass and through the Toltec Gorge into Colorado, with views of the San Juan and Sangre de Cristo mountains. Traveling at a top speed of 7 miles (12 km) per hour, you'll have ample time to take in the beautiful scenery.

Cumbres and Toltec Scenic Railroad

⊗ 🄰 Hwy 17 ⊙ Late May–mid-Oct: 7:30am–6pm daily 🆆 cumbrestoltec.com

GEORGIA O'KEEFFE

Georgia O'Keeffe (1887–1986) enjoyed both critical and popular acclaim for her paintings, which, either as studies of single blooms or the sun-washed landscapes of the Southwest, are universally loved. Wisconsin-born and raised, she studied art in Chicago and New York but fell in love with the light of New Mexico. O'Keeffe bought an old adobe in Abiquiu and created art that brought the beauty of the state to national attention.

A DRIVING TOUR
NORTHERN PUEBLOS

Length 45 miles (72 km) **Starting point** Tesuque Pueblo, N of Santa Fe on Hwy 84

The fertile valley of the Rio Grande between Santa Fe and Taos is home to eight pueblos of the 19 Native American pueblos in New Mexico. Although geographically close, each pueblo has its own government and traditions, and many offer attractions to visitors. Nambe gives stunning views of the surrounding mountains, mesas, and high desert. San Idelfonso is famous for its fine pottery, while other villages produce handcrafted jewelry or rugs. Visitors are welcome, but must respect the local laws and etiquette (p279).

This small pueblo is known for its artisans and their work. As in many pueblos, it contains a number of craft shops and small studios, often run by the Native American artisans themselves.

El Guacho

Rio Grande

74

84

Española

Guachupangue

Santa Clara Pueblo

30

Puye Cliffs Welcome Center

*Now deserted, the **Puye Cliff Dwellings** contain over 700 rooms, complete with stone carvings, that were home to indigenous peoples until 1500.*

Rio Grande

△ Black Mesa 6,092 ft (1,857 m)

Pajarito

Rio Grande

*Occupied since 1300, the **San Ildefonso Pueblo** is best known for its etched black pottery, the proceeds of which saved its people from the Depression of the 1930s.*

30

502   San Ildefonso Pueblo   502

Otowi

← Characteristic adobe buildings found in San Ildefonso Pueblo

Declared the first capital of New Mexico in 1598, and known until 2005 as San Juan Pueblo, the village of **Ohkay Owingeh** is a center for the visual arts and has an arts cooperative.

Ohkay Owingeh

FINISH

74

68

Ranchitos

291

El Llano

583

Fairview

291

Santa Cruz

La Puebla

76

Riverside

76

Cuartelez

369

San Pedro

581 399

Sombrillo

El Valle De Arroyo Seco

Black Mesa Golf Club

La Mesilla

84

Northern Pueblos Tour

SANTA FE AND NORTHERN NEW MEXICO

Locator Map
For more detail see p190

↑ Traditional corn dancers at Nambe Pueblo during July 4 celebrations

Nambe Pueblo

503

Pojoaque

El Rancho

Jacona 502

Jaconita

Cuyamungue

The Poeh Museum at **Pojoaque Pueblo** is an excellent introduction to the pueblo way of life in these small communities.

Set in a beautiful fertile valley, the village of **Nambe Pueblo** is bordered by a lakeside hiking trail with waterfall views and a buffalo ranch.

84

The Tewa people at **Tesuque Pueblo** have a centuries-long tradition of farming and pottery-making.

Tesuque Pueblo
● **START**

0 kilometers   3

0 miles   3

N
↑

A DRIVING TOUR
ENCHANTED CIRCLE

Questa *hamlet is the gateway to Carson National Forest, with rivers, mountains, and lakes set against a rocky backdrop.*

Distance 111 miles (179 km) **Starting point** North of Taos on Hwy 522, continuing east and south on Hwys 38 & 64 **Stopping-off point** Eagle Nest **Terrain** While the main roads offer smooth driving, bear in mind that many sights are located on dirt tracks and minor roads

The scenery around Taos rises from high desert plateau with its sagebrush and yucca plants to the forested Sangre de Cristo Mountains. The Enchanted Circle tour follows a National Forest Scenic Byway through some of the area's most breathtaking landscapes. Circumnavigating the highest point in New Mexico, Wheeler Peak (13,161 ft/4,011 m), it continues through the ruggedly beautiful Carson National Forest. Lakes and hiking trails lie off the tour, which passes through a number of small towns.

Cerro

Questa

Flag Mountain 11,939 ft (3,639m)

Lama

Lobo Peak 12,087 ft (3,684 m)

Rio Grande del Norte National Monument

Arroyo Hondo

Valdez

Arroyo Seco

Rio Grande del Norte National Monument

Taos Municipal Airport

Taos Pueblo

Taos

Ranchos De Taos

Talpa

START

Pilar

FINISH

Rio Grande del Norte Visitors Center

↑ River flowing through the Rio Grande Gorge, Rio Grande del Norte National Monument

Established in 2013 by President Obama, the **Rio Grande del Norte National Monument** *stretches up the Rio Grande Gorge to Colorado. The visitor center has information on hiking and is a launch point for rafting trips.*

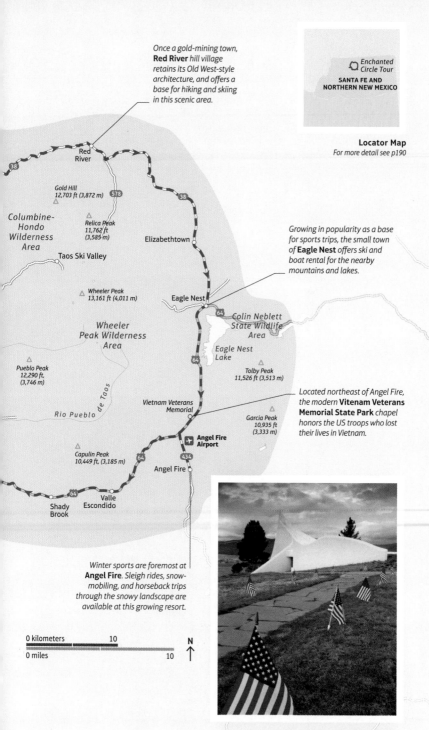

Once a gold-mining town, **Red River** hill village retains its Old West-style architecture, and offers a base for hiking and skiing in this scenic area.

Enchanted Circle Tour
SANTA FE AND NORTHERN NEW MEXICO

Locator Map
For more detail see p190

Growing in popularity as a base for sports trips, the small town of **Eagle Nest** offers ski and boat rental for the nearby mountains and lakes.

Located northeast of Angel Fire, the modern **Vietnam Veterans Memorial State Park** chapel honors the US troops who lost their lives in Vietnam.

Winter sports are foremost at **Angel Fire**. Sleigh rides, snowmobiling, and horseback trips through the snowy landscape are available at this growing resort.

Red River

Gold Hill
12,703 ft (3,872 m)

Columbine-Hondo Wilderness Area

Relica Peak
11,762 ft
(3,585 m)

Elizabethtown

Taos Ski Valley

Wheeler Peak
13,161 ft (4,011 m)

Wheeler Peak Wilderness Area

Pueblo Peak
12,290 ft,
(3,746 m)

Eagle Nest

Colin Neblett State Wildlife Area

Eagle Nest Lake

Tolby Peak
11,526 ft (3,513 m)

Rio Pueblo

de Taos

Vietnam Veterans Memorial

Garcia Peak
10,935 ft
(3,333 m)

Angel Fire Airport

Capulin Peak
10,449 ft, (3,185 m)

Angel Fire

Shady Brook

Valle Escondido

0 kilometers ——— 10
0 miles ——— 10

N ↑

↑ The chapel and US Flags at the Vietnam Veterans Memorial State Park.

ALBUQUERQUE AND SOUTHERN NEW MEXICO

Southern New Mexico is home to natural wonders such as the Carlsbad Caverns, as well as modern cities thriving on hi-tech research industries. Albuquerque is the state's largest city, with an Old Town plaza and fine museums. West of here is Acoma Pueblo, the oldest continuously inhabited settlement in the US. The southern third of the state is dominated by the Chihuahua Desert, which is one of the driest in the region. Despite this, the area was cultivated by Hohokam farmers for centuries. The Gila Cliff Dwellings preserve a remarkable settlement built by the Mogollon people between 1275 and 1300. In the 17th century Apaches occupied much of the region, with its reputation as a Wild West outpost stemming from the 19th-century exploits of characters such as Billy the Kid.

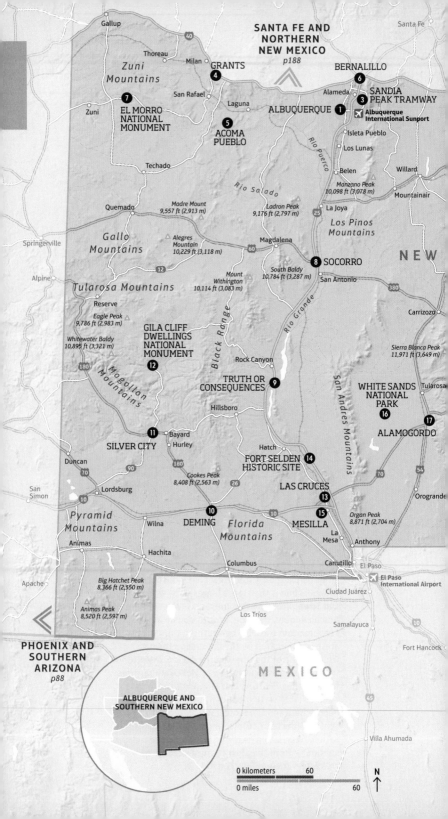

ALBUQUERQUE AND SOUTHERN NEW MEXICO

Must Sees

1. Albuquerque
2. Carlsbad Caverns National Park

Experience More

3. Sandia Peak Tramway
4. Grants
5. Acoma Pueblo
6. Bernalillo
7. El Morro National Monument
8. Socorro
9. Truth or Consequences
10. Deming
11. Silver City
12. Gila Cliff Dwellings National Monument
13. Las Cruces
14. Fort Selden Historic Site
15. Mesilla
16. White Sands National Park
17. Alamogordo
18. Cloudcroft
19. Roswell
20. Ruidoso
21. Lincoln Historic Site
22. Carlsbad

Gift and craft shops
on Albuquerque's
Old Town Plaza ↑

1

ALBUQUERQUE

🅰E4 ✈5 miles (8 km) S of downtown 🚉🚌100 First St SW
ℹ303 Romero St NW; www.visitalbuquerque.org

New Mexico's largest city fills the valley that stretches westward from
the foothills of the Manzano and Sandia Mountains and across the
banks of the Rio Grande. Its modern downtown with its high-tech
industries contrasts with Old Town, filled with historic adobe buildings.

① ⌖ 🅼 🖵 🎒

New Mexico Museum of Natural History and Science

🏠1801 Mountain Rd NW
🕐9am–5pm daily 🔒Jan 1, Thanksgiving, Dec 25
Ⓦnmnaturalhistory.org

This fascinating museum has a series of excellent interactive exhibits. Visitors can stand inside a simulated volcano or explore an ice cave. The "Evolator"is a six-minute ride through 38 million years of the region's evolution using the latest video technology.

Replica dinosaurs, a state-of-the-art planetarium, and a large-screen film theater are all highly popular with families.

② ⌖ 🅼 🎒

Turquoise Museum

🏠400 2nd St SW
🕐Times vary, check website Ⓦturquoise museum.com

Housed in a castle with beautiful grounds, this museum contains an unsurpassed collection of rare and varied turquoise specimens and jewelry from all around the world. Exhibits include 400 pieces of Native American turquoise art and displays relating to science, turquoise mines and mining, and the mystical qualities of the stones.

←

Dinosaur skeletons in the New Mexico Museum of Natural History and Science

③ 🎨 🏛

Explora! Science Center and Children's Museum

📍 1701 Mountain Rd NW
🕐 10am–6pm Mon–Sat, noon–6pm Sun 🔒 Public hols 🌐 explora.us

Explora!'s child-oriented science center is enjoyable for adults and children alike with its many interactive exhibits, such as stepping inside a soap bubble. In the Children's Museum, youngsters can look through kaleidoscopes, build wind cars, or practice weaving.

④ 🎨 🖥 🏛

Aquarium and Botanic Garden

📍 2601 Central Ave NW
🕐 9am–5pm daily
🔒 Jan 1, Thanksgiving, Dec 25 🌐 cabq.gov

The Albuquerque Aquarium in the ABQ BioPark focuses on the marine life of the Rio Grande (*p206*) and features a fascinating walk-through eel cave and an impressive floor-to-ceiling shark tank. The park also encompasses the Botanic Garden, the ABQ BioPark Zoo, and Tingley Beach, where boats can be rented.

⑤ 🎨 🏛

American International Rattlesnake Museum

📍 202 San Felipe Ave N
🕐 10am–6pm Mon–Sat (Sep–May: 11:30am–5:30pm), 1–5pm Sun 🔒 Public hols
🌐 rattlesnakes.com

This animal conservation museum explains the life cycles and ecological importance of some of Earth's most misunderstood creatures. It contains the world's largest collection of different species of live rattlesnakes, including natives of North, Central, and South America.

EAT

Church Street Café
This renowned café in an 1800s adobe building is filled with Native American art and rugs, and serves superb regional dishes.

📍 2111 Church St NW
🌐 churchstreetcafe.com

$⑤$⑤$

Antiquity
Consistently voted one of the best restaurants in Albuquerque, this gem serves clever takes on classic American and European dishes.

📍 112 Romero St NW
🕐 Lunch 🌐 antiquity restaurant.com

$⑤$⑤$⑤$

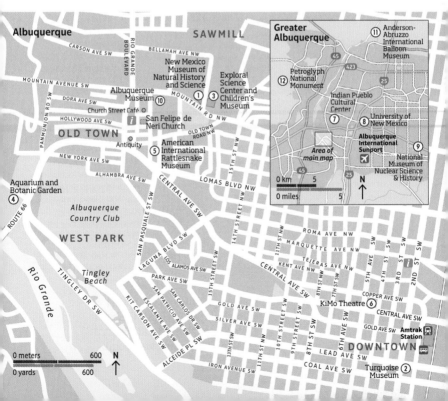

↑ The Art Deco and Pueblo Revival-style facade of the KiMo Theatre

⑥ Ⓜ

KiMo Theatre

⌂ 423 Central Ave NW
ⓦ kimotickets.com

The three-story KiMo Theatre was built in 1927, its design inspired by that of the nearby Native American pueblos. It presents a fusion of extravagant Pueblo Revival and American Art Deco styles. The theater stages a superb, eclectic range of musical and theatrical performances.

⑦ Ⓜ Ⓨ 🛍

Indian Pueblo Cultural Center

⌂ 2401 12th St NW
🕒 9am–5pm daily 🚫 Public hols ⓦ indianpueblo.org

This impressive cultural center is run by New Mexico's 19 Native American Pueblos,

which are largely concentrated along the Rio Grande north of Albuquerque, but also occupy lands as far west as the border with Arizona. The complex history and varied culture of the Puebloan peoples is traced through their oral testimony and is presented from their viewpoint. The building is designed to resemble Pueblo Bonito at Chaco Canyon (p168), one of the largest pueblo dwellings from the pre-Columbian era. The center also has a restaurant with fusion cuisine and an excellent gift shop of Native American arts and crafts. Every weekend exuberant dance performances are held in the Puebloan central courtyard.

⑧

University of New Mexico

ℹ Welcome Center, Central and Cornell; www.unm.edu

New Mexico's largest university is known for its Pueblo Revival-style architecture and its museums. The **University Art Museum** contains one of the largest fine art collections in the state, including Old Master paintings, sculpture, and other works from the 17th to the 20th centuries.

The **Maxwell Museum of Anthropology** concentrates on the culture of the Southwest, with an important collection of art and artifacts. There are also traveling exhibits on regional and international themes, as well as a permanent exhibition that traces human development through the ages.

University Art Museum
⌂ 1 University of New Mexico
🕒 10am–4pm Tue–Fri, 10am–8pm Sat 🚫 Public hols
ⓦ artmuseum.unm.edu

Maxwell Museum of Anthropology
⌂ 500 University Blvd NE
🕒 10am–4pm Tue–Sat
🚫 Public hols ⓦ maxwellmuseum.unm.edu

⑨ 🛍

National Museum of Nuclear Science & History

⌂ 601 Eubank Blvd SE at Southern Blvd 🕒 9am–5pm daily 🚫 Jan 1, Easter, Thanksgiving, Dec 25
ⓦ nuclearmuseum.org

This museum presents the stories of nuclear pioneers

> **The complex history and varied culture of the Puebloan peoples is traced through their oral history and presented from their viewpoint.**

and the history of nuclear development (*p208*). The exhibits explore the many applications of nuclear energy in the past, present, and into the future. "Energy Encounter" illustrates the amount of wind, solar, or hydro power required to match the output from one nuclear reactor, while "Little Albert's Lab" introduces children to the concepts of physics. Outdoors, the Heritage Park displays unique military missile systems, rockets, and historic planes including a B-52 bomber.

---

⑩ ⊘ Ⓜ 🏛

Albuquerque Museum

🏠 2000 Mountain Rd NW
🕐 9am–5pm Tue–Sun
🚫 Public hols 🌐 cabq.gov/museum

This excellent museum showcases the art and history of New Mexico. "Only in Albuquerque" tells an inter-active story of the city from before written history to the present. "Common Ground" celebrates the diversity of artists living in or influenced by this region. The museum also offers walking tours of the historic Old Town (Mar–Nov).

⑪ ⊘ 🏛

Anderson-Abruzzo International Balloon Museum

🏠 9201 Balloon Museum Dr NE 🕐 9am–5pm Tue–Sun
🚫 Jan 1, Thanksgiving, Dec 25 🌐 balloonmuseum.com

The soaring gallery spaces at this museum contain the world's most extensive coll-ection of modern and historic balloons and ballooning memorabilia. Named after two of Albuquerque's legendary balloonists, the museum shows how balloons have been used in adventurous exploits, warfare, and space exploration. Exhibits include artifacts that date from the earliest days of ballooning.

---

⑫ ⊘

Petroglyph National Monument

🏠 6510 Western Trail NW
🕐 8:30am–4:30pm daily
🚫 Jan 1, Thanksgiving, Dec 25 🌐 nps.gov/petr

Lying on the western outskirts of Albuquerque, this site was established in 1990 to preserve nearly 20,000 images carved into rock

The world's largest hot air balloon festival takes place in Albuquerque in October (p54).

Did You Know?

The world's largest hot air balloon festival takes place in Albuquerque in October (*p54*).

along the 17-mile (27-km) West Mesa escarpment. The earliest petroglyphs date back to 1000 BC, but the most prolific period is thought to have been between AD 1300 and 1680. The depictions from this period range from human figures such as musicians and dancers to animals, including snakes, birds, and insects. Spirals and other geometric symbols are also common. Though the meaning of many of the petroglyphs has been lost over time, others continue to have great cultural significance to today's Puebloan population.

Hundreds of petroglyphs are accessible along Boca Negra Canyon, 2 miles (3 km) north of the park visitor center, where three self-guided trails wind past them. Touching the petroglyphs is strictly forbidden.

Exterior of the Albuquerque Museum, located in the heart of Old Town ↑

A SHORT WALK
ALBUQUERQUE OLD TOWN

Distance 0.5 mile (1 km) **Time** 15 minutes
Nearest bus 36, 66, 766

Occupied by indigenous peoples from AD 1100 to 1300, Albuquerque grew up from a small colonial settlement of pioneers who first inhabited the banks of the Rio Grande in the wake of late 16th-century explorers of the region. Today's multicultural Old Town still has many original adobe buildings dating from the 1790s and is a pleasant area to walk around. The city's first civic structure, the San Felipe de Neri church, was completed in 1793. Despite many renovations, the church retains its original adobe walls. The adjacent plaza forms the heart of the Old Town. Here people relax on benches, surrounded by lovely adobe buildings that house numerous craft shops, restaurants, galleries, and museums.

START

The **Agape Southwest Pueblo Pottery** store features a selection of handcrafted pottery from pueblos.

Christmas shop

Said to occupy the oldest house in the city, **Church Street Café** (p223) serves excellent New Mexican cuisine and is famous for its spicy chili.

San Felipe de Neri church

The **Old Town Plaza** was the center of Albuquerque for over 200 years. Today, this charming square makes a pleasant rest stop for visitors strolling around the nearby streets lined with museums and colorful stores.

CHURCH ST NW

ROMERO ST NW

NORTH PLAZ

RIO GRANDE BOULEVARD NW

SOUTH PLAZ

Did You Know?

The town was named after the Spanish Duke of Alburquerque (the first "r" was later dropped).

Exterior of the renowned Church Street Café

ALBUQUERQUE

Old Town

Locator Map
See pp220–221

MOUNTAIN ROAD NW

19TH STREET

FINISH

The space-age dome of the Astronomy Center in the **New Mexico Museum of Natural History and Science** *(p222) houses a planetarium and observatory.*

Works by artists living in or influenced by New Mexico and local historical objects are displayed at the superb **Albuquerque Museum** *(p225).*

SAN FELIPE ST NW

The **American International Rattlesnake Museum** *(p223) has displays on many species of rattler and includes information about their role in medicine, history, and Native American culture.*

0 meters   50
0 yards   50

San Felipe de Neri church, built during the Spanish Colonial period

2

CARLSBAD CAVERNS NATIONAL PARK

🅐 G6 🅟 727 Carlsbad Caverns Hwy, Carlsbad 🅞 Winter: 8am–5pm daily; summer: 8am–7pm daily 🅠 Jan 1, Thanksgiving, Dec 25 🅦 nps.gov/cave

Located in the Chihuahuan Desert in remote southeastern New Mexico, Carlsbad Caverns National Park protects one of the world's largest cave systems. Over the millennia dripping water has built an awe-inspiring array of formations in the caves.

Pictographs near the Natural Entrance indicate that the caves had been visited by indigenous peoples, but it was 16-year-old cowboy Jim White who brought them to national attention in 1898. While tending cattle, White noticed a cloud of bats rising from the desert hills, which led him to the cave entrance. He explored the caverns over the next few years, naming many of the rooms and rock formations. As tales of the wondrous subterranean world spread, White used an old guano mining bucket to transport early visitors down into the cave. The caverns were made a national park in 1930, and a United Nations World Heritage Site in 1995.

> 💬 INSIDER TIP
> **Cool Caverns**
>
> Temperatures are cool in the caves year round, and even in summer remain in the mid-50s Fahrenheit (about 13°C). Dress in long-sleeved shirts and trousers.

↑ The Doll's Theater cave, filled with soda-straw formations, and resembling a fairy grotto

↑ The zig zag path leading to the entrance to the Carlsbad Caverns

↑ A visitor sitting in an underground amphitheater at Carlsbad Caverns

FORMATION OF THE CAVES

Over time, fractures in the ancient limestone sedimentation started to appear, allowing mineral-laden water to cut through the rock and form the caverns. Within the national park there are more than 119 known caves, including some of the biggest and longest in the world. The main attraction is Carlsbad Cavern, which is over 1,000 ft (305 m) deep, with 30 miles (48 km) of mapped passages. Over the centuries, drip by drip, rain and snow-melt soaking through the limestone rock above created marvelous, massive speleothems (cave decorations), including top-down stalactites, soda straws and curtains, and bottom-up stalagmites, columns, flowstone, and totem poles.

Exploring Carlsbad Cavern

To enter the cavern, either take the elevator directly to the Big Room, or follow the Natural Entrance Trail. This moderate but steep route descends 750 ft (229 m), passing such formations as the Boneyard, Devil's Den, and Iceberg Rock. It connects to the Big Room Trail, a relatively flat, 1.25-mile (2-km) pathway leading to the Big Room, the largest underground cave chamber in the USA, with such massive formations as the Rock of Ages and Twin Domes. Both of these tours are self-guided; pick up audio guides at the visitor center. Several ranger-led tours are also available. The King's Palace Tour takes you to the deepest part of the cave open to the public, where there are more amazing cave formations.

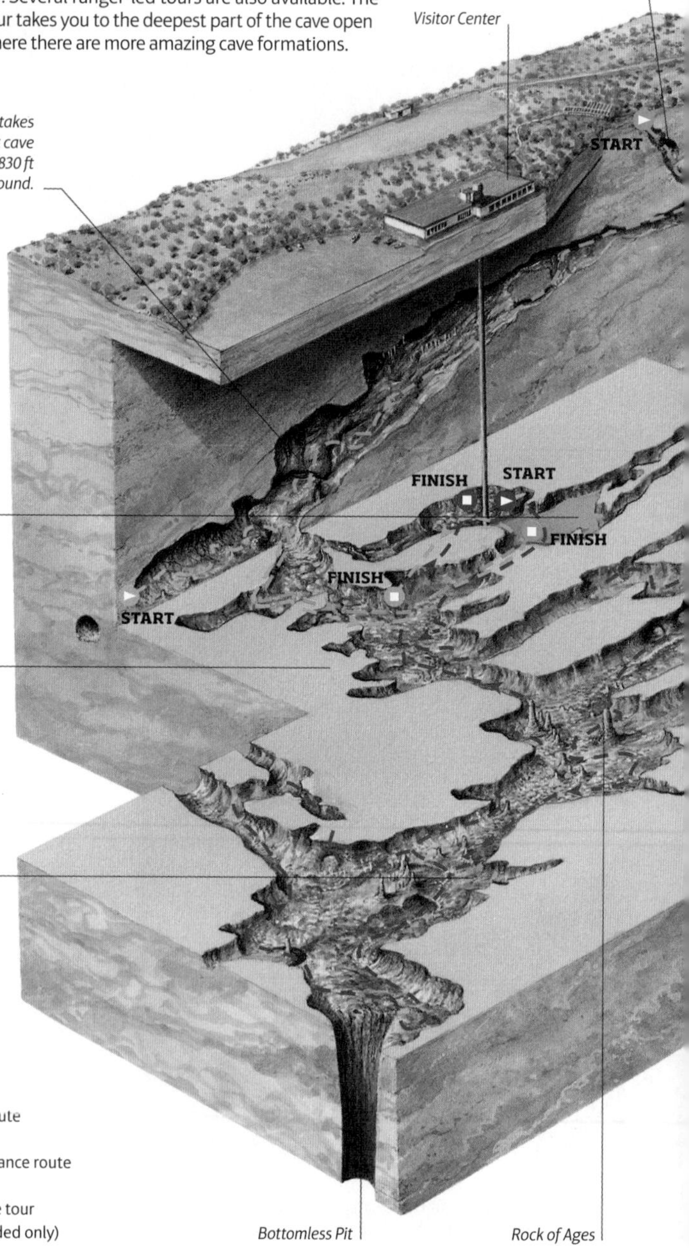

Most summer evenings at dusk, clouds of free-tailed bats emerge from the Bat Cave to cross the desert in search of food.
Visitor Center
START
King's Palace Tour takes in the deepest cave open to the public, 830 ft (250 m) below ground.
A paved section of the cavern is home to a popular underground snack bar, and restrooms.
FINISH
START
FINISH
FINISH
START
The Boneyard is a complex maze of dissolved limestone rock.
A self-guided tour takes in the 14-acre (5.6-ha) Big Room and passes features such as the Bottomless Pit.
TOURS
Big Room route
Natural Entrance route
King's Palace tour (Ranger-guided only)
Bottomless Pit
Rock of Ages

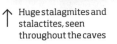

↑ Huge stalagmites and stalactites, seen throughout the caves

↑ The mighty spectacle of thousands of bats emerging at sundown from the Natural Entrance of Carlsbad Cavern

← Cross-section of Carlsbad Cavern showing tour routes through the main caves

The small Doll's Theater cave is named for its size and is filled with fine, luminous soda-straw formations.

ABOVE GROUND

The park has plenty to do above ground too. The Rattlesnake Springs Picnic Area is a natural wetland with cottonwood trees, where you can spot many of the 357 bird species that find an oasis here. The Walnut Canyon Desert Loop is a scenic 9-mile (15-km) drive with the backdrop of the Guadalupe Mountains. There are also several hiking trails through the surrounding desert wilderness.

← A car on the Sandia Peak Tramway overlooking the stunning Rio Grande valley

Grants is well placed along Highway 40/Route 66 for exploring the area, including the badlands of El Malpais National Monument.

New Mexico Mining Museum

 🏠100 Iron Ave 🕐9am-4pm Mon-Sat 🚫Public hols

EXPERIENCE MORE

❸ 🈂️🖨️🛍️
Sandia Peak Tramway

🅰F4 🏠30 Tramway Rd NE 🕐Late May-early Sep: 9am-9pm daily; early Sep-late May: 9am-8pm Wed-Mon, 5-8pm Tue 🚫2 weeks spring & fall for mainten-ance 🌐sandiapeak.com

The Sandia Peak Tramway is a breathtaking ride from the foothills of northeastern Albuquerque to Sandia Peak. The tram was constructed in the mid-1960s, and carries you to the summit's viewing platform. The 15-minute ride passes through desert, pon-derosa pine forests, and mountains, with outstanding views of Albuquerque and the surrounding landscape.

🔍 HIDDEN GEM
El Malpais National Monument

The dramatic lava flows, cinder cones, and lava tube caves make the volcanic landscape of El Malpais ("The Badlands" in Spanish) a fascinating place to explore. Stop at the visitor center near Grants for information.

---

❹
Grants

🅰E4 🛈100 Iron Ave; www.grants.org

Between the 1950s and the 1980s, Grants was famous as a center for uranium mining. The mineral was found in 1951 by Navajo farmer Paddy Martinez on top of Haystack Mountain, 10 miles (16 km) from town. The industry has now declined, but visitors can relive its heyday at the **New Mexico Mining Museum**; the tours go underground to see a re-created mine.

❺ 🈂️🈁
Acoma Pueblo

🅰E4 🏠Rte 23, off I-40

The incredible beauty of Acoma Pueblo's setting on the top of a 357-ft- (107-m-) high mesa has earned it the sobriquet "Sky City." Looking out over a stunning panorama of distant mountains, mesas, and plains, it gave the Puebloans a natural defense against enemies and helped delay submission to Spanish rule. Acoma is one of the oldest continuously inhab-ited towns in the US, occupied since before the 12th century. Today, fewer than 30 people live on the mesa top year round; 6,000 others from local towns return to their ancestral home for festivals and celebrations.

As well as original pueblo buildings, the village has a 1629 mission church, San

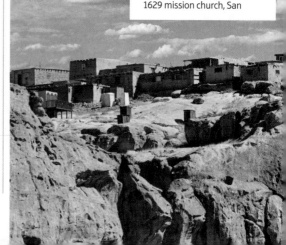

Esteben del Rey. There are also seven ceremonial kivas (*p176*). Acoma can be visited only on a guided tour (arranged at the **Sky City Cultural Center and Haak'u Museum**), where expert guides explain its rich history.

Sky City Cultural Center and Haak'u Museum

⊕⊕☺☺ 🄿 Base of the mesa ⏲ Mid-Mar-Oct: 9am-5pm daily; Nov-mid-Mar: 9am-4pm Fri-Sun ⓦ acomaskycity.org

Bernalillo

🄰 F4 🛈 264 Camino del Pueblo; www.townof bernalillo.org

This small farming community was settled by the Spanish in 1698. Here, against a striking backdrop on the banks of the Rio Grande, is the **Coronado Historic Site**, which encompasses the partially restored ruins of the Kuaua Pueblo. Spanish explorer Francisco Vázquez de Coronado is believed to have been here in 1540 seeking the fabled cities of gold (*p57*).

Nearby Sandia Pueblo is home to some 300 people, who take part in tribal dancing on San Antonio's Day in June (*p55*). Around 16 miles (25 km)

northwest of Bernaillo, Zia Pueblo is famous for its redware pottery. Visitors are welcome to buy the pottery and woven baskets made in this small community.

Coronado Historic Site

⊛ 🄿 485 Kuaua Rd ⏲ 8:30am-5pm Wed-Mon ⏲ Jan 1, Easter, Thanksgiving, Dec 25 ⓦ nmhistoricsites.org/coronado

---

⑦ ⊛ Ⓜ

El Morro National Monument

🄰 E4 ⏲ 9am-5pm daily (to 6pm in summer); trails shut 1 hour before closing time ⏲ Jan 1, Thanksgiving, Dec 25 ⓦ nps.gov/elmo

Rising dramatically from the surrounding plain, El Morro is a long sandstone cliff that slopes gently upward to a high bluff, where it suddenly drops off. Its centerpiece is the 200-ft- (61-m-) tall Inscription Rock, which is covered with more than 300 petroglyphs and pictographs from early Pueblo people, as well as thousands of inscriptions left by Spanish and Anglo travelers.

For centuries people were drawn to this remote spot by a pool of fresh water, formed by runoff and snowmelt.

> ### ZIA SUN SYMBOL
>
> The distinctive red Zia sun symbol, which was adopted in 1925 by the state of New Mexico and is used on the state flag and license plate, originated in Zia Pueblo in ancient times. The symbol has sacred meaning to the Zia. It symbolizes the circle of life - the four seasons, the four cardinal directions, the four periods of each day, and the four seasons of life - bound together by a circle.

Here they carved their initials into the rock. Among the signatures is that of the Spanish colonizer Juan de Oñate (*p58*), who, in 1605, wrote "pasó por aquí," meaning "I passed by here." An easy half-mile (1-km) trail leads past the pool and the inscriptions on the rock.

The people of Zuni Pueblo, 32 miles (51 km) west of El Morro, are the descendants of the early mesa dwellers of the region. Today, Zuni artists are known for their fine pottery and jewelry. Murals depicting Zuni history can be seen in the pueblo's 17th-century mission church.

← Acoma Pueblo, or Sky City, perched on top of the mesa

8

Socorro

E5 🛈 217 Fisher Ave;
www.socorronm.org

Socorro, meaning "aid" or "help" in Spanish, was named by conquistador and explorer Juan de Oñate. As his traveling party emerged from the desert in 1598, they were given food and water by the people of Pilabo Pueblo, which once stood here. The area was resettled in the early 1800s, and it was during the silver boom of the 1880s that many of its Victorian buildings were built. Just north of here is the 1821 San Miguel Mission, featuring massive adobe walls, supported by curved arches.

The **Bosque del Apache National Wildlife Refuge**, a renowned bird-watching area, lies 18 miles (29 km) south of Socorro. The 90-sq-mile (233-sq-km) refuge attracts many thousands of migrating waterfowl in winter, including snow geese, cormorants, and sandhill cranes.

Bosque del Apache National Wildlife Refuge

♿ 🚗 Hwy 1 🕐 8am–4pm daily (Jun–Aug: Thu–Mon only) 🚫 Jan 1, Thanksgiving, Dec 25 🌐 fws.gov/refuge/Bosque_del_Apache

9

Truth or Consequences

E5 🛈 301 S Foch St;
www.sierracounty
newmexico.info/truth-
or-consequences

Known by locals as "T-or-C," this town changed its name from Hot Springs to Truth or Consequences for the tenth anniversary of the game show of the same name, held here in 1950. The original hot springs still exist in the form of the bathhouses dotted around the town. For centuries the thermal springs drew Native Americans to the area, notably the prominent Apache leader Geronimo. **Geronimo Springs Museum** has displays on Apache history, including a life-size statue of the Apache warrior and information on other Native American famous figures. Warm mineral water from an underground spring flows down the ceramic mountains of an elaborate fountain in the plaza next to the museum. Nowadays, the town is a mecca for artists and free spirits.

Truth or Consequences is a popular summer resort, close to both the **Elephant Butte Lake State Park** (New Mexico's largest body of water) and the Caballo Lake state parks. These are famous for their numerous water sports, such as fishing, jet skiing, boating, and windsurfing.

Geronimo Springs Museum

♿ 🏛 🚗 211 Main St 📞 (575) 894-6600 🕐 9am–5pm Mon-Sat, noon–4pm Sun 🚫 Public hols

Elephant Butte Lake State Park

♿ 🚗 Off I-25 🌐 emnrd.state.nm.us

←

Sandhill cranes at Bosque del Apache National Wildlife Refuge near Socorro

SPACEPORT AMERICA

In the desert 30 miles (50 km) southeast of Truth or Consquences is the world's very first purpose-built commercial spaceport, designed for privately operated space flights. Space tourism is still a long way off, but the site is open every Saturday for guided tours, which include a white-knuckle ride in a G-force machine. Book online *(spaceport americatour.com)*.

10

Deming

E6 🏛 📷 🛈 800 E Pine St; www.demingvisitorcenter.webs.com

Situated 60 miles (97 km) west of Las Cruces, Deming is home to the Deming Luna Mimbres Museum, which houses an excellent collection of Mimbres pottery, frontier artifacts, and a fine gem and mineral display. Rockhounding (amateur rock and mineral collecting) often takes place in **Rockhound State Park**, where quartz, jasper, agate, and many other minerals can be found. The town is also known for its Great American Duck Race, run every August.

Rockhound State Park

♿ 🚗 Hwy 141 📞 (575) 546-6182 🕐 7am–sunset daily

11

Silver City

E6 🚌 🛈 201 N Hudson St; www.visitsilvercity.org

As its name suggests, Silver City was once a mining town. Located in the foothills of the Pinos Altos Mountains, Silver City's ornate architecture dates from its boom period between 1870 and the 1890s.

↑ Colorful galleries and cafés lining West Yankie Street in downtown Silver City

In 1895, a flood washed away the city's main street, and in its place today is Big Ditch Park, an *arroyo* (or waterway) running some 50 ft (15 m) deep through the town. This area was the site of the cabin where Billy the Kid *(p239)* spent much of his youth.

Silver City has three defined historic districts – Chihuahua Hill, Gospel Hill, and the old downtown district – all of which contain buildings that evoke its Wild West boomtown past. Downtown is also home to a vibrant arts scene. Painters, potters, weavers, and other artisans have made it their home, and the area is overflowing with art galleries.

The **Silver City Museum** is located in the beautiful 1881 H. B. Ailman House, and houses a huge collection (some 20,000 objects) of frontier-era memorabilia. The **Western New Mexico University Museum** holds the world's largest and most complete collection of Mimbres artifacts.

Silver City is a good base for exploring the area. The nearby forest is home to wildlife such as elk, deer, and bear, and there are several hiking trails and picnic areas.

Silver City Museum

🏠 312 W Broadway ◷ 9am–4:30pm Tue–Fri, 10am–4pm Sat & Sun ⏳ Public hols
🖥 silvercitymuseum.org

Western New Mexico University Museum

🏠 1000 W College Ave ◷ 9am–4:30pm Mon–Fri
⏳ Public hols 🖥 wnmu.edu/univ/museum.shtml

12

Gila Cliff Dwellings National Monument

🗺 E5 ◷ Late May–early Sep: 8am–5pm daily; early Sep–late May: 8am–4:30pm daily ⏳ Jan 1, Dec 25
🖥 nps.gov/gicl

The Gila (pronounced "hee-la") Cliff Dwellings are one of the most remote archaeological sites in the Southwest, situated among the piñon, juniper, and ponderosa evergreens of the Gila National Forest. The dwellings occupy five natural caves in the side of a sandstone bluff high above the Gila River.

Hunter-gatherers and farmers called the Tularosa Mogollon established their 40-room village here in the late 13th century. The Mimbres Mogollon people, famous for their abstract black-and-white pottery designs, also lived in the area *(p56)*. The ruins are accessed by a 1-mile (1.5-km) round-trip hike from the footbridge crossing the Gila River's West Fork. Allow about two hours to drive to the site from Silver City along the road winding through mountains and canyons.

→ Exploring the ruins of the sandstone Gila Cliff Dwellings

Majestic sandhill cranes at Bosque del Apache National Wildlife Refuge

13 Las Cruces

E6 336 S Main St; www.lascrucescvb.org

Spreading out at the foot of the Organ Mountains, Las Cruces, or "The Crosses", was named for the graves of early settlers ambushed here by the Apache in 1787 and again in 1830. It has always been a crossroads – of frontier trails, of the railroads, and now two Interstate highways (10 and 25). Today, it is New Mexico's second-largest city and home to New Mexico State University.

While the town is best used as a base for exploring the region, there are also a number of interesting museums to be found here. They include the **Branigan Cultural Complex**, which houses a cultural center with a historical museum, and the Las Cruces Museum of Art. Tours can also be arranged here of the nearby Bicentennial Log Cabin, a late 19th-century pioneer house of hand-hewn timber furnished with period antiques and artifacts.

Branigan Cultural Complex
501 N Main St 10am-4:30pm Tue-Fri, 9am-4:30pm Sat Public hols las-cruces.org/1523/Museums

14 Fort Selden Historic Site

E6 1280 Fort Selden Rd, Radium Springs 8:30am-5pm Wed-Sun Jan 1, Easter, Thanksgiving, Dec 25 nmhistoric-sites.org/fort-selden

This adobe fort was built in 1865 to protect settlers and railroad construction crews in the Mesilla Valley from attacks by Apaches and outlaws. Its buildings once housed the 125th Infantry, a unit of African Americans known as Buffalo Soldiers. Douglas MacArthur, who was to command Allied troops in the Pacific in World War II, lived here for two years as a boy in the 1880s, when his father was post commander. The fort was abandoned in 1891. Living history demonstrations are sometimes held on weekends, with rangers in period uniforms portraying 19th-century army life. There are also exhibits on frontier life in the visitor center.

15 Mesilla

E6 2231 Avenida de Mesilla; www.old mesilla.org

It was in the courthouse of this 19th-century frontier town that Billy the Kid was sentenced to hang in 1881. The **Gadsden Museum** contains exhibits on local history and cultures.

Gadsden Museum
1875 Boutz Rd By appt Wed-Sat gadsden museummesilla.com

→

A statue honoring the Buffalo Soldiers Black infantry at Fort Selden

←
Strolling across the glistening dunes at White Sands National Park

16 (image icons)

White Sands National Park

A E6 **O** Times vary, check website; Dune Drive: 7am–sunset daily **C** Dec 25 **W** nps.gov/whsa

The glistening dunes of the White Sands National Park rise up from the Tularosa Basin at the northern end of the Chihuahuan Desert. It is the world's largest gypsum dune field, covering around 300 sq miles (800 sq km).

BILLY THE KID

Billy the Kid was one of the Old West's most notorious outlaws. Born in 1859, he killed his first victim in 1877 and fled to Lincoln. In 1878, Billy helped form a vigilante group called the Regulators. After the Lincoln County War, Billy was captured by Sheriff Pat Garrett, escaped, and was eventually shot by Garrett on July 14, 1881. In spite of his violent life, Billy was a local hero whose story and deeds are now legendary (p241).

Gypsum is a water-soluble mineral, rarely found as sand. But here, with no drainage outlet to the sea, the sediment washed by the rain into the basin becomes trapped. As the rain evaporates, dry lakes form, and strong winds blow the gypsum up into the vast fields of rippling dunes.

Visitors can explore White Sands by car on the Dunes Drive, a 16-mile (25-km) loop. There are also five signposted hiking trails that will lead you around the park, including the wheelchair-accessible Interdune Boardwalk. Year-round ranger-led walks introduce visitors to the dunes' flora and fauna. Only plants that grow fast enough not to be buried survive, such as the soaptree yucca. Most animals here are nocturnal, and include coyotes and porcupines.

The park is surrounded by the White Sands Missile Range. For safety, the park and road leading to it (Highway 70) may shut for up to two hours during testing. **White Sands Missile Range Museum** displays many of the missiles tested here.

White Sands Missile Range Museum

A Hwy 70, 25 miles (40 km) E of Las Cruces **O** 8am–4pm Mon–Fri, 10am–3pm Sat **C** Sun, public hols **W** wsmr-history.org

17

Alamogordo

A F6 **O** **1** 1301 N White Sands Blvd; www.alamogordo.com

Alamogordo was established as a railroad town in 1898. Its streets are lined with cotton-wood trees, which reflect its origins – *alamo gordo* means "fat cottonwood" in Spanish. Located at the foot of the Sacramento Mountains, the town was a sleepy backwater until World War II, when it became a major defense research center.

The town is only 13 miles (21 km) from White Sands and offers many opportunities for outdoor activities, especially in the Lincoln National Forest on the eastern border. In town the **New Mexico Museum of Space History**, housed in a golden-glass, cube-shaped building, focuses on the history of the space race, with exhibits detailing living conditions inside a space station, a full-size replica of Sputnik I, the first space satellite, and a simulated space walk.

New Mexico Museum of Space History

(image icon) **A** Scenic Dr **O** 10am–5pm Mon, Wed–Sat; noon–5pm Sun **C** Thanksgiving, Dec 25 **W** nmspacemuseum.org

↑ A rocket on display outside the glass cube of the New Mexico Museum of Space History in Alamogordo

↑ Mexican Canyon Trestle near Cloudcroft in the Sacramento Mountains

> Once just a small ranching town, Roswell has become a byword for aliens and UFOs, due to the now legendary Roswell Incident.

Roswell Incident. The **International UFO Museum and Research Center** is devoted to the investigation of visitors from outer space and features an extensive collection of newspaper clippings, photographs, and maps of the crash site. A 70-minute film contains over 400 interviews with people connected to the crash.

The **Roswell Museum and Art Center** houses a collection of 2,000 artifacts on the history of the American West. The fascinating Robert H. Goddard Collection details 11 years of his experiments (p208).

International UFO Museum and Research Center

⊗⊕ ⬛114 N Main St ⬛9am–5pm daily ⬛roswell ufomuseum.com

Roswell Museum and Art Center

⬛ ⬛1011 N Richardson Ave ⬛9am–5pm Tue–Sun, 1–5pm Sun ⬛roswell museum.org

⑱

Cloudcroft

⬛F6 ⬛Cloudcroft Chamber of Commerce, Hwy 82; www.coolcloudcroft.com

The picturesque mountain town of Cloudcroft was established in 1898 as a center for the lumber trade. Perched up in the Sacramento Mountains, the village became a favorite spot for escaping the summer heat of the valley below. Burro Avenue, running parallel to the main highway, looks much as it did at the turn of the 20th century, with its rustic timber buildings. Surrounded by the Lincoln National Forest, the town offers many outdoor sports. Just outside town is a trail to the restored Mexican Canyon Trestle, part of the 19th-century railroad that ran from Alamogordo to Cloudcroft.

⑲

Roswell

⬛G5 ⬛426 N Main St; www.seeroswell.com

Once just a small ranching town, Roswell has become a byword for aliens and UFOs, due to the now legendary

⑳

Ruidoso

⬛F5 ⬛720 Sudderth Dr; www.visitruidoso.com

Nestled high in the Sacramento Mountains, surrounded by cool pine forest, Ruidoso is one of New Mexico's fastest-growing resorts. Sudderth Drive is lined with shops, art galleries, cafés, and restaurants. Here, specialty shops sell everything from candles to cowboy boots.

Outdoor activities are the area's major attraction, with hiking, horseback riding, and

---

THE ROSWELL INCIDENT

On July 4, 1947, an unidentified airborne object crash-landed in the Capitan Mountains, 75 miles (120 km) northwest of town. Jim Ragsdale was camping nearby and claims to have seen a craft hurtling through the trees and the bodies of four "little people," with skin like snakeskin. The US Air Force issued a statement that a flying disc had been recovered. By July 9, however, they said it was just a weather balloon. Witnesses were allegedly sworn to secrecy, fueling alien conspiracy theories to this day.

fishing. There are several golf courses, including the **Links at Sierra Blanca**, a top-rated 18-hole course. Northwest of the town is **Ski Apache**. Owned and operated by the Mescalero Apache Tribe, it is famous for its warm-weather powder snow. The town is best known for the horse racing at **Ruidoso Downs Racetrack**, which also has exhibits of racing artifacts. The **Hubbard Museum of the American West** has a collection of more than 10,000 pieces, ranging from fine art to horse-drawn carriages. Outside is the fabulous *Free Spirits at Noisy Water* (1995), a monument with seven larger-than-life horses. Every October, the town celebrates life in the Old West with the Lincoln County Cowboy Symposium, which features music and dancing, celebrity roping, and a cook-off.

A few miles north at Alto is the state-of-the-art **Spencer Theater for the Performing Arts**, a venue in a sandstone building with a spectacular mountain backdrop.

Links at Sierra Blanca
🏠 105 Sierra Blanca Dr
📞 (575) 258-5330

Ski Apache
🏠 1286 Ski Run Rd
🌐 skiapache.com

Ruidoso Downs Racetrack
⊘ 🏠 Hwy 70 📞 (575) 378-4431 🕐 May-early Sep

Hubbard Museum of the American West
⊘ 🏠 26301 Hwy 70 W
🕐 9am-5pm Thu-Mon
🌐 hubbardmuseum.org

Spencer Theater for the Performing Arts
⊘ 🏠 108 Spencer Dr
🌐 spencertheater.com

Lincoln Historic Site

🅰 F5 🏠 Hwy 380 🕐 9am-5pm daily 🕐 Jan 1, Easter, Thanksgiving, Dec 25 🌐 nmhistoricsites.org/lincoln

The peacefulness of this small town, surrounded by the beautiful Capitan Mountains, belies its violent past. It was at the center of the 1878 Lincoln County War, a battle between rival ranchers involving the

↑ A re-enactment of Billy the Kid's escape from Lincoln County Jail

legendary Billy the Kid *(p239)*. It is now a State Historic Site, with 11 buildings kept as they were in the late 1800s. At the Lincoln County Courthouse you can see where Billy the Kid was held, and the bullet hole made in the wall during his escape. The Tunstall Store is stocked with original 19th-century merchandise. The Historic Lincoln Visitor Center and Museum has displays on the Apache people, the early Hispanic settlers, and the Buffalo Soldiers all-Black regiment from Fort Stanton, as well as the Lincoln County War.

㉒
Carlsbad

🅰 G6 🛈 302 S Canal St; www.carlsbadchamber.com

The town of Carlsbad lies 20 miles (32 km) northeast of Carlsbad Caverns National Park *(p228)*. It has a relaxed, small-town atmosphere, with plenty of hotels and outdoor activities. The Pecos River winds through town; there are three lakes, and fishing, boating, and water-skiing are popular pastimes. At the northern edge of town, the Living Desert Zoo and Gardens State Park offers numerous exhibits focusing on the varied plants and animals of the Chihuahuan Desert.

← A vintage carriage at the Hubbard Museum in Ruidoso

A DRIVING TOUR
THE TURQUOISE TRAIL

Distance 52 miles (84 km) **Stopping-off points** Golden, Madrid, Los Cerrillos

The Turquoise Trail National Scenic Byway is a gem of a short drive. It provides an alternative route between Albuquerque and Santa Fe, following Highway 14 through the picturesque landscape on the east side of the Sandia Mountains and Cibola National Forest. This surrounding scenic and historic area covers 15,000 sq miles (39,000 sq km). Named after the precious gemstone, the drive takes in the old mining towns of Golden, Madrid, and Cerrillos, as well as other scenic spots that are easily reached by short detours off the highway. You can drive the trail in about an hour nonstop. Alternatively, make a day of it, stopping off to photograph the atmospheric ghost towns and browse the art galleries, craft shops, and antiques stores that have given the quaint towns a new livelihood.

The Turquoise Trail

ALBUQUERQUE AND SOUTHERN NEW MEXICO

Locator Map
For more detail see p220

Budaghers

*The **Sandia Mountains and Cibola National Forest** is a prime recreation area for hiking, cycling, horseback riding, climbing, and skiing. The hawk and eagle migrations in this diverse landscape draw bird-watchers from around the world.*

Algodones

Ranchito

Sundance Mesa

Diamond Tail Ranch

*Highway 536 winds its way to the top of **Sandia Crest**, the highest point on the Turquoise Trail. At 10,678 ft (3,255 m) high, you'll have spectacular views across Albuquerque and the Rio Grande Valley from the observation deck.*

Placitas

Tecolote

Bernalillo

Village de las Huertas

Sandia Mountains

Palomas Peak
8,684 ft (2,647 m)

*Just outside of Sandia Park, the **Tinkertown Museum** sits along the Sandia Crest National Scenic Byway (Highway 536). Its miniature, hand-carved figures and animated dioramas were the life work of folk artist Ross Ward.*

Sandia Crest
10,678 ft
(3,255 m)

Tinkertown Museum

Cedar Crest *has a variety of shops, restaurants, and lodging options, including a campground.*

Cibola National Forest Sandia Park San Antonio

Los Pinos

Albuquerque

Cedar Crest Zamora

Turquoise Museum **START**

Tijeras

*The **Turquoise Museum** in Old Town Albuquerque, where you can learn about the history and qualities of this precious gemstone, makes a good starting point for the drive. Head east from the city on I-40.*

Tijeras Pueblo Archaeological Site

Monticello

Tijeras *is the gateway to the Turquoise Trail. Visit the Tijeras Pueblo Archaeological Site to learn about the Pueblo people who lived here.*

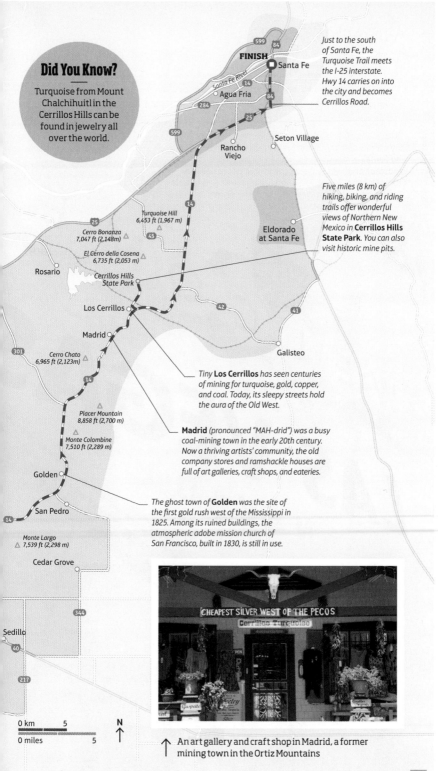

Did You Know?

Turquoise from Mount Chalchihuitl in the Cerrillos Hills can be found in jewelry all over the world.

FINISH

Santa Fe

Just to the south of Santa Fe, the Turquoise Trail meets the I-25 interstate. Hwy 14 carries on into the city and becomes Cerrillos Road.

Agua Fria

Seton Village

Rancho Viejo

Eldorado at Santa Fe

*Five miles (8 km) of hiking, biking, and riding trails offer wonderful views of Northern New Mexico in **Cerrillos Hills State Park**. You can also visit historic mine pits.*

Turquoise Hill
6,453 ft (1,967 m)

Cerro Bonanza
7,047 ft (2,148 m)

El Cerro della Cosena
6,735 ft (2,053 m)

Rosario

Cerrillos Hills State Park

Los Cerrillos

Galisteo

Madrid

Cerro Chato
6,965 ft (2,123 m)

*Tiny **Los Cerrillos** has seen centuries of mining for turquoise, gold, copper, and coal. Today, its sleepy streets hold the aura of the Old West.*

Madrid (pronounced "MAH-drid") was a busy coal-mining town in the early 20th century. Now a thriving artists' community, the old company stores and ramshackle houses are full of art galleries, craft shops, and eateries.

Placer Mountain
8,858 ft (2,700 m)

Monte Colombine
7,510 ft (2,289 m)

Golden

San Pedro

*The ghost town of **Golden** was the site of the first gold rush west of the Mississippi in 1825. Among its ruined buildings, the atmospheric adobe mission church of San Francisco, built in 1830, is still in use.*

Monte Largo
7,539 ft (2,298 m)

Cedar Grove

Sedilla

CHEAPEST SILVER WEST OF THE PECOS

Cerrillos Turquoise

0 km   5
0 miles   5

N ↑

↑ An art gallery and craft shop in Madrid, a former mining town in the Ortiz Mountains

LAS VEGAS

Occupied by the Ancestral Puebloans until around AD 1150, the Las Vegas area later became the home of several Native American tribes, including the Paiute, until Mexican traders arrived in the early 19th century. Mormon pioneers built a fort here in 1855, establishing the beginnings of a settlement in the area, which gradually developed.

Officially founded in 1905, the city of Las Vegas expanded in the 1930s with the building of the Hoover Dam across the Colorado River, some 30 miles (48 km) away, and the legalization of gambling in 1931. The influx of construction workers with money to burn, and the electricity and water provided by the dam, paved the way for the casino-based growth that took place in the 1940s and 1950s. Since the 1990s, ever more extravagant resorts have been built in Las Vegas, including the impressive Bellagio, Venetian, and Cosmopolitan – the city has six of the ten largest hotels in the world – and this brilliant expansion shows few signs of slowing.

LAS VEGAS

Experience

1. The Strip
2. Mandalay Bay
3. Excalibur
4. New York New York
5. Luxor
6. Cosmopolitan of Las Vegas
7. MGM Grand
8. Tropicana
9. Aria
10. Showcase Mall
11. Planet Hollywood
12. Paris Las Vegas
13. Bellagio
14. Flamingo Las Vegas
15. Caesars Palace
16. The LINQ Hotel + Experience
17. The Venetian
18. Treasure Island
19. Mirage
20. Wynn Las Vegas & Encore
21. Circus Circus
22. The STRAT
23. Sahara
24. Fremont Street Experience
25. Mob Museum
26. Discovery Children's Museum
27. The Las Vegas Natural History Museum
28. Neon Museum
29. Old Las Vegas Mormon State Historic Park
30. Valley of Fire State Park
31. Lake Mead National Recreation Area
32. Red Rock Canyon
33. Mount Charleston
34. Hoover Dam

Eat

1. Picasso
2. Restaurant Guy Savoy
3. Siegel's 41
4. Oscar's Steakhouse
5. Top Of Binion's Steakhouse

▽ Headliners

When the Colosseum theater was built at Caesar's Palace *(p259)* in 2003 to showcase Celine Dion, other casinos followed suit. Today, casino showrooms stage shows by pop stars such as Lady Gaga and Jennifer Lopez, or other top artists like Elton John and Robbie Williams, who often take up long-running residencies.

ENTERTAINMENT IN
LAS VEGAS

Las Vegas shines as one of the great entertainment capitals of the world. There are dozens of shows, from casino lounge acts to lavish productions in purpose-built theaters. Sinatra and Elvis may be gone, but today's headliners appear regularly in the city's showrooms.

💬 INSIDER TIP
Buying tickets

The easiest way to book tickets to major shows is via the venue or hotel, using their website or toll-free number. Dinner and show packages are also available. Vegas. com *(www.vegas.com/ shows)* sell discounted tickets. Prices range from around $30 to over $250 for big-name artists. Tix4Tonight *(www.tix4tonight.com)* sells same-day tickets up to half price from multiple outlets. Book well in advance for popular shows.

△ Sports and Concert Arenas

The enormous T-Mobile Arena *(3780 Las Vegas Blvd S)* and the MGM Grand Garden Arena *(p255)* host concerts by major stars such as Michael Bublé, Barbra Streisand, and Justin Timberlake. Sports fans can see professional sporting events such as boxing, wrestling, and basketball here as well.

▽ Production Shows

Performances by Cirque du Soleil® in a custom-built theatre are one of Vegas's highlights. The mix of circus-like acrobatics, music, costumes, technology, and theatrical storytelling creates mind-blowing entertainment. Other top shows include the phenomenal Blue Man Group and Le Rêve, an aquatic theater in the ground.

△ Lounges

The time-honored tradition of the Las Vegas lounge – providing free entertainment with a bar open to the casino floor – is still going strong in many venues along the Strip. Lively lounges with dueling-piano shows include New York New York's Bar at Times Square *(p253)* and Napoleon's in Paris Las Vegas *(p257)*.

▷ Magic, Comedy, and Tribute Acts

Magicians, puppets, showgirls... Las Vegas's entertainment talent knows no bounds. Jimmy Kimmel's Comedy Club at the LINQ Promenade *(p260)* is just one of many comedy shows. Magic shows with the likes of David Copperfield and Penn & Teller are highly popular. *Vegas! The Show* and other fantastic tribute acts honoring Elvis and the Rat Pack take you back to the days of classic Vegas entertainment.

VEGAS SHOPPING MALLS

The Forum Shops
Marble columns form a classical backdrop for luxury brands and more than 100 shops at Caesars Palace *(p259)*.

The Shops at Crystals
City Center glimmers with art installations and a range of chic and luxury designer stores *(p256)*.

Fashion Show Mall
ⓦ thefashionshow.com
This huge shopping mall has regular runway shows to showcase the hottest fashion brands.

◁ Clubs and Bars

From clubs with light shows, LED screens, and celebrity DJs to pool parties, boisterous saloons, hipster bars, and glamorous cocktail lounges, Vegas's dazzling nightclub scene rivals any of the world's top party destinations.

CASINOS IN LAS VEGAS

Despite its reputation as an all-round adult amusement park, Las Vegas remains famous for its casinos. Do not come expecting to make your fortune; with a combined annual income from gaming of over $10 billion, the casinos have the advantage. Casinos know this and aim to keep you playing for as long as possible. Before you start, it is wise to decide on an amount that you can afford to lose and stick to it.

Nearly 70 percent of the city's 43 million annual visitors gamble. For a first timer, a casino can seem daunting, but, with a basic understanding of the rules, most of the games are relatively simple to play. Some hotels have gaming guides on their in-house TV channels, and the Las Vegas visitor center supplies helpful printed guides. Several large casinos give free lessons at the tables. Blackjack is one of the most popular games, craps is often the most fun game on the floor, offering a sense of camaraderie, while roulette is a simple game but with a variety of bets. Keno, one of the easiest games to play, is a close relative of bingo. Out of the 80 numbers on a keno ticket, players may choose up to 20. A range of bets is possible; winning depends on your chosen numbers coming up.

→ A Las Vegas casino gambling chip

KNOW BEFORE YOU GO

It is illegal to gamble under the age of 21, so always carry ID if you are young-looking. Children are not welcome on the casino floor. Be aware that if you are winning, it is casino etiquette to tip the dealers. It can also be to your advantage to tip when you first sit down at a table. Dealers can prevent inexperienced gamblers from making silly mistakes and will usually explain the finer points of the games, if asked. It is a good idea to collect Player Club cards at each casino you visit; these offer a range of rewards from cashback to worthwhile discounts on hotel rooms and meals.

Slot machines inside the Wynn Las Vegas ↑

GAMES

① Slot Machines

Slots of every kind dominate Las Vegas casinos. Computerized push-button and touchscreen machines offer a bewildering variety of plays. Most machines use prepaid electronic cards, but there are a few coin machines left in the downtown casinos.

② Blackjack

The aim is to get as close to 21 without going over, and to beat the dealer. Cards are worth their numerical value, with all the face cards worth 10 and an ace worth 1 or 11. Each player receives two cards face up, while the dealer's second card is face down. Players must use hand signals to indicate if they wish to take another card, or "hit" (scratch the table with their forefinger) or not take a card, "stand" (wave a flat hand over their cards). Once each player has decided to stand or hit the 21 limit, the dealer turns over his second card and plays his hand, hitting 16 or less and standing with 17 or more.

③ Craps

Players bet either with or against the "shooter" (whoever has the dice) on what the next number rolled will be. The aim of the shooter's first roll is to make 7 or 11 in any combination (say 3/4, 5/6) to win. A roll of 2, 3, or 12 is craps; everyone loses, and the shooter rolls the dice again. If a total of 4, 5, 6, 8, 9, or 10 is rolled, this becomes the "point" number, and the shooter must roll this number again before rolling a 7 to win. Always roll with one hand; the dice must hit the end of the table.

④ Roulette

A ball is spun on a wheel containing numbers 1 to 36 divided equally between red and black, plus a single and a double zero, colored green. Each player's chips are a different color. The aim is to guess the number that will come up on the spin of the wheel. Bets are placed on the table, which has a grid marked out with the numbers and a choice of betting options. The highest payout odds are 35 to 1 for a straight bet on one number such as 10 black.

⑤ Baccarat

Baccarat is played at a leisurely pace with eight decks of cards, the deal rotating from player to player. Each card has a point value. The object of the game is to guess which hand will be closest to a point value of 9: the player's or the banker's.

1

The Strip

A4 visitlasvegas.com

The heart of Las Vegas lies along Las Vegas Boulevard, a sparkling vista of neon known simply as "the Strip." Running for over 4 miles (7 km) south of downtown, it is home to a cluster of vast, lavishly themed hotels, including Caesar's Palace, New York New York, and the Bellagio, all buzzing with restaurants, shops, and casinos. This is the Vegas you've come to see, especially at night, when the lights come on and these mega-resorts become a fantasyland of riotous extravaganza. Strolling the Strip, soaking up the gaudy, giddy ambience, is thoroughly entertaining. In spite of the crowds, it can be faster to walk than sit in snail-like traffic. Distances between casinos can be farther than they seem, so take advantage of the free monorail that connects several of the resorts here. Change is constant along the Strip, where hotels get ever larger, acclaimed chefs open new restaurants, and long-running shows close to make room for the latest stars. The first casino resort to open on Las Vegas's Strip in 1941 was the El Rancho Vegas Hotel-Casino, which was located in the northern section, on the corner of Sahara Avenue. A building boom followed in the 1950s, resulting in a swathe of resorts that turned the Strip into a high-rise adult theme park. Most are now gone or utterly transformed. Today, resorts such as the Venetian and Mirage have established the Strip's reputation for upscale quality, and almost nothing remains of the spit-and-sawdust atmosphere the city once had.

2

Mandalay Bay

A5 3950 Las Vegas Blvd S 24 hours mandalaybay.com

The Mandalay Bay resort aims to re-create the tropics of the late 19th century. Located at the south end of the Strip, it has over 3,000 rooms. Tropical plants and stunning white stucco architectural features such as arches and decorative cornices evoke an old-world atmosphere. Even the vast 135,000-sq-ft (12,550-sq- m) casino manages to suggest elegant 1890s Singapore. One highlight is the enormous lagoon-style swimming pool with its sandy beach and wave machine, plus a water ride that travels around the pool. More restrained than other Strip resorts, the Mandalay Bay includes over 20 restaurants and lounges, and the House of Blues Music Hall, which features live performances of many musical genres. It was also the first resort on the Strip to feature a non-gaming hotel, the Four Seasons, which is located on the Mandalay's top four floors.

The Strip is the Vegas you've come to see, especially at night, when the lights come on and these mega-resorts become a fantasyland.

WEDDINGS IN LAS VEGAS

A Las Vegas wedding comes second only to the lure of gaming. The kitsch style of a range of ceremonies - from a drive-in chapel to themed medieval receptions or an Elvis Presley special - persuades more than 100,000 couples to tie the knot here each year. One brave couple said their vows on a high platform in front of Circus Circus before performing a spectacular bungee jump. A host of celebrities have married here, including Elvis and Priscilla Presley, and pop star Britney Spears to Jason Alexander. Packages start at $100. Both parties must also first appear in person to obtain a $77 marriage license at the County of Clark Marriage Bureau *(201 E Clark Ave; open 8am-midnight daily; www.clarkcountynv.gov).*

---

❸ 🍴 🛍️

Excalibur

📍 A5 🏛️ 3850 Las Vegas Blvd S 🕐 24 hours
🌐 excalibur.com

The inspiration of the medieval world of King Arthur is obvious at the first sight of this castle-like, family-friendly theme resort, with its white towers, turrets, moat, and drawbridge. Grand suits of armor line the main entrance to the casino where even the one-armed bandits have themed sign-posts such as "Medieval Slot Fantasy."

The second floor houses the Medieval Village, where quaint alleyways are lined with shops and restaurants, such as Dick's Last Resort, Buffet at Excalibur, and Steakhouse at Camelot. The shops and kiosks on Castle Walk offer merchandise and souvenirs based on the hotel's medieval theme.

Fun Dungeon, the in-house games arcade offering more than 200 exciting games, is a good option for families. There is a huge selection of arcade machines, redemption games, and sports challenges, such as the Mega Stacker, Big Bass, and Key Master.

❹ 🍴 🍸 🛍️

New York New York

📍 A5 🏛️ 3790 Las Vegas Blvd S 🕐 24 hours
🌐 newyorknewyork.com

This hotel's re-creation of the Manhattan skyline dominates the Tropicana Avenue corner of the Strip. One of Las Vegas's most appealing sights, New York New York is fronted by a replica of the Statue of Liberty, behind which are some of Manhattan's most famous landmark buildings, including the Empire State, the Chrysler, and the Seagram. Every detail reflects a part of New York City, including Times Square and the Brooklyn Bridge.

Roaring around the complex is a Coney Island-style roller coaster that twists and dives at speeds of 67 mph (108 km/h) around and through the casino.

Adding to the Manhattan flavor are many popular New York-style eateries. Set among Greenwich Village brownstones is a wide variety of cafés, bars, and restaurants offering a choice of live music from swing and jazz to Motown and rock.

←

The Bellagio and Paris Las Vegas amid the glitzy fantasyland of the Strip

Luxor

📍A5 🏠3900 Las Vegas Blvd S ⏰24 hours 🌐luxor.com

The Luxor's famous 30-story bronze pyramid opened in 1993 and quickly became a Las Vegas icon. Despite the fact that the resort is named after the Egyptian city of Luxor, which has no pyramid, there is impressive attention to detail in the Ancient Egyptian architectural features. Painted pillars adorn the casino, and a reproduction Cleopatra's Needle graces the entrance. Visitors enter the pyramid through the legs of a sphinx to find themselves inside the casino, where ringing slot machines are surrounded by walls decorated with copies of paintings and hieroglyphs from the original Karnak temple in Luxor.

As a tribute to the ancient religions of Egypt, the Luxor Sky Beam, the strongest beam of light in the world, is projected from the pyramid's apex nightly. It is so powerful that it can be seen from planes cruising above Los Angeles 250 miles (400 km) away.

Among the attractions, a free ride in the guest elevators (named "inclinators") ranks high; they travel along the inclines of the pyramid at an angle of 39 degrees.

Bodies: The Exhibition showcases whole bodies and hundreds of organs that have been preserved through an innovative process in which bodily liquids are replaced with a polymer mixture. The resulting specimens provide a unique, 3D view of the human form and its skeletal, muscular, and circulatory systems. Also on display are organs that have been damaged by over-eating and lack of exercise.

Titanic: The Artifact Exhibition tells the story of the Titanic, an ocean liner that sank on a calm night in 1912 when it struck an iceberg in the North Atlantic. Actual artifacts recovered from the ship are on show, including luggage, the ship's whistles, and an unopened bottle of champagne from 1900. Visitors can walk through re-created first- and third-class rooms.

Bodies: The Exhibition
⊛ 🏠Luxor ⏰10am–10pm daily

Titanic: The Artifact Exhibition
⊛ 🏠Luxor ⏰10am–10pm daily

6 Cosmopolitan of Las Vegas

📍A4 🏠3708 Las Vegas Blvd S ⏰24 hours 🌐cosmopolitanlas vegas.com

Situated within two high-rise towers on the Strip, the Cosmopolitan offers a huge casino, an oasis-inspired spa, and three pools. There are 2,995 hotel rooms, most with marble bathrooms and sliding glass doors that open onto a large terrace. Some suites even have their own kitchenettes. Guests will find a wide variety of cuisines among the two-dozen restaurants here, including Chinese-Mexican fusion at

Did You Know?

The Cosmopolitan's Vesper Bar is named after the cocktail James Bond drinks in *Casino Royale*.

Sphinx surrounded by palm trees outside the 30-story pyramid of the Luxor hotel

7  🕏 🍴

MGM Grand

📍 A5 🏠 3799 Las Vegas Blvd S 🕐 24 hours
🌐 mgmgrand.com

The emerald-green MGM Grand building is fronted by the famous Leo, a 45-ft- (14-m-) tall bronze lion that serves as the symbol of the MGM film studio in Hollywood. The original MGM hotel was built in the 1970s farther down the strip, where Bally's now stands, and was named for the 1920s film, *Grand Hotel*. In 1980 the worst fire in Las Vegas history destroyed the building. The MGM Grand reopened in 1993 at its current location at the corner of the Strip and Tropicana Avenue, themed on *The Wizard of Oz*. Subsequent refurbishments have removed most of its associations with MGM movies.

The 5,000 or so rooms that originally made the Grand the world's largest hotel have been supplemented by a further 1,728 suites in its three Signature towers, not to mention 51 ultra-luxurious Sky Lofts. It also features a 171,500-sq-ft (16,000-sq-m) casino, and big-name restaurants that include the Morimoto, and the Joël Robuchon Restaurant.

MGM is also home to night-spots such as Wet Republic, held in the hotel's huge pool complex. In the daytime, the major attraction is **The Hunger Games: The Exhibition**, in which participants join the rebellion portrayed in the blockbuster film series.

Above all, though, the MGM Grand is known for its entertainment. The Grand Garden Arena is famous for hosting big-name acts such as Barbra Streisand, Andrea Bocelli, and Kanye West. It also hosts major sports events and world championship boxing, most memorably the 1997 fight in which Mike Tyson bit Evander Holyfield's ear. The intimate David Copperfield Theater attracts many top entertainers, such as comedians Drew Carey and Lewis Black.

The Hunger Games: The Exhibition
♿ 🏠 MGM Grand 🕐 11am–6pm Wed–Sun 🌐 mgmgrand. mgmresorts.com/en/ entertainment.html

China Poblana and Spanish tapas at Jaleo, both from chef José Andrés, as well as New American options at Beauty & Essex. The Chandelier, one of several bars, spans three levels, while Vesper is particularly classy in silver and white, and the Marquee combines clubbing with great poolside entertainment with its infinity pools and a cabana.

Beaded curtains of light at the Chandelier bar in the Cosmopolitan ↑

Tropicana

A5 **3801 Las Vegas Blvd S** **24 hours** **troplv.com**

One of the few 1950s boom hotels still on the Strip, the Tropicana was built in 1957. Las Vegas's famous illusionist double act Siegfried & Roy first appeared here at the Folies Bergères in 1973. In 2009 the resort was restyled with lush tropical gardens and a fine South Beach facade. One of the most delightful attractions is the water park, featuring waterfalls and exotic flowers and foliage. The huge main pool has a bar alongside and offers an unusual casino experience with "swim-up" blackjack tables, which have waterproof surfaces.

The resort also has several outdoor spas for the ultimate in relaxation. It's the ideal place to escape from the bright lights and full-on action of the city and to enjoy luxurious spa treatments amid tropical greenery.

Aria

A5 **3730 Las Vegas Blvd S** **24 hours** **aria.com**

Set away from the Strip, the Aria resort and casino is a sleek monolith far removed from Las Vegas's usual ostentatious style. It has a collection of modern and contemporary sculpture ranging from Maya Lin and Henry Moore to Jenny Holzer, and holds restaurants run by some of the top chefs in the country, such as Julian Serrano and Michael Mina, and the

---

The Eiffel Tower of Paris Las Vegas across the Strip from the Bellagio Fountains

ultrahip Jewel nightclub. There are more than 4,000 high-tech guest rooms, each with floor-to-ceiling windows providing panoramic city views.

Several unique water features, designed by the same team that was behind the fountains at the Bellagio, grace the front of Aria. The centerpiece is *Lumia*, a fountain adjacent to the main entrance, where jets of "liquid light" flit about and collide in glorious patterns.

The entire complex was built with sustainability in mind, using natural lighting and reclaimed water. Even the slot machines promote conservation, as the bases serve as air-conditioning units, efficiently cooling guests from the ground up.

The Aria is the centerpiece of CityCenter, a development designed as a city within a city to exploit the vast acreage of unused land west of the Strip. Encompassing five separate hotel-casinos, CityCenter stretches between the Monte Carlo to the south and the Bellagio to the north. It includes Aria, Vdara, and the Oriental Mandarin. A free, futuristic tram, the Aria Express, runs from one end of CityCenter to the other in just under three minutes. The most striking component is the quartz-shaped Shops at Crystals, a high-end retail mall characterized by dazzling architecture, indoor gardens, sculptures, and water features, as well as upmarket boutiques including Tom Ford, Tiffany & Co., and the largest branch of Louis Vuitton in North

---

4,500

The number of lights that the Bellagio Fountains use.

America. The mall also houses a number of gourmet restaurants and art galleries.

Showcase Mall

A5 **3785 Las Vegas Blvd S** **(702) 597-3122** **Varies for each attraction**

Dominated by a 100-ft (30-m) neon Coca-Cola bottle, the Showcase Mall entertainment and retail complex is best known as the home of M&M's® World. This promotional exhibit, spread over four stories, offers fun chocolate-themed displays for kids and abundant opportunities to buy chocolate in a rainbow of colors.

> **The Tropicana is the ideal place to escape from the bright lights and full-on action of the city and to enjoy luxurious spa treatments amid tropical greenery.**

⑪ Planet Hollywood

⦿ A4 🏠 3667 Las Vegas Blvd S ⏱ 24 hours ⓦ caesars.com/planet-hollywood

In 2007, Planet Hollywood (then known as Planet Hollywood Resort & Casino) opened on the site formerly occupied by the Aladdin, scene of the 1967 wedding of Elvis and Priscilla Presley. The glamorous, 1930s-style lobby features eight sparkling crystal chandelier columns, and the hotel's two pools offer alfresco poolside cocktails.

Planet Hollywood focuses firmly on entertainment. Major headliners sign up for long-term residencies and regularly appear at the property's main theater, the Zappos, while a separate showroom hosts the burlesque show *Crazy Girls*.

The Miracle Mile shopping mall, so called as it snakes for a full mile convent around the casino, still features Arabian Nights touches dating back to the Aladdin era, and offers 170 shops and more than 30 bars and restaurants, as well as its own theater with an ever-changing line-up of shows.

---

⑫ Paris Las Vegas

⦿ A4 🏠 3655 Las Vegas Blvd S ⏱ 24 hours ⓦ parislv.com

Be transported to Paris at this hotel and casino resembling a Hollywood film set of the real French capital. The facade is composed of replicas of Paris landmarks such as the Louvre, the Hôtel de Ville, and the Arc de Triomphe. A 50-story, half-scale Eiffel Tower dominates the complex, and visitors can ride an elevator to the observation deck at the top or dine in its gourmet restaurant 100 ft (33 m) above the Strip. The casino contains architectural details that re-create Parisian streetlife, including cast-iron street lamps, and everything is set beneath a fabulous painted sky.

Cobblestone streets wind along the edge of the casino and are filled with shops selling an array of fine French goods including clothes, wine, and chocolate. The resort also has five lounges, two wedding chapels, and 15 restaurants.

> **🏔 GREAT VIEW**
> **Mon Ami Gabi**
>
> Enjoy fine French cuisine in true Parisian style at the casual Mon Ami Gabi bistro at Paris Las Vegas. Eat and drink alfresco while admiring the Strip and the Bellagio fountain display.

Bellagio

📍 A4 🏠 3600 Las Vegas Blvd S 🕐 24 hours
🌐 bellagio.com

This $1.6 billion luxury resort opened in 1998 on the site of the former Dunes hotel, which faltered badly after a long run and was demolished in 1993. Its design is based on the northern Italian town of Bellagio, with terracotta- and ocher-colored Mediterranean buildings set back from the Strip behind a lake modeled on Italy's Lake Como. One of the hotel's many attractions is the sublime fountain display on the lake that springs into action at regular intervals through the day and evening. Crowds gather to watch the show – a choreographed water dance set to music, accompanied by visual effects including a rolling mist and, at night, stunning light effects.

No expense has been spared on the Bellagio's interior either; delicate marble mosaics adorn the entrance hall floors, and the main lobby ceiling is hung with sculpted glass flowers of every color. Even the casino manages to be light and airy.

Another popular part of the Bellagio is its Conservatory, adjoining the lobby, which is planted with ever-changing

displays of seasonal plants. Set farther back from the Strip, the hotel's **Gallery of Fine Art** features exhibitions from big-name international artists.

Gallery of Fine Art
🏠 Bellagio 📞 (702) 693-7871
🕐 10am–8pm daily

___

Flamingo Las Vegas

📍 A4 🏠 3555 Las Vegas Blvd S 🕐 24 hours
🌐 caesars.com/flamingo-las-vegas

The brilliant pink and orange neon plume on the Flamingo

↑ The bright neon plume outside the Flamingo, a famous Las Vegas icon

hotel's facade is, to many, the archetypal Las Vegas icon. However, nothing remains of the original 1946 casino: the last vestiges of this building, including mobster Bugsy Siegel's private suite, were bulldozed in 1976. One of the few remaining signs of this notorious gangster's involvement in the hotel is a small monument located near the lavishly landscaped outdoor wedding chapels, marking the spot of the original hotel.

The Flamingo has one of the most elegant pool areas in Vegas. Nestled among exquisitely landscaped gardens, the two Olympic-sized pools are veiled by tropical plants and palm trees. There is also a kids' pool, two Jacuzzis, and a water slide leading to three more pools.

Set within the hotel's large grounds, the Flamingo Wildlife Habitat is a lush, peaceful area with streams, waterfalls, and an island with Chilean flamingos, ringed teal ducks, pelicans, and sacred ibis, living alongside turtles and koi fish. A popular Las Vegas attraction, it is open to the public, not just to hotel guests.

BUGSY SIEGEL

Nicknamed "Bugsy", Benjamin Siegel was a New York City gangster. He moved to Los Angeles in the 1930s and created the luxurious Flamingo hotel and casino in Las Vegas. He was killed by fellow investors only six months after the casino opened in 1946, probably because other mobsters disliked his high profile. The original structure has been replaced by a modern luxury hotel and casino on the same spot.

> The Wildlife Habitat at the Flamingo is a lush, peaceful area with streams, waterfalls, and an island with Chilean flamingos, ringed teal ducks, and sacred ibis.

15 🍴 🛍️

Caesars Palace

📍 A4   🏠 3570 Las Vegas Blvd S   🕐 24 hours   🌐 caesars.com/caesars-palace

Roman statues, Greek columns, and cocktail waitresses in togas could all be found at Caesars Palace when it opened in 1966. Today the decor and waitresses remain part of the ambience here, but in a less kitsch, more upscale way ever since the resort was refurbished and expanded in the mid-1990s.

This classic Vegas casino was the first themed hotel on the Strip and quickly established a reputation for attracting top artists to its 4,000-seat Colosseum, from Andy Williams in the 1960s to Celine Dion and Elton John in the 2010s. Since the 1980s Caesars has also hosted international sports events, including tennis, featuring stars such as John McEnroe and Andre Agassi, and boxing, with such names as world champions Muhammad Ali and Mike Tyson.

Today the hotel houses a lavish casino with race and sports betting, four lounges, a health spa, and the Garden of the Gods – an oasis with seven pools. Caesars' elegant facade is fronted by fountains and cypress trees as well as a 20-ft (6-m) statue of Augustus Caesar near the entrance. The high ceilings and light decor in the casinos create an elegant and upbeat atmosphere.

The entrance to the highly exclusive Forum Shops shopping mall continues the ancient Greek and Roman iconography and is as impressive as the hotel and casinos. The mall's grand portico features a modern-day trompe-l'oeil sky ceiling, which changes appearance depending on the time of day and the weather, and is adorned with further statues and relief sculpture. Replicas of the Trevi and Triton fountains in Rome adorn a sweeping plaza topped by a glass-dome ceiling. There is even a small aquarium. A majestic spiral escalator leads up to the mall itself, which has some 160 specialty stores and fine restaurants, including Italian, Asian, French, and American steakhouse cuisines.

→

The opulent Forum Shops at Caesars Palace, with a glass-dome ceiling

EAT

Picasso
Julian Serrano's creative menu explores French-Mediterranean flavors.

📍 A4   🏠 Bellagio   🕐 Lunch, Tue   🌐 bellagio.com

💲💲💲

Restaurant Guy Savoy
Michelin-starred Guy Savoy serves classic dishes in an emulation of his Paris restaurant.

📍 A4   🏠 Caesars Palace   🕐 Lunch, Mon & Tue   🌐 caesars.com/caesars-palace

💲💲💲

🔟6️⃣ 🍴 🍹 🛍

The LINQ Hotel + Experience

📍 A4 🏨 3535 Las Vegas Blvd S 🕐 24 hours
🌐 caesars.com/linq

The LINQ Hotel + Experience and casino is a relative newcomer to the Strip. It originated in 1959 as the Flamingo Capri (adjacent to the Flamingo proper) and was remodeled into the Imperial Palace in 1979, which became the LINQ Hotel + Experience in 2014.

The 2,640 sleek, modern rooms with accents of color are supplemented with casual eateries offering everything from doughnuts to Mexican fare and brunch favorites.

There's also a theater for shows, a pool for day parties, and a futuristic bar.

As with many resorts, the hotel contains its own shopping district, the LINQ Promenade, but more notably, also features the mind-boggling High Roller ferris wheel and the Fly LINQ zipline, where guests soar 12 stories over the Promenade.

1️⃣7️⃣ 🚊 🍴 🛍

The Venetian

📍 A4 🏨 3355 Las Vegas Blvd S 🕐 24 hours
🌐 venetian.com

An astounding piece of architecture that re-creates the city of Venice, the Venetian hotel holds, along with its sister resort the Palazzo, over 7,000 suites. Together they typify the luxury mega-resorts of Vegas. The Venetian opened in 1999 on the site of the legendary Sands Hotel – former home of the "Rat Pack" (p264) and a famous swim-up craps table – which was demolished in 1996.

The Venetian's Strip facade consists of facsimiles of the Doge's Palace, the Campanile, and the Ca' d'Oro, which overlook the blue waters of the Grand Canal – complete with a gondola park beneath the Rialto Bridge. Craftsmen have made sure that every detail looks as authentic as possible – even the concrete is aged to look like 400-year-old stone. The colonnade of the Doge's Palace offers visitors one of the best views of the Strip.

Inside the building, and up the stairs, another separate section of canal, winds through a large upscale shopping mall known as the Grand Canal Shoppes. The Venetian fantasy continues with high-quality stores and restaurants set among cobblestone walkways and bridges beneath a painted blue sky that resembles a Renaissance painting. Acres of marble flooring, statues, and replicas of Venetian artworks are found throughout. The front lobby has a dome decorated with scenes from paintings by the Venetian masters, and the entrance to the Grand Canal Shoppes boasts a copy of Veronese's 1585 painting, *The Apotheosis of Venice*.

At the far end of the mall, a series of walkways lead into the Palazzo hotel and casino, completed in 2008, which has the largest rooms on the Strip as well as more upscale stores, restaurants, and nightclubs.

←
A performance of *Mystère*™ by the Cirque du Soleil® troupe at Treasure Island

Treasure Island

📍 A4 🏠 3300 Las Vegas Blvd S 🕐 24 hours
🌐 treasureisland.com

This hotel resort and casino offers luxurious accommodations and award-winning service. Originally pirate-themed, the hotel is now a more generic young-adult resort, and often abbreviates its name to the less piratical TI. Guests can relax in the hotel spa or sip cocktails by the heated outdoor pool. There are eight restaurants to choose from, including a branch of the Mexican-themed Señor Frog's, as well as several bars and lounges; nightclubs include the honky tonk Gilley's Saloon.

The hotel is also host to the exhilarating contemporary circus *Mystère*™ by Cirque du Soleil®, which is performed regularly in a specially customized showroom.

Mirage

📍 A4 🏠 3400 Las Vegas Blvd S 🕐 24 hours
🌐 mirage.com

The Mirage hotel and casino opened in the fall of 1989 at a staggering cost of $620 million. At the time it was the largest hotel in the US, with over 3,000 rooms. This mega-resort aimed to cater not only to gamblers but to vacationers and conventioneers. Perhaps more than any other hotel, the Mirage revolutionized the Strip, setting out to draw visitors with attractions other than just the casino – a kind of fantasyland for adults.

←
Gondolas gliding through the Grand Canal Shoppes under a painted sky at the Venetian

Occupying an entire block along Las Vegas Boulevard between Caesars Palace and Treasure Island, Mirage offers a range of attractions to its own guests and Vegas visitors alike. Its traffic-stopping facade introduces the complex's South Sea island theme, with tropical gardens, waterfalls, and a lagoon. But the star of the show is undoubtedly a volcano outside the main entrance that erupts, spewing fire and smoke, daily at 8pm and 9pm, and at 10pm on Friday and Saturday. Inside the complex, an atrium filled with exotic plants (some real, some fake) is kept suitably steamy by computerized misters. Behind the main desk an aquarium is filled with 85 species of tropical fish.

As well as gaming, visitors can shop in designer stores, eat in one of 16 restaurants and bars, walk in the hotel's lush, landscaped gardens, or see one of the many shows staged here nightly – past performances have included *LOVE*™ and Cirque du Soleil®'s tribute to the Beatles.

> **GOLF IN LAS VEGAS**
>
> Las Vegas has dozens of superb golf courses, surrounded by spectacular scenery. As well as exclusive championship courses there are many public ones, some just a short hop from the Strip. Your hotel concierge desk will book you a slot. The Mirage and some other resorts partner with specific golf clubs, so enquire when booking. If you want to play a particular course it's best to get a combined golf-hotel package.

↑ A tree-lined walkway under the glass ceiling of the Wynn's Atrium

The summit of The STRAT Tower has indoor and outdoor observation decks, which offer unparalleled views of the city and the surrounding desert and mountains.

20

Wynn Las Vegas & Encore

⦿ B3 ⌂ 3131 Las Vegas Blvd S ⊙ 24 hours ⓦ wynn lasvegas.com

While the exteriors are not as flamboyant as other hotels on the Strip, the bronze-glass facades of the Wynn Las Vegas and its sister resort, Encore, are nevertheless stunning. Set against the desert and a forest-clad mountain range, the hotel offers wonderful views.

Within the two gigantic 60-story towers, opulence and exclusivity reign. The resort carries a reputation as the most expensive and fashionable place in town.

Upon arriving at the main entrance of the Wynn, visitors are guided to the Atrium, with its tree-lined walkways. At the center of the hotel is the Lake of Dreams and a man-made mountain that soars over the lake, while curtains of water cascade in a dramatic waterfall. There is also a majestic

18-hole golf course, which has hosted PGA and LGPA tour events, in addition to award-winning restaurants and spas.

Encore ranks among the city's most prominent nightlife destinations. The indoor-outdoor Encore Beach Club achieved worldwide notoriety thanks to Prince Harry in 2012, while the acclaimed XS nightclub has a 10-ft (3-m) rotating chandelier and a patio with poolside bars. The resorts' casinos are known for high gambling stakes: the Sky Casino only takes bets over $300,000. However, for the less serious gamer, there are slot machines, table games, and poker tournaments.

---

21 Ⓨ 🍽

Circus Circus

⦿ B3 ⌂ 2880 Las Vegas Blvd S ⊙ 24 hours ⓦ circus circus.com

Located at the north end of the Strip, Circus Circus opened in 1968 and is a themed resort

offering family entertainment. The hotel has an impressive choice of reasonably priced restaurants and buffets, including a delicious steakhouse.

This vast property has one of the largest indoor theme parks in Nevada. The huge pink **Adventuredome** is decorated with a re-created Southwest landscape of sandstone cliffs, caves, and a waterfall, and is maintained at a temperature of 22° C (72° F) year round. It includes an FX 4D theater, a range of family rides, and two fabulous coaster rides: El Loco twists, turns, and

LAS VEGAS FOR KIDS

There's plenty of fun for children in Vegas. Lots of shows are family-friendly. Many resorts, like Excalibur and Circus Circus, have fantastic family swimming pools with slides. Circus Circus's Adventuredome under its Big Top is a fun amusement park and the resort also features daily clown shows. North of the Strip is the Discovery Children's Museum (p267).

drops 90 ft (27 m), providing a 1.5 vertical G-force, while the Canyon Blaster is a double-loop, double-corkscrew roller coaster.

The four casinos here cover an incredible 100,000 sq ft (9,300 sq m). Above the main casino is the Big Top, with its circular walkway of traditional games where the children are the winners. This is also the place to find seating for the live circus acts that perform half-hourly from 11am to midnight, with world-class acrobats flying high above the heads of gamblers at the slot machines below.

Adventuredome

⊛ ⬛ Circus Circus ⬛ Daily; times vary, check website ⬛ adventuredome.com

---

㉒ 🍴 🏛

The STRAT

📍 B2 🏠 2000 Las Vegas Blvd S ⬛ 24 hours ⬛ thestrat.com

Located at the north end of the Strip, away from the main attractions, this resort hotel has the tallest building in the city. The summit of The STRAT Tower has both indoor and outdoor observation decks, which offer unparalleled views of the city and the surrounding desert and mountains,

and are the highest of their kind in the USA. There is also the popular Top of the World revolving restaurant, which rotates 360 degrees over the course of an hour.

The tower elevators take just 30 seconds to whisk you up to the top, where you will find several thrilling rides, including **X-Scream**, a giant teeter-totter that propels riders 27 ft (8 m) over the tower edge; **Insanity**, where a giant mechanical arm suspends you 900 ft (275 m) above the Strip; and **SkyJump**, a terrifying 855-ft (260-m) free-fall (the highest controlled free-fall in the world).

The STRAT hotel itself offers two shows, a comedy club, and several restaurants and stores.

X-Scream, Insanity, and SkyJump

⊛ ⬛ The STRAT ⬛ 10am–1am Sun–Thu, 10am–2am Fri, Sat & public hols

---

㉓ 🍴

Sahara

📍 B3 🏠 2535 Las Vegas Blvd S ⬛ 24 hours ⬛ saharalasvegas.com

Once the favored destination of the Beatles, Frank Sinatra, and the "Rat Pack" (p264), the legendary former Sahara Hotel and Casino reopened

↑ The warm interior of the Casbar Lounge at the Sahara

as the sleek, modern SLS Las Vegas in 2014 following a $415-million renovation. Having undergone a further $100-million upgrade in 2018, this upscale property changed its name back to Sahara. The hotel today is characterized by the striking contemporary and artistically whimsical interior decor by Parisian designer Philippe Starck, creating a sophisticated environment. Over 1,600 guest rooms and suites are spread across three towers, and the rooms in each tower are decorated in varying styles.

The Sahara is home to plenty of bars and lounges, and also hosts a changing line up of popular comedy and adult entertainment shows. The hotel also features two rooftop pools: the Alexandria Pool with panoramic views over downtown Las Vegas and the mountains beyond, and a glamorous Retro Pool Lounge. You can also rent cabanas and daybeds.

In addition, there are six restaurants to choose from, including Bazaar Meat, run by James Beard Award-winning chef José Andrés. The comfortable and inviting 60,000-sq-ft (5,574-sq-m) casino offers over 600 slot machines, dozens of classic table games, and a high-limit room and sports book.

↑ Visitors enjoying an Insanity thrill ride far above the Strip at The STRAT

THE CHANGING FACE OF LAS VEGAS

No other city in the US has reinvented itself as often and as successfully as Las Vegas. The city's early growth is linked to some of the biggest names in 20th-century show business, such as Elvis Presley, and personalities like the eccentric millionaire Howard Hughes, not to mention mobsters like the notorious Bugsy Siegel *(p258)*. Today, more than ever, Las Vegas is a dazzling city that fires the imagination – a playground of limos, star-studded entertainment, and an "anything goes" ethos for those who can pay for it.

BIRTH OF A CITY

Las Vegas grew up around Fremont Street *(p266)* in the early 1900s, but by the early 1920s the city's population fell to 2,300. Beginning in 1931, the construction of the Hoover Dam *(p269)* nearby brought a rise in Las Vegas's fortunes and by the early 1930s the population had grown to around 7,500. Tens of thousands of visitors arrived to see the building of the dam and to enjoy the new gambling clubs springing up, and the city became a hedonistic escape from the 1930s' Depression. In the 1950s, the Rat Pack, which included Peter Lawford, Sammy Davis Jr., Frank Sinatra, Joey Bishop, and Dean Martin, sealed Las Vegas' reputation as an entertainment mecca. By the 1980s Fremont Street had begun to suffer from competition from the Strip *(p252)*. From a few low-rise buildings along a desert road in the 1960s to the glittering neon canyon of today, the Strip's transformation was remarkable.

↑ The Hoover Dam being constructed on the Colorado River, around 1934

HOWARD HUGHES

Billionaire Howard Hughes arrived in Las Vegas in November 1966, moving into a luxurious suite on the ninth floor of the Desert Inn hotel. When the hotel's management tried to move him out a few months later, Hughes bought the place for $13.2 million. Although he never left his room in four years, he spent some $300 million buying Vegas properties. These included the Silver Slipper hotel and casino across the Strip, whose blinking neon slipper disturbed him – as the owner he had it switched off. Hughes is credited with bringing legitimate business and a sanitized image to Vegas, sounding the death knell of mob investment in the city.

↑ Fremont Street in 1953, lined with numerous casinos and hotels

Timeline of events

1905

Las Vegas is founded as a stopover on the railroad between Los Angeles and Salt Lake City.

1931

Gambling is legalized in Nevada; casinos are licensed on Fremont Street, which becomes the first paved street in the city.

1931–35

Construction of the Hoover Dam nearby spurs the building of casinos and showgirl theaters to entertain dam workers and visitors.

1941

Thomas Hull builds the luxury El Rancho Vegas, the first hotel resort on the Strip.

1946

Mobster Bugsy Siegel builds The Flamingo, a high-class casino; mafia money increasingly fuels the development of new casinos.

1950s

Las Vegas becomes an entertainment mecca with an influx of Hollywood stars.

1966

Billionaire Howard Hughes arrives and begins investing in Las Vegas properties, bringing legitimate business to the city.

1989

The opening of Steve Wynn's Mirage ushers in the era of mega-resorts; MGM Grand, Luxor, New York New York, and others follow.

1993

The first Cirque du Soleil® show, *Mystère*™, opens at Treasure Island.

2009

CityCenter is built on the Strip, featuring a mega-resort and luxury shops.

2014

The High Roller, the world's tallest Ferris wheel, opens on the Strip.

24 Fremont Street Experience

📍C1 ⏰Light shows: hourly, 6pm-midnight daily
🌐vegasexperience.com

Long known as "Glitter Gulch," Fremont Street has been at the heart of downtown Las Vegas since the city was founded in 1905. This is where the first casinos were built, complete with neon signs, and where famous illuminated icons such as Vegas Vic and Vickie lit up the night sky. However, as the Strip boomed in the 1980s and early 1990s, Fremont Street became ever more run-down.

The spectacular Fremont Street Experience, an ambitious $70-million project to revitalize the area, was unveiled in 1994. A vast steel canopy was erected over the central stretch of downtown. Light shows are projected onto the canopy after sunset every night, on the hour, using over 12 million synchronized LED modules backed by a huge sound system.

Fremont is pedestrianized, so you can easily stroll from casino to casino, stopping to snack and shop along the way. Some of the famous signs have gone, but many of the dazzling old facades remain. One way to see them is from the Slotzilla zipline, allowing you to fly the full length of the street.

Did You Know?

The length of the steel canopy that stretches above Fremont Street for five blocks is 1,500 ft (457 m.)

For many years the landmark casino in Vegas was Binion's Horseshoe, established by the legendary Benny Binion, who is said to have arrived in town in 1946 wearing a ten-gallon hat and carrying $2 million in cash. **Binion's**, as it is known today, is famous for its poker heritage; the World Series of Poker started here in 1970, and the Hall of Fame Poker Room is lined with photos of historic poker games and players. You can even pose next to a stack of $1 million in banknotes.

The dazzling **Golden Nugget** has its eponymous nugget on display in the lobby. The "Hand of Faith" is the world's largest nugget, weighing an incredible 61 lb 11 oz (28 kg). The nearby **El Cortez** is one of the very few casinos to retain its original 1950s features. Built in 1966, the **Four Queens** has mirrors and chandeliers evoking 19th-century New Orleans.

Binion's

🏠128 E Fremont St ⏰24 hrs
🌐binions.com

Golden Nugget

🏠129 E Fremont St ⏰24 hrs
🌐goldennugget.com

El Cortez

🏠600 E Fremont St ⏰24 hrs
🌐elcortezhotelcasino.com

Four Queens

🏠202 E Fremont St ⏰24 hrs
🌐fourqueens.com

25 Mob Museum

📍C1 🏠300 Stewart Ave
⏰9am-9pm daily
🌐themobmuseum.org

Las Vegas these days is a far cry from the city of the 1950s and 1960s, when many casino owners had close links with organized crime, and profits were "skimmed" to line the pockets of mobsters. That era is recalled at the Mob Museum, a pet project of former mayor Oscar Goodman, who, as a lawyer, defended many Mob-associated figures. Three floors of displays tell the story of the gory deeds and flamboyant lifestyles of the city's gangsters, and of the dedicated lawmen and politicians who eventually brought them to justice.

→

The Neon Museum on Las Vegas Boulevard, lit up in green at night

26

Discovery Children's Museum

📍B1 🏠360 Promenade Place ⏰10am-6pm Tue, 10am-5pm Wed-Sat (Jun-early Sep: also Mon), noon-5pm Sun ❌Jan 1, Easter, Thanksgiving, Dec 24 & 25 🌐discoverykidslv.org

Located in Symphony Park, on the western edge of downtown, this excellent museum is devoted to interactive exhibits that are fun for both adults and children. It centers on a 12-level tower known as the Summit, where visitors can experiment with exhibits that show the connections between scientific concepts and real-life applications. Other displays include a laboratory for young inventors; a water tank that replicates and explains the Hoover Dam and Lake Mead; Eco City, a child-sized environmentally friendly city laid out along a boulevard complete with banks, grocery stores, and a wind turbine; and a glorified desert sandpit called Toddler Town with role-play activities for kids under the age of five. Changing exhibitions cover a range of interesting subjects from world cultures to art and wildlife.

27

The Las Vegas Natural History Museum

📍C1 🏠900 Las Vegas Blvd N ⏰9am-4pm daily ❌Jan 1, Thanksgiving, Dec 24 & 25 🌐lvnhm.org

A popular choice with families who need a break from the Strip, this museum has an appealing range of exhibits. Dioramas re-create the African savanna and display a variety of wildlife from leopards and cheetahs to several African antelope species such as bush boks, nyalas, and duikers.

The International Wildlife gallery showcases mammals' ability to adapt and survive. Animatronic dinosaurs include a 35-ft- (11-m-) long Tyrannosaurus rex, while the marine exhibit has live eels and sharks. Try digging for fossils and exploring the five senses in the discovery room.

28

Neon Museum

📍C1 🏠770 Las Vegas Blvd N ⏰Daily; times vary, check website ❌Jan 1, Jul 4, Thanksgiving, Dec 25 🌐neonmuseum.org

This museum is dedicated to the iconic glowing neon signs that once dominated the Las Vegas skyline before most of the mega-resorts switched to LED lighting. The history of neon stretches back to 1910, when French inventor Georges Claude discovered that passing an electric current through a glass tube filled with neon gas results in a brilliant light. In the 1940s and 1950s, the craft of neon sign-making was elevated to the status of art form in Las Vegas.

The site includes a visitor center, gallery, and the outdoor Neon Boneyard, where you can take a guided tour of 200 retired signs, including those from the Stardust, Moulin Rouge, and Flamingo. The museum also traces changes and trends in sign design and technology from the 1930s to the present day. Although the museum is open during the daytime, an evening visit has the authentic feeling of the glitzy Las Vegas of old.

EAT

Siegel's 1941
Enjoy classic American dishes and prime ribs in an old-Vegas setting.

📍C1 🏠600 E Fremont St 🌐elcortezhotelcasino.com

$$$ (S)(S)

Oscar's Steakhouse
The former mayor's one-of-a-kind eatery in a futuristic glass bubble.

📍C1 🏠The Plaza, 1 Main St ❌Lunch 🌐plazahotelcasino.com

$$$

Top Of Binion's Steakhouse
Spectacular views of the Strip, plus live piano music on weekends.

📍C1 🏠128 E Fremont St ❌Lunch 🌐topofbinions steakhouse.com

$$$

29

Old Las Vegas Mormon State Historic Park

📍C1 🏠500 E Washington Blvd 🕐8am–4:30pm Tue–Sat 🌐parks.nv.gov/parks/old-las-vegas-mormon-fort

This diminutive, pink adobe building in downtown is the oldest in Las Vegas and all that remains of a fort built by a group of Mormon settlers, who established themselves permanently in the area in 1855. The fort, built on the banks of Las Vegas Creek, consisted of two bas-tions and a row of two-story buildings arranged around a 150-ft-(46-m-) long, rectangular *placita* (small plaza) with 14-ft- (4-m-) high walls. After crop failures, disappointing mining yields, and dissension among the group, the settlers abandoned the site around three years later. It became part of a ranch in the 1880s and was run by Las Vegas pioneer Helen Stewart.

Today, the visitor center is a reconstruction of the original adobe house, with its simply furnished interior much as it would have been when the Mormon settlers lived here. The building also contains an exhibition that describes the Mormon missions and their impact on Las Vegas.

30

Valley of Fire State Park

📍F4 🚌Las Vegas 🌐parks.nv.gov/parks/valley-of-fire

This spectacularly scenic state park sits in a remote desert location some 60 miles (97 km) northeast of Las Vegas. Its name derives from the red sandstone formations that began as huge, shifting sand dunes about 150 million years ago. There are several well-maintained trails across this wilderness, including the Petroglyph Canyon Trail, an easy half-mile (1-km) loop that takes in a series of Ancestral Puebloan rock carvings. Summer temperatures often reach 44° C (112° F). The best time to visit is in spring or fall.

The nearby town of Overton lies along the Muddy River. The Ancestral Puebloans settled here around 300 BC but left some 1,500 years later, perhaps because of a long drought. Archaeologists have unearthed hundreds of prehistoric artifacts in the area since the first digs in the 1920s. The **Lost City Museum of Archaeology**, just outside the town, has a large collection of pottery, beads, woven baskets, and delicate turquoise jewelry.

Lost City Museum of Archaeology

🏠721 S Moapa Valley Blvd, Overton 🕐8:30am–4:30pm daily 🚫Jan 1, Thanksgiving, Dec 25 & 26 🌐nvculture.org/lostcitymuseum

31

Lake Mead National Recreation Area

📍F4 🚌Las Vegas ℹ️Alan Bible Visitor Center; www.nps.gov/lake

After the completion of the Hoover Dam, the waters of the Colorado River filled its deep canyons to create a huge reservoir. This lake, with its 700 miles (1,130 km) of shoreline, is the centerpiece of the Lake Mead National Recreation Area. The focus is on water sports, especially sailing, waterskiing, and fishing. Striped bass and rainbow trout are popular catches. You'll also find many campgrounds and marinas.

32

Red Rock Canyon

📍E4 🚌Las Vegas 🕐Scenic Drive: 6am–dusk daily 🌐redrockcanyonlv.org

From downtown Las Vegas, a short, 10-mile (16-km) drive west will take you to the low hills and steep gullies of the Red Rock Canyon. A gnarled escarpment rises out of the desert, its gray limestone and red sandstone the geological residue of an ancient ocean and the huge sand dunes that succeeded it. Red Rock is easily explored on an enjoyable 13-mile (21-km) scenic road that loops off Highway 159. Beside the road are picnic spots and short hikes that cover the area's winding canyons. The visitor center at the start of the road has informative displays on the canyon's range of flora and fauna. There are some 80 to 100 bighorn sheep in the conservation area.

㉝ Mount Charleston

⦿ E4 **🚌 Las Vegas**
🅦 gomtcharleston.com

About 45 miles (72 km) northwest of Las Vegas, Mount Charleston rises to 11,918 ft (3,633 m) out of Toiyabe National Forest, clad with pine, mountain mahogany, fir, and aspen. Also known as the Spring Mountain Recreation Area, it offers refuge from the Vegas summer heat, with a variety of hiking trails and picnic areas.

↑ Visitors taking in the spectacular views from the visitor center at the Hoover Dam

Skiing and snowboarding are popular in the winter. A range of hikes is available, including two demanding trails that snake up to the summit: the 11-mile (18-km) North Loop and the 9-mile (14-km) South Loop. Easier walks on the forested slopes include a one-hour hike up Cathedral Rock, which starts from a picnic area at the end of Highway 157. This is the more southerly of the two by-roads leading to Mount Charleston off Highway 95; the other is Highway 156, which runs to Lee Canyon Ski Area.

㉞ 🚲 🅼 Hoover Dam

⦿ F4 **🚹🚌 ⓣ 9am–5pm daily**
🅦 usbr.gov/lc/hooverdam

The Hoover Dam was built between 1931 and 1935 across the Colorado River's Black Canyon, 30 miles (48 km) east of Las Vegas. An engineering marvel, the dam gave the desert region a reliable water supply and provided inexpensive electricity. Today, the dam supplies water and power to Nevada, Arizona, and California,

← Exploring the red sandstone formations in the Valley of Fire State Park

and has created Lake Mead. Visitors to the dam can take the Hoover Dam Powerplant Tour, which includes a trip to the observation deck, where there are panoramic views of the dam's huge generators. Guided tours lead through old construction tunnels and explain how the dam was built.

Just 8 miles (13 km) west of the dam, Boulder City was built as a community to house dam construction workers and is one of Nevada's most attractive towns. Its founders banned casinos, and there are still none here today. Several of its original 1930s buildings remain, including the 1933 Boulder Dam Hotel, which houses the Hoover Dam Museum.

Hoover Dam Museum

 🏠 1305 Arizona St, Boulder City ⓣ 7am–7pm daily ⓓ Public hols
🅦 bcmha.org

△ GREAT VIEW
Helicopter Ride

To truly appreciate the vast scale of the Hoover Dam, see it from the air. Helicopter and plane trips from Las Vegas fly directly over the dam on their way to the Grand Canyon, giving you a splendid bird's-eye view.

NEED TO KNOW

Monument Valley Navajo Tribal Park

BEFORE
YOU GO

Things change, so plan ahead to make the most of your trip. Be prepared for all eventualities by considering the following points before you travel.

AT A GLANCE

CURRENCY
US dollar (USD)

AVERAGE DAILY SPEND

SAVE
$100

SPEND
$200

SPLURGE
$300+

BOTTLED WATER
$1.00

COFFEE
$2.50

BEER
$5.00

DINNER FOR TWO
$80

CLIMATE

 The Southwest averages 14–15 hours of daylight in summer and 9–10 hours of daylight in winter.

 Mountain regions average 36°F (2°C) in winter, 75°F (24°C) in summer; desert regions 70°F (21°C) in winter, 105°F (41°C) in summer.

 Short, heavy monsoon rains occur in the desert June to August. Thunderstorms are common.

ELECTRICITY SUPPLY
Plug sockets are type A and B, fitting plugs with two and three flat pins. Standard voltage is 100–120 volts AC.

Passports and Visas

For entry requirements, including visas, consult your nearest US embassy or check with the **US Department of State**. Canadians and Mexicans need valid passports to enter the US. Citizens of Australia, New Zealand, and the EU do not need a visa, but must apply in advance for the Electronic System for Travel Authorization (**ESTA**) permit and have a valid passport. All other visitors need a passport and tourist visa, and will be photographed and have their fingerprints taken. A return ticket is required to enter the US.
ESTA
W esta.cbp.dhs.gov
US Department of State
W travel.state.gov

Travel Safety Advice

Now more than ever, it is important to consult both your and the US government's advice before travelling. The **UK Foreign and Commonwealth Office**, the **US State Department**, and the **Australian Department of Foreign Affairs and Trade** offer the latest information on security, health, and local regulations.
Australia
W smartraveller.gov.au
UK
W gov.uk/foreign-travel-advice
US
W state.gov

Customs Information

Find information on the laws relating to goods and currency taken in or out of the US on the **US Customs and Border Protection Agency** website.
US Customs and Border Protection Agency
W cbp.gov

Insurance

We recommend that you take out a comprehensive insurance policy covering theft, loss of belongings, medical and dental care, cancellations and delays, and read the small print carefully.

Vaccinations

No inoculations are required for visiting the US.

Money

Most retailers will accept card or cash payments. It is common to sign for purchases rather than entering a pin into an electronic reader. While contactless payments are not yet the norm, they have become more common following the COVID-19 pandemic. Cities and most towns have ATMs. Carry cash when traveling in remote areas as card and ATM facilities may not be available.

Check your bank's withdrawal fees before traveling; the ATM may also charge $2.50 to $3.50 per transaction. You can exchange currency in larger branches of Bank of America, Wells Fargo, and Chase, as well as at bureaux de change. Prepaid currency cards can be used to withdraw money, and act like debit cards in shops and restaurants.

Note that tipping is expected in the US. Around 15–20 per cent is normal when dining out or travelling by taxi; hotel porters and housekeeping will expect $2 per bag or day.

Booking Accommodation

Booking a package deal or fly-drive holiday is often the most inexpensive way of visiting the Southwest. Websites offer air fares, hotels, and car rentals. Book in advance if visiting during spring break (March/April) or summer vacation (June–August). Prices also spike around holidays and local festivals and events. National park lodges have limited accommodations and must be booked well ahead.

Accommodations include luxury hotels and resorts, historic inns and B&Bs, dude ranches, and inexpensive chain motels. Campgrounds and RV parks are widespread.

Travelers with Specific Requirements

Hotels, restaurants, galleries, museums, and other public buildings, as well as public transportation, generally have excellent facilities for travelers with specific requirements. Some historic buildings and sites may have limited accessibility. Many national parks and archaeological sites have paved walkways suitable for wheelchairs. The

National Park Service offers an **Access Pass** to US citizens and permanent residents with permanent disabilities. It is best to contact accommodations and attractions in advance to verify their ability to meet your specific requirements.
Access Pass
w store.usgs.gov/access-pass

Language

The official language of the US is English. Spanish is widely spoken throughout the Southwest, and bilingual signage is common at attractions and stores. Phone information usually has a Spanish option. At pueblos and reservations, you may hear a variety of Native American languages.

Opening Hours

COVID-19 The pandemic continues to affect Southwest USA. Some museums, tourist attractions, and hospitality venues are operating on reduced or temporary opening hours, and require visitors to make advance bookings for a specific date and time. In addition, all Native American lands may be closed to visitors. Always check ahead before visiting.

Monday and Tuesday Some museums close.
Sunday Most banks are closed.
November–March Businesses, restaurants, museums, and shops close early.
Public holidays Some museums close.

PUBLIC HOLIDAYS	
Jan 1	New Year's Day
3rd Mon in Jan	Martin Luther King Jr. Day
3rd Mon in Feb	President's Day
Last Mon in May	Memorial Day
Jul 4	Independence Day
1st Mon in Sep	Labor Day
2nd Mon in Oct	Columbus Day
Nov 11	Veterans Day
4th Thu in Nov	Thanksgiving
Dec 25	Christmas Day

GETTING AROUND

Whether you are visiting for a short city break or exploring the desert, discover how best to reach your destination and travel like a pro.

AT A GLANCE

PUBLIC TRANSPORT COSTS

PHOENIX: BUS AND LIGHT RAIL

$2.00

single ticket
1-day ticket :$4.00

TUCSON: BUS AND LIGHT RAIL

$1.75

single ticket
1-day ticket: $4.50

ALBUQUERQUE: BUS

$1.00

single ticket
1-day ticket: $2.00

TOP TIP
Santa Fe and Flagstaff's downtown areas are compact and best explored on foot.

SPEED LIMIT

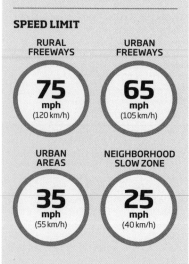

RURAL FREEWAYS

75 mph
(120 km/h)

URBAN FREEWAYS

65 mph
(105 km/h)

URBAN AREAS

35 mph
(55 km/h)

NEIGHBORHOOD SLOW ZONE

25 mph
(40 km/h)

Arriving by Air

Phoenix and Las Vegas are served by a number of direct international flights. For other Southwest destinations, international visitors and many domestic travelers will have to connect via one of the country's major hubs, such as Los Angeles, Dallas, Denver, or Chicago.

Each state in the Southwest has at least one major airport; these include Phoenix Sky Harbor and Tucson International (Arizona), Albuquerque International Sunport (New Mexico), Salt Lake City International Airport (Utah), Denver International Airport (Colorado), and Las Vegas's McCarran International Airport (Nevada). There are regional airports at many locations.

The major airports offer car rental, taxi and private shuttle services such as **SuperShuttle** and the **Groome Transportation**.
Groome Transportation
W groometransportation.com
SuperShuttle
W supershuttle.com

Train Travel

Long-Distance Trains
Three **Amtrak** routes running east to west across the USA make stops in the Southwest. The Southwest Chief runs daily between Chicago and Los Angeles, stopping at Lamy (with a bus link to Santa Fe) and at Albuquerque, before heading west, via Navajo and Hopi country at Gallup and Winslow, to Flagstaff and Kingman. Running between Chicago and San Francisco, the California Zephyr stops at Green River in southern Utah, about 40 miles (65 km) northwest of Arches and Canyonlands national parks. The Sunset Limited travels from New Orleans through Texas and along the southern sections of New Mexico and Arizona. Stops include Tucson, Maricopa (which has a connecting bus service to Tempe and Phoenix), and Yuma. All three trains are Amtrak Superliners, with two-tier cars, full-length domed windows for viewing the scenery, as well as lounge, restaurant, and snack cars.
Amtrak
W amtrak.com

GETTING TO AND FROM THE AIRPORT

Airport	Distance to city	Taxi fare	Public Transport	Journey time
Phoenix	4 miles (6 km)	$30	Bus, light rail	10 mins
Tucson	9 miles (14 km)	$27	Bus	15 mins
Albuquerque	5 miles (8 km)	$15	Bus	15 mins
Las Vegas	10 miles (16 km)	$27	Bus, tram	20 mins

RAIL JOURNEY PLANNER

Plotting the main train routes according to journey time, this map is a handy reference for traveling between the Southwest's main cities, towns, and sights by rail. The times reflect the fastest and most direct routes available.

Albuquerque to Santa Fe	1 hr
Flagstaff to Albuquerque	4 hrs 75 mins
Flagstaff to Grand Canyon	1 hr 30 mins
Las Cruces to Albuquerque	3 hrs 25 mins
Phoenix to Flagstaff	2 hrs 25 mins
Phoenix to Tucson	1 hr 75 mins
Tucson to Las Cruces	4 hrs

••• Direct train routes

Grand Canyon

Santa Fe

Flagstaff • Albuquerque

Phoenix

Tucson • Las Cruces

Scenic Train Trips

Three historic railroads allow you to enjoy some of the region's most delightful scenery. The **Cumbres and Toltec Scenic Railroad** runs between Chama in New Mexico (*p213*) and Antonito in Colorado through 64 miles (103 km) of peaks, tunnels, and gorges on a narrow gauge steam locomotive during the summer months. Colorado's **Durango and Silverton Narrow Gauge Railroad** (*p185*) travels through Rocky Mountain scenery, while the **Grand Canyon Railway** offers scenic diesel and steam rail trips from Williams (*p81*) to the Grand Canyon.

Cumbres and Toltec Scenic Railroad
w cumbrestoltec.com

Durango and Silverton Narrow Gauge Railroad
w durangotrain.com

Grand Canyon Railway
w thetrain.com

Long-Distance Bus Travel

Greyhound, and a few affiliated companies, links most of the major and many of the smaller towns and cities across the Southwest. They also provide essential links with the major airports and Amtrak services. The Amtrak Thruway is a van and bus service connecting train stops with the major cities. Other useful routes run from Albuquerque and Phoenix airports to places in New Mexico and Arizona. Greyhound and other specialist companies, including **Gray Line Tucson**, also offer package tours, which provide a leisurely way of exploring the area without the need to drive long distances.

Greyhound
w greyhound.com

Gray Line Tucson
w graylinearizona.com

Public Transportation

Several public transport organizations operate in the region – see individual websites for information on safety and hygiene measures, timetables, ticket information, and transport maps.

Albuquerque's metropolitan bus system, **ABQ Ride**, covers most parts of the city, including the airport, Old Town, and University District. New Mexico's **Rail Runner Express** runs between Albuquerque and Santa Fe, with connections to Sunport International Airport in Albuquerque. In Phoenix, the **Valley Metro** light rail system passes through the heart of downtown as part of its 26-mile (42-km) run from Camelback Road to the outlying areas of Tempe and Mesa, while downtown Phoenix also has the convenient and free **Downtown Dash**, which travels between the State Capitol, Arizona Center, and the Civic Plaza from Monday to Friday. Phoenix, Scottsdale, and the rest of the Valley of the Sun are covered by the Valley Metro bus system. In Tucson, the **Sun Link** Streetcar light rail connects five downtown districts, while the **Sun Tran** bus system runs through the rest of the city. The **Las Vegas Monorail** connects to several casinos, shopping centers, and the convention center, while **The Deuce** bus runs along the Strip and to downtown.

ABQ Ride
w cabq.gov/transit

The Deuce
w rtcsnv.com

Las Vegas Monorail
w lvmonorail.com

Rail Runner Express
w riometro.org

Sun Link and Sun Tran
w suntran.com

Valley Metro and Downtown Dash
w valleymetro.org

Tickets

Check the public transportation websites above for each city for fare options and ticket information. Some, such as the Sun Link streetcar in Tucson, do not accept cash on board and tickets must be bought in advance from ticket machines at the stops. Most machines accept both cash and card, but if paying with cash you will need to have the exact change. Buying pre-paid cards can also give you a reduced fare.

Taxis

Taxi fares can quickly mount up in large metropolitan areas like Phoenix, especially when there is traffic congestion, and are best confined to a short distance. The main companies are **ABQ** and **zTrip** in Albuquerque, **Yellow Cab** in Arizona, and **Desert Cab** in Las Vegas. Pickup fees range from $2.50 to $4.50, and fares from $2 per mile and up. Uber and Lyft operate in most cities.

Albuquerque
w ztrip.com/new-mexico
w abqtaxi.com

Arizona
w yellowcabaz.com

Las Vegas
w desertcabinc.com

Driving

Driving is a pleasure in this spectacular region. It's often the only means of reaching remote backcountry areas where you'll find some of the most interesting archaeological sites and natural geological formations. The entire region is served by a network of well-maintained roads.

Car Rental

Visitors from abroad must have a full driver's license that has been issued for at least two years before the date of travel. International Driving Licenses are not required for many countries if your current driver's license is in Roman script. Some rental companies charge extra to those under 25 years and limit the type of vehicle that can be rented. It is essential to have a credit card to pay the rental deposit.

There are rental car companies all over the Southwest. Most of the major businesses, such as Alamo, Avis, Hertz, Budget, Dollar Rent-A-Car, and Thrifty, have outlets at airports and in towns and cities across the region. If you are planning to arrive at one of the major hubs such as Phoenix or Las Vegas, the least expensive option is to arrange a fly-drive deal. Rates vary from state to state. Be aware that the cheapest rates do not always mean the best deal. Check that the price includes unlimited mileage and basic liability insurance, which is a legal requirement and covers any damage to another car. There is also a rental tax of 10 per cent or more.

Collision damage waiver (CDW) saves you from being charged for accidents or any visible defects on the car. Note that this is seldom included when booking your car rental in the US, and adding it can easily double the price of your rental. American drivers are usually covered for CDW on their rental car through their personal car insurance. Foreign drivers should consider booking their car rental before they leave home, as CDW is often included in the package.

Most rental cars have automatic transmission, although some companies offer a stick shift. Child seats or cars for travelers with specific requirements must be arranged in advance.

Rules of the Road

Highway speed limits are set by each state. In the Southwest the speed limit on the major highways varies between 55 mph (90 km/h) and 75 mph (120 km/h) for interstate highways (freeways). Anyone caught speeding will be fined. In cities and in small towns especially, watch for speed limit signs as they can vary from 45 mph (70 km/h) to as little as 15 mph (25 km/h) in school zones. It is illegal to pass a stationary school bus. Heed road signs, especially in remote areas where they may issue warnings about local hazards. There are heavy penalties for those who drink and drive, and the alcohol limit is low.

Get information on US traffic rules from your rental company or the **AAA** (American Automobile Association). Americans drive on the right. Unless signposted otherwise, you can turn right on a red light if there is no oncoming traffic. At a four-way stop sign, the first vehicle to reach the junction has the right of way. The AAA provides maps.

AAA
ⓦ aaa.com

Backcountry Driving

For travel in remote parts of the Southwest, such as the desert regions of Arizona and New Mexico, it is very important to check your route to see if a 4WD-vehicle is required. Although some backcountry areas now have roads able to carry conventional cars, a 4WD is essential in some wild and remote areas. Motoring organizations and tourist centers can provide information.

There are basic safety points to be observed on any trip of this kind. Plan your route and carry up-to-date maps. When traveling between remote destinations, inform the police or park wardens of your departure and expected arrival times. Check road conditions before you start, and be aware of seasonal dangers such as flash floods in Utah's canyonlands. Carry plenty of food and water, and a cell (mobile) phone as an added precaution. If you run out of gas or break down, stay with your vehicle, as it offers protection from the elements. If you fail to arrive at the expected time, a search party will look for you.

It is forbidden to remove or damage native flora and fauna. Do not drive off-road, unless in a designated area and especially not on reservation land. If driving an RV, you must stop overnight in designated campgrounds. Be aware that gas stations can be few and far between, so fill your tank before driving across remote areas.

Parking

In cities, street parking is generally metered and free spaces can be hard to find. Fees vary. Some parking meters may be coin-operated only, but many take credit cards. Parking lots and garages are another option, and can range from $1 for 30 minutes to $30 per day. Residential areas may require a permit. Yellow and red lines along the curb means parking is prohibited.

Cycling

Cycling is popular throughout the Southwest. Bike rentals are widely available. University cities such as Tucson and Tempe are particularly bike-friendly. You'll find bike trails in most national and state parks and other recreation areas. Be aware that the strong sun and high desert heat can be debilitating, especially in the summer months. A high-factor sunscreen and sun hat are recommended, as well as carrying plenty of water. Mountain biking is popular too – Moab (p146) and Durango (p185) are the main centers for this sport. Be sure to acclimatize yourself to a higher altitude if coming from a lower elevation.

Walking

There are plenty of great hiking trails scattered throughout the Southwest's state and national parks. While some urban areas are not particularly pedestrian-friendly, others are more walkable: Santa Fe's downtown area, Tempe's riverside, and Las Vegas's iconic Strip are all good walking spots.

PRACTICAL
INFORMATION

A little local know-how goes a long way in the Southwest. Here you will find all the essential advice and information you will need during your stay.

AT A GLANCE

EMERGENCY NUMBER

GENERAL EMERGENCY

911

TIME ZONE
MDT/DST Daylight Saving Time runs first Sunday in March to first Sunday in November except in Arizona.

TAP WATER
Unless otherwise stated, tap water is safe to drink, but bottled water is widely available.

WEBSITES AND APPS

GoSkyWatch
With this astronomy app, point your phone at the sky and discover which stars, constellations, and planets are above you.

GasBuddy
This app helps you find the cheapest gas stations while on your road trip.

Discover Navajo
Find out about the national monuments, parks, and historical sites of the Navajo peoples on www.disccovernavajo.com.

Personal Security

The Southwest is generally a safe place to visit. Pickpocketing can occur in busy tourist areas, so always be alert to your surroundings, especially on public transportation and in crowded areas.

If you have anything stolen, report the crime within 24 hours to the nearest police station and take ID with you. Get a copy of the crime report in order to claim on your insurance. Contact your embassy if you have your passport stolen, or in the event of a serious crime or accident.

As a rule, the Southwest is generally accepting of all people, regardless of their race, gender, or sexuality. The region celebrates its multicultural heritage, particularly its Native American and Hispanic influences which have deep historic roots. Same-sex marriage is legal in all five states in the area, and in late 2020, Nevada was the first US state to protect this right in its constitution.

When traveling along remote country roads, take a reliable map and follow the advice of local rangers and visitor information centers. These sources also offer invaluable information on survival in the wilderness for hikers and on the safety procedures that should be followed by anyone engaging in outdoor activities. Check the local media for current weather and safety conditions.

Health

The US has a world-class healthcare system but it is costly. Ensure you have full medical and dental cover prior to your visit, and keep receipts to claim on your insurance if needed.

Walgreens and **CVS** pharmacies can be found all over the Southwest. Certain medications available over the counter in other countries require a prescription in the US. If you are already taking prescribed medication, be sure to take enough supplies for your trip.

Hospital emergency rooms are open 24 hours. For non-emergencies, there are Urgent Care centers in most cities where you can see a doctor on a walk-in basis. You may be required to provide evidence of your ability to pay before a doctor will agree to treat you, hence the importance of adequate medical insurance.

CVS
w cvs.com
Walgreens
w walgreens.com

Smoking, Alcohol, and Drugs

You must be over 21 to buy and drink alcohol, and to buy tobacco products; expect to show photo ID. Drinking alcohol is not allowed in most public areas, especially from open containers. Driving while under the influence of alcohol or any drug is prohibited. It is illegal to smoke in public buildings, workplaces, restaurants, and bars. It is also illegal to smoke anywhere that exposes others to second-hand smoke, including parks, beaches, and bus stops. These laws extend to e-cigarettes.

ID

There is no requirement for visitors to carry ID in the US. However, remember to take some form of photo identification when buying alcohol or tobacco, as bars, clubs, restaurants, and shops are required by law to check it.

Local Customs

The Southwest is generally a very laid-back region. Casual clothing, such as jeans, T-shirts, and trainers, is quite acceptable in all but the most upmarket restaurants and nightclubs.

Some of the region's most famous sites, such as Canyon de Chelly (p164) and Monument Valley (p160), are located on Native American reservation land. Visitors are welcome but should be respectful, dress modestly, and ask about the local laws before visiting. It is illegal for alcohol to be brought onto many reservations. Some reservations have restrictions on photography. Always ask before photographing anything, especially ceremonial dances or homes, and take into consideration that a tip may be requested. Do not wander off marked trails as this is forbidden.

Cell Phones and Wi-Fi

Cellphone service in the Southwest is strong in the cities, but you may not be able to get a signal in remote areas. The main US network providers are AT&T, Sprint, T-Mobile US, and Verizon. Most of these offer prepaid, pay-as-you-go phones and US SIM cards, starting at around $30 (plus tax), which you can purchase upon arrival. Calls within the US are cheap, but international calls may be pricey. Free Wi-Fi is widely available in public areas in cities, and in many cafés and hotels.

Post

Stamps can be purchased at post offices, hotel reception desks, and some grocery stores. Check current postal rates at the **US Postal Services** website. Letters can be mailed from post offices, your hotel, and street mailboxes. Express services are offered by couriers such as DHL and UPS.
US Postal Services
w usps.com

Taxes and Refunds

Sales tax in cities and towns across the region ranges from 7 to 8.6 per cent. Tax is charged on everything except groceries, plants used for food, and prescription drugs, with a few other exemptions. Tourists cannot claim sales tax refunds, as none of these taxes are levied at a national level.

Discount Cards

Visitors with proof of student status receive discounts at many museums and other attractions. Apply for an International Student Identity Card (**ISIC**) prior to traveling. Seniors can also receive discounts at many attractions, so always carry ID with proof of age.

Over-50s should look into buying an **AARP** membership (open to non-Americans), which can provide discounts at hotels and on car rentals.

If you are planning to visit several national parks, you can save money with an annual America the Beautiful pass. This pass covers entrance fees for a driver and all passengers in a personal vehicle when visiting any of the country's national parks – further details can be found on the **National Park Service** website.

Many cities offer passes that include admission to several attractions at a discounted rate.
AARP
w aarp.org/membership
National Park Service
w nps.gov
ISIC
w isic.org

INDEX

Page numbers in **bold** refer to main entries.

N

O

P

ACKNOWLEDGMENTS

DK would like to thank the following for their contribution to the previous edition: Donna Dailey, Paul Franklin, Michelle de Larrabeiti, Philip Lee

The publisher would like to thank the following for their kind permission to reproduce their photographs:

Key: a-above; b-below/bottom; c-centre; f-far; l-left; r-right; t-top

123RF.com: Lukas Bischoff 126-7b; fotoluminate 80b; jakobradlgruber 146-7b, 150-1t; Mariusz Jurgielewicz 107tl; Anna Yakimova 115tr.

4Corners: Jordan Banks 83b; Monica Goslin 44tl; Susanne Kremer 266t.

Alamy Stock Photo: AB Forces News Collection 35tr; AF archive 258bc; AlphaAndOmega 78-9b; America 11br, 155tl, 227br; Aurora Photos 147tl; Tom Bean 74cr, 185cra; BHammond 199tr, 227tl, 238br; blickwinkel 135tl; steve bly 79tl; Stockimo / Ceri Breeze 248crb; Ed Callaert 28t; John Cancalosi 47cr; Cannon Photography LLC 28bl; Pat Canova 8clb; Yvette Cardozo 167br; Naum Chayer 77tl, 97tr; Mark Chivers 208-9b; David Cobb 139cr; Judith Collins 250c; B Christopher 57cr; Yaacov Dagan 255b; Ian Dagnall 94-5b, 104tl, 167c, 211br, 259br, 260-1b, 268-9b; John Dambik 212clb; Danita Delimont / Julien McRoberts 207t; Sam Dao 261tl; David L. Moore - US SW 201bl; Phil Degginger 103bl, 231cra; Danita Delimont 107ca, 140tr; Cody Duncan 72bl; Jonathan Eden 145tr; Chad Ehlers 12tl, 51cl; Richard Ellis 26-7c; Everett Collection Inc 265cl; eye35 24tr; Michele Falzone 73cra; FAY 2018 203tr; Nick Fox 182-3; Zachary Frank 210-1t; Dennis Frates 26tr; Glasshouse Images 167bc; Paul Christian Gordon 212b; Granger Historical Picture Archive 56br, 213br; Richard Green 81tl; Guillen Photo LLC / Amar and Isabelle Guillen 175bc; Steve Hamblin 47tl; Gavin Hellier 249tr; hemis.fr / LEMAIRE Stéphane 255t; Historic Images 59br; Wild Places Photography / Chris Howes 231br; George H.H. Huey 123, 179br; John Elk III 185t, 194tl; Richard Ellis 55br; Images-USA 235t; Tetra Images 51tr; Eric James 222t; Janice and Nolan Braud 186cl; Inge Johnsson 26tl; Jon Arnold Images Ltd 28cr; Jon Bower USA 49t; Julie Diebolt-Price 113tr; Ruslan Kalnitsky 133b; Niels van Kampenhout 166-7t; SCPhotos / James Kay 144tr; Scott Kemper 51br; kravka 24tl; John Lambing 175crb; Dan Leeth 175br; Simon Leigh 173tl; TIN LIEU 152-3b; LOOK Die Bildagentur der Fotografen GmbH 239b; Charles Mann 222bl, 241bl; Benny Marty 250b; Buddy Mays 48tr; Angel McNall 82t; MediaPunch / Erik Kabik Photography 248t; Moviestore collection Ltd 48cla, 49bl; National Geographic Image Collection / works by © Agnes Martin / DACS 2019 202br; Native American - Indian culture 13br, 215cra; Ron Niebrugge Images 100t, 145br, 145c; imageBROKER / Norbert Eisele-Hein 22cr; imageBROKER / Thomas Sbampato 37cl; North Wind Picture Archives 57tl, 193cla; Novarc Images 30bl; George Ostertag 167tr, 179tr, 234bl; Efrain Padro 39br, 41cl, 52t, 53tr, 53cla, 58bl, 167crb, 184b, 196tr, 209crb, 210cla, 241tr; Panther Media GmbH 71br; parkerphotography 205b, 232tl; Sean Pavone 61cra, 76-7b, 92-3t; Jamie Pham 141cr; Photo 12 48b; Mostardi Photography 177; Pictorial Press Ltd 49cr, 155cr; PictureLux / The Hollywood Archive / John Bramley 36b; Portis Imaging 30cr; Media Punch / Gdp Photos 249br; Robertharding / Walter Rawlings 176b; SuperStock / RGB Ventures 165crb; RidingMetaphor 202-3tl; Juergen Ritterbach 151br; RooM the Agency 107tr; RosalreneBetancourt 14 251cr; Sumiko Scott 71t; SDM Images 22crb; Adrian Seal 262t; Robert Shantz 235br; Dmitriy Shironosov 35cl; Marc De Simone 4; Witold Skrypczak 169bl; Solarsysys 253tr; Pierre Steenberg 77cr; SW Travel Imagery 30t; TCD / Prod.DB 160bl; Mason Vranish 269tr; Ron Watts 194br; Leon Werdinger 50tl; Jim West 27tl, 240tl; Scott Wilson 148-9; Richard Wong 47bl, 217br; World History Archive 193tc; YAY Media AS 33c; Marek Zuk 45crb, 153tr.

Arcosanti: Hanne Sue Kirsch 44-5b.

AWL Images: Danita Delimont Stock 45cl, 129, 139bl; Mark Sykes 206bl.

Bridgeman Images: Private Collection / Currier, N. (1813-88) and Ives, J.M. (1824-95) 58-9t; / Wood Ronsavile Harlin, Inc. USA / Rob Wood 56bl; National Geographic Image Collection / Scott S. Warren 59clb; Granger 59tr, 60tl; UIG / Ewing Galloway 61bl; / Universal History Archive 46br.

courtesy of Cirque du Soleil: 249cla; Matt Beard Photography 34-5b.

Depositphotos Inc: bhofack2 43cla; tang90246 107br.

Dillinger Brewing: 42bl.

Dorling Kindersley: University of Pennsylvania Museum of Archaeology and Anthropology / Angela Coppola 176cl, Bradbury Science Museum, Los Alamos / Francesca Yorke 208cra.

Dreamstime.com: Allison14 143cl; Amineah 11cr; Giuseppe Anello 251br; Bennymarty 166br; bhofack2 41tr, 41crb; Bonita Cheshier 86bl; Chris Curtis 95tl; Kobby Dagan 263bl; Anna Dudko 135cra; F11photo 252-3b; Golasza 171tr; Grian12 168-9t; Kojihirano 32-3b; Kravka 162tl; Steve Lagreca 224tl; Mykola Lukash 84-5t; Florence Mcginn 107cb; Derrick Neill 115bl Oscity 131bl; Sean Pavone 102-3t; Aaron Rayburn 110bl; Robin Runck 135tr; Pere Sanz 75t; Mykola Slavik 122b; Swisshippo 39c; Trebro 132cla; Edwin Verin 137br; Brian Welker 181br, 213t; Wilsilver77 170bl; Zhiwei Zhou 2-3.

Georgia O'Keeffe Museum: Insight Foto Inc. 38tl.

Getty Images: 500px Prime / Anastasios Vourekas 112-3b; Adventure_Photo 33br; Robert Alexander 169br, 195bl; AzmanL 11t; Aurora Photos / HagePhoto 122clb; benedek 24-5c, 69tl; Bettmann 58tl, 209tr; Peter V. Bianchi 57tr; Kevin Boutwell 8cl; Frederic J. Brown 61tr; Ernesto Burciaga 53cr; W. Buss 254-5t; Cavan Images 217cla; Jeff Clow 160cra; Matteo Colombo 22t, 124, 163cr; Corbis Documentary / Scott Smith 127cra; Charles Davies 136cl; DEA Picture Library 154-5b; Danita Delimont 109cl, 109cr; Dougberry 53b; Lonnie Duka 258tr; EyeEm / Daniel Cicivizzo 68-9b, / Benedikt Helmhagen 138, / Stephanie Hohmann 131br; David Epperson 143clb; Lola L. Falantes 20t, 156-7; Michele Falzone 238-9t; C Flanigan 54br; Michael Freeman 214bl; Bill Heinsohn 55bl; Historical 60bl; Ingram Publishing 21tl; 218-9; JannHuizenga 20bl, 188-9; Jupiterimages 251cra; Glenn van der Knijff 174-5t; Keith Ladzinski 140-1b; Gene Lester 264-5b; LGeoffroy 105b; LordRunar 154-5b; Eric Lowenbach 160cr; LPETTET 21cb, 244-5; Mark Brodkin Photography 33tr, 142-3t; Michael Marquand 30crb; MCT / Doug Merriam 50b; Aaron Meyers 19cb, 118-9; Minden Pictures / Tim Fitzharris 163c, 216bl; Daniele Molineris 161; Moment / Thomas Roche 32tl; Mona Makela Photography 204-5t; MPI 57cra; Bryan Mullennix 10clb; Richard T. Nowitz 101b; Glenn Oakley 172-3b; Onfokus 256-7t; Praveen P.N 178t; PBNJ Productions 131crb; Photography by Deb Snelson 180t; Design Pics / Mark Newman 55c; Popperfoto 264cra; powerofforever 162-3b; Robertharding / Alan Copson 187crb; Witold Skrypczak 165cra; Sam Spicer 13t; Starcevic 62-3; Steve Peterson Photography 164; Mike Theiss 229tl; Mark Theriot 236-7; Jason Todd 251tr; Peter Unger 229tr; UIG / Education Images 13cr; Universal History Archive 56t; wanderluster 164-5b; John Wang 130-1t; YinYang 10ca.

Gruet Winery: 43tr.

Heard Museum Collection: 38-9b.

iStockphoto.com: adwalsh 144-5b; David Arment 87br; AZCat 117b; benedek 35br, 77br, 108, 111tr; bpperry 100cl; CrackerClips 116tr; csfotoimages 201tl; Davel5957 96b; DenisTangneyJr 19zt; DOUGBERRY 84b, 180cla; E+ / pchoui 109br, / Ron and Patty Thomas 54bl; Ericliu08 77tr; EunikaSopotnicka 169tb; f11photo 6-7; gnagel 267bl; grandriver 46tl; ivanastar 197b, 232-3b; JurgaR 143br; Milehightraveler 228-9b; Moment / Charles Harker 19tl, 88-9; Onfokus 10-1b; Sean Pavone 18c, 64-5; Poike 251crb; RichLegg 36-7t; c_sorvillo 70bl; Tashka 52bl; tonda 12t, 114t; Peter Unger 231tr; wanderluster 163tr.

La Entrada and Tubac /Oxford Capital Partners: Darshan Phillips 39tr.

La Fonda on the Plaza: 42tl; Gabriella Marks 43br.

MIM—Musical Instrument Museum: 25tr, 98bl, 99tr; Jessica Savidge 98-9br, 99tl, 99cra.

NASA: 61br, 209cr.

Rex by Shutterstock: EPA / Mohamed Omar 249crb; Glasshouse Images 57cb; Granger 208cr.

Robert Harding Picture Library: Wendy Connett 225b, 243br' James Hager 107cr; Christian Heinrich 74b; Gavin Hellier 37ca; Frans Lanting 128bl; Bryan Mullennix 174bl; Michael Nolan 106-7b; Geoff Renner 12-3b.

Sahara Las Vegas: 263tr.

Science Photo Library: NASA 209cra.

Shutterstock: Blazg 28crb; Everett Historical 154cra; iacomino FRiMAGES 8-9; Bill Perry 127tl; Craig Zerbe 22bl.

SITE Santa Fe: *The Storm on the Sea of Galilee,* 2015, one of the works in his lightbox, series Gardner Museum Revisited, 2016, Courtesy of the artist and Christopher Grimes Gallery, Santa, Monica 198cr; Nick Merrick, Hall + Merrick Photography 198-9bl.

SuperStock: Visions of America 57br.

Taliesin West: Andrew Pielage 45tr.

The Santa Fe Opera: Kate Russell 34tl.

TopFoto.co.uk: Classicstock / Charles Phelps Cushing 60br; The Image Works 58br, / © Marilyn Genter 27tr; World History Archive 60-1t.

Tourism Santa Fe: Genevieve Russell 40-1b.

Visit Tucson: 40-1t.

Front flap:
Alamy Stock Photo: George Ostertag t; **Dreamstime.com:** Trebro cla; **Getty Images:** Kevin Boutwell cb; Bill Heinsohn br; **iStockphoto.com:** f11photo cra. **Shutterstock:** Blazg bl.

Cover images:
Front and spine: **Shutterstock.com:** Checubus.
Back: **Alamy Stock Photo:** Cannon Photography LLC cla; **iStockphoto.com:** E+ / YinYang tr; tonda c; **Shutterstock. com:** Checubus b.

For further information see: www.dkimages.com

Illustrators: Gary Cross, Eugene Fleurey, Claire Littlejohn, Chris Orr & Associates, Mel Pickering, Robbie Polley, John Woodcock

Penguin Random House

This edition updated by
Contributer Donna Dailey
Senior Editor Alison McGill
Senior Designers Laura O'Brien,
Vinita Venugopal
Project Editors Parnika Bagla, Rachel Laidler
Editor Anuroop Sanwalia
Picture Research Coordinator
Sumita Khatwani
Assistant Picture Research Administrator
Vagisha Pushp
Jacket Coordinator Bella Talbot
Jacket Designer Laura O'Brien
Senior Cartographic Editor Casper Morris
Cartography Manager Suresh Kumar
Cartographer Ashif
DTP Designers Rohit Rojal, Tanveer Zaidi
Senior Production Editor Jason Little
Production Controller Kariss Ainsworth
Managing Editors Shikha Kulkarni,
Hollie Teague
Deputy Managing Editor Beverly Smart
Managing Art Editors Bess Daly,
Priyanka Thakur
Art Director Maxine Pedliham
Publishing Director Georgina Dee

First edition 2001

Published in Great Britain by Dorling Kindersley Limited,
One Embassy Gardens, 8 Viaduct Gardens, London SW11 7BW

Published in the United States by DK Publishing,
1450 Broadway, Suite 801, New York, NY 10018

Copyright © 2001, 2021 Dorling Kindersley Limited
A Penguin Random House Company
21 22 23 24 10 9 8 7 6 5 4 3 2 1

A CIP catalog record for this book
is available from the British Library.

A catalog record for this book is available
from the Library of Congress.

ISSN: 1542 1554
ISBN: 978 0 2414 6264 5

Printed and bound in China.

www.dk.com

MIX
Paper from
responsible sources
FSC™ C018179
www.fsc.org

This book was made with Forest Stewardship Council™ certified paper – one small step in DK's commitment to a sustainable future. For more information go to www.dk.com/our-green-pledge

A NOTE FROM DK EYEWITNESS

The rapid rate at which the world is changing is constantly keeping the DK Eyewitness team on our toes. While we've worked hard to ensure that this edition of Southwest USA and National Parks is accurate and up-to-date, we know that opening hours alter, standards shift, prices fluctuate, places close and new ones pop up in their stead. So, if you notice we've got something wrong or left something out, we want to hear about it. Please get in touch at travelguides@dk.com